Developing Adoption
Support and Therapy

of related interest

Supporting Parents
Messages from Research
David Quinton
Foreword by the Right Honourable Margaret Hodge,
Minister for Children, Young People and Families
ISBN 1 84310 210 2

Trauma, Attachment and Family Permanence
Fear Can Stop You Loving
Edited by Caroline Archer and Alan Burnell for Family Futures
Foreword by Daniel A. Hughes
ISBN 1 84310 021 5

The Dynamics of Adoption
Social and Personal Perspectives
Edited by Amal Treacher and Ilan Katz
ISBN 1 85302 782 0

Fostering Now
Messages from Research
Ian Sinclair
Foreword by Tom Jeffreys, Director General, Children,
Families and Young People Directorate, DfES
ISBN 1 84310 362 1

The Adoption Experience
Families Who Give Children a Second Chance
Ann Morris
Adoption UK
Published in association with The Daily Telegraph
ISBN 1 85302 783 9

New Families, Old Scripts
A Guide to the Language of Trauma and Attachment
in Adoptive Families
Caroline Archer and Christine Gordon
Foreword by Alan Burnell
ISBN 1 84310 258 7

Babies and Young Children in Care
Life Pathways, Decision-making and Practice
Harriet Ward, Emily R. Munro and Chris Dearden
ISBN 1 84310 272 2

Foster Children
Where They Go and How They Get On
Ian Sinclair, Claire Baker, Kate Wilson and Ian Gibbs
ISBN 1 84310 278 1

Lesbian and Gay Fostering and Adoption
Extraordinary Yet Ordinary
Edited by Stephen Hicks and Janet McDermott
ISBN 1 85302 600 X

Foster Placements
Why They Succeed and Why They Fail
Ian Sinclair, Kate Wilson and Ian Gibbs
ISBN 1 84310 173 4

Developing Adoption Support and Therapy

New Approaches for Practice

Angie Hart and Barry Luckock

Jessica Kingsley Publishers
London and Philadelphia

First published in 2004
by Jessica Kingsley Publishers
116 Pentonville Road
London N1 9JB, England
and
400 Market Street, Suite 400
Philadelphia, PA 19106, USA

www.jkp.com

Copyright © Angie Hart and Barry Luckock 2004
Digitally printed in 2006

Library of Congress Cataloging in Publication Data
Hart, Angie.
Developing adoption support and therapy : new approaches for practice / Angie Hart and Barry Luckock.
p. cm.
Includes bibliographical references and index.
ISBN 1-84310-146-7 (pbk.)
1. Adoption—Great Britain. 2. Adoption—United States. 3. Adopted children—Great Britain. 4. Adopted children—United States. 5. Adoptive parents—Services for—Great Britain. 6. Adoptive parents—Services for—United States. I. Luckock, Barry, 1953- II. Title.
HV875.58.G7H37 2004
362.734—dc22

2004015124

British Library Cataloguing in Publication Data
A CIP catalogue record for this book is available from the British Library

ISBN-10: 84310 146 7
ISBN-13: 978 1 84310 146 8

Contents

List of Tables

List of Figures

Acknowledgements

This book has two authors, and we are jointly responsible for its contents. However, like most books, we suspect, something of a team effort lies behind it. The ideas we develop in *Developing Adoption Support and Therapy* have evolved from a research study we undertook with Chloe Gerhardt in 2001. We thank her for assisting us with that research, and for her enthusiasm in helping us to bring this book to fruition. Chloe undertook the mammoth job of organising our references. As well as reading and commenting on the entire manuscript, she also helped with other editorial tasks.

Our thanks are also due to Brighton and Hove Council and South Downs Health Care NHS Trust for commissioning the original research study and to the Department of Health for funding it. In particular, we thank Derek Blincow, Sue Boiling, Yvonne Ely, Fiona Johnson and Paul Holmes, and also members of the Brighton and Hove Attachment Team, who gave generously of their thoughts about service development in this area. The administrative and secretarial support of Sarah Gardner and Sally Smith has been invaluable to us.

We are grateful to very many colleagues and friends for reading through chapter drafts. Caroline Archer, John Simmonds and Helen Thomas read through the entire manuscript prior to publication and gave us extremely helpful feedback. Alex Saunders also deserves a particular mention for his insightful comments on different chapters. Leslie Ironside and Jenny Kenrick have also helped us enormously by providing valuable comments on current practice in relation to child psychotherapy. Trudy Ward gave us some specialist medical advice. Anne Foulger at the Department of Health provided us with some useful statistics. Alan Simpson taught us a lot about key working. Alan Rushton and Julie Selwyn shared the findings of their research in progress.

We cannot begin to list the names of those many friends and colleagues with whom we have had inspiring conversations about adoption support. Celia Balbernie, Alan Burnell, Jenny Clifton, Mary Dozier, Monica Duck, Sheila Fearnley, Alison Field, Barbara Fleetwood, Marnie Freeman, Alec Grant, David Howe, Karen Irving, Jeanne Kaniuk and colleagues at Coram Family, Rachael Lockey, Gillian Luckock, Carolyn Miller, Philly Morrall, Ginny Morrow, Imogen Taylor, Beth Neil and Michael, Edward and Becky Street Hartfield have all given us particular insights. Some of them have commented on chapter drafts.

We thank the staff at Adoption UK for answering our many adoption-related queries, and for allowing us to recruit parents to our research through *Adoption Today*. The staff at Jessica Kingsley Publishers deserve our thanks for their patient editorial support.

We are particularly grateful for the co-operation we have received from adoptive and foster parents (both locally and nationally), and those adoption supporters we interviewed for our original research study. Although for reasons of confidentiality we cannot name any of these people here, we thank all our research participants for giving us their time and sharing their views with us.

Finally we thank our own families for the very valuable support they provided to us so that we could write this book.

Chapter 1

Adoption Today

This book is about adoptive family life and how it might best be supported, particularly when abused and neglected children have come to adoption via public care. Adoption support is now firmly on the policy and practice agenda. And judging from the dissatisfaction or desperation of so many parents and children involved, this is not before time. But what is it about the nature and experience of adoption that leads to demands that this particular type of family should have a specific claim for support? What sort of support would help most in any case and why is it so difficult for it to be achieved? And why write a book just on support for adoptive families? We return regularly to these key questions in later chapters, but we want to begin in this introduction by outlining our own general approach to them. We also want to say something about how and why we have gone about the task of writing this book in the way we have.

The challenge of adoption and its support: Evidence from experience, research and practice

This book is the result of three years' collaborative work. The ideas for it have their origins in the local research evaluation of adoption support services that we conducted in Brighton and Hove (Hart, Luckock and Gerhardt 2002). However, as well as drawing on our work as academic adoption researchers, our experiences of adoption and parenting come from other sources too. One of us (Barry) is a former social worker, social work educator and a biological parent. The other (Angie) is an adoptive parent and a research lecturer in health and social care. She is also a therapist in a Child and Adolescent Mental Health Service.

Between us we have quite a range of different perspectives on adoption from which to draw. Our shared starting point, however, is the recognition that there is something about adoptive childhood and parenting that makes it difficult. Somehow in adoption the process of making 'the family' work seems to take that much more care, deliberation and plain hard work. Family life, through whatever means we choose to do it, invariably confounds the initial romance and expectation. In adoption the surprises, and sometimes the disillusion, can seem just that much more intense. Often, of course, there can be a good deal of fun and joy on the way but in many cases this is hard to come by. And sometimes the struggle is lost and things fall apart.

We know about all these difficulties from our own experiences of adoptive family life. We also know it from accounts of people whom adoption brings together. Any adoptive parent, adopted child or other person involved who has picked up this book out of interest will probably have done so because some part of this has been their experience too.

We also know about the difficulties because the rather different evidence of empirical research, with representative samples of children and parents, confirms the impression. The original adversities of birth family life make it hard for children to settle happily and develop ordinarily in their new adoptive home (Dance, Rushton and Quinton 2002). The longer it takes for them to be permanently placed the worse the effect on adoptive childhood and family life (Howe, Shemmings and Feast 2001; Rutter 2000). At the same time the early child and family experiences of adoptive parents affects their sensitivity and capability in looking after these difficult children effectively (Dozier 2003; Steele et al. 2003). And the way the family transition is managed is known to be important too. In particular it is essential to remember that children are, in the now famous phrase, more than just 'objects of concern' (Butler Sloss 1988). If the adults forget to find out and respect their views, because they are too busy assessing their needs, it is not surprising that children sometimes resist the new family future chosen for them (Thoburn 2001).

These dual sources of evidence – from experience and from research – are important for understanding the dynamics and outcomes of adoptive family life. We have benefited enormously, in doing our own research for this book, from the insights provided by both. We have also, however, been struck by the effect of the different experiences and voices of researchers and family members, on the way the question of adoption support practice is approached. For example, the measured tones of the academic paper, advising continued caution about the selection of interventions until trials are completed, contrast dramatically with the urgency of the demand from the family front room that something useful be done immediately to provide relief and support. In this latter respect, as we know from larger surveys (Lowe et al. 1999) and small-scale studies (Hart, Luckock and Gerhardt 2002), the routine practices of local professionals continue, more or less, to disappoint and frustrate.

Unsurprisingly, in the circumstances, the evidence of daily life tends to be particularly influential. It is apparent that the practitioners and agencies who capture the sense of the lived experience of the adoptive family find people beating a path to their door. Sometimes these practitioners are to be found in local mainstream agencies (see, for example, Hart and Thomas 2000), established voluntary adoption agencies like the Coram Family (Kaniuk 1992) and specialist national centres such as the Tavistock Clinic (Kenrick 2000). Often they are not. Thus in addition to empirical research findings and personal accounts we have been able to draw on the views and experiences of the new breed of therapeutic practitioners working in independent agencies such as the Post-Adoption Centre, Family Futures, and Keys Attachment Centre. Practitioner-developed models of therapy in the US private sector (Hughes 1997, 2003; Levy and Orlans 1998) and parent-devised strategies in this country (Archer 1999a, 1999b; Cairns 2002) are now having a direct and significant impact on parents and professionals. These two traditions have been mutually influential for some time now in the US, since many adoption therapists are explicit about the fact that they are themselves foster or adoptive parents (Keck and Kupecky 2002; Pavao 1998; Thomas 1997, 2000). In this country now too, practitioner models and parent-developed strategies have recently been explicitly combined in a book edited by Caroline Archer and Alan Burnell (2003).

On the face of it this is a rich diversity of evidence for practice. And yet our experience is that the different standpoints have led to the establishment of very little common ground on which a shared approach to adoption support might be built (Steele 2003). For example, whilst the charismatic US therapists fill lecture halls and training events with adoptive parents who carry home their videos and self-help manuals, the sober analysts of research do tend to speak overwhelmingly to other professionals in their seminars and talks. This is regrettable because adoption depends on dialogue and collaboration across the conventional professional and family divide.

The distinctive nature of adoptive family life and its support: Theory for effective practice

Adoptive family life tends to have about it the quality of being 'in' but not fully 'of' the wider community of families, however diverse in itself that community now is. As an approach to doing family it is not simply more difficult than many others due to the characteristics of the people involved. It is also made distinctive as a result of the social status of adoption and the way in which family is established. Uniquely in family life, whilst the adoptive family must be formed through a process of professional sponsorship and orchestration, it has traditionally been expected to go fully its own way thereafter. This unusual means of creation of family life has significant implications for the process and experience of support and for the way in which it is thought about, both in theory and practice.

In shaping our own approach to these questions we have been influenced by sociological and anthropological as well as developmental psychological perspectives. In particular we have drawn on ideas developed in recent years by David Morgan (Morgan 1996, 1999) and used recently in research on divorce and separation (Smart and Neale 1999; Smart, Neale and Wade 2001). This work suggests that childhood and family life are helpfully seen as 'practices' developed in the context of daily experience rather than set pathways on which people are embarked, or life-stages they move through together. We like this theoretical approach to understanding adoption and its support because it can be used to bridge the gap we have identified, between what Bill Jordan calls the 'blood and guts codes' (Jordan with Jordan 2000, p.5) of everyday family life, as it is lived in the moment, and the relationship patterns and developmental associations that are laid out in the more distanced accounts of the academic researchers. Reflecting on our own exploratory studies (Hart and Thomas 2000; Hart *et al.* 2002; Luckock 1997, 2000), which involved talking with adoptive parents and their social work and therapeutic supporters, has confirmed the importance of this. We realised that success in getting and giving support that was really supportive depended on the negotiation of a shared understanding and vision of the realities and possibilities of family life in adoption. In the terms of the new sociology of the family, it was best therefore to see children, parents and professionals coming together in the joint 'practice' of constructing adoptive family life. Our use of the term 'practitioner' needs to be spelt out at this early stage in our book. For us, 'practitioner' is not simply another word for agency workers. Rather, we see children, parents and professionals all as adoption practitioners. Our understanding of the term then, is grounded in a sociological understanding of 'practice'.

From this 'practice' perspective we can see that things tend to go awry when too little attention is given to the process of establishing mutual understanding and respect, and when, consequently, the prescription of standard remedies substitutes for the negotiation of a tailor-made strategy. It is important not to see this as a one-way street. We are not simply setting 'user-led' approaches against 'profession-centred' service models and interventions. Instead we use the evidence of experience to challenge professional assumptions and methods that end up putting family life under more rather than less pressure. Children and parents have a right to expect accessible and responsive local services that leave them feeling they are personally respected and cared for as well as skilfully and efficiently advised and supported. They should also expect flexible therapeutic approaches that are carefully designed to enhance family relationships and routines when things go more seriously wrong. All too often the services are either lacking (Rushton and Dance 2002) or are unreliable, inefficient and ineffective (Parker 1999), the therapy unavailable, inappropriate or uncomprehending of the dynamics of adoption (McDaniel and Jennings 1997). The process of getting support can simply add to the stress of family life rather than relieve it, as parents and children get caught up in the bureaucracy, inflexibility and buck-passing of the professional world. New adoption legislation, policy and funding has kick-started change and improvement but no one should think there are any standard 'models' of support to take off the peg and apply.

However the evidence of the longitudinal research presents challenges to parents too. Unsurprisingly, we now have confirmation that adoption works best when adoptive parents have the emotional capacity to empathise with the trauma and grief of the abused and neglected children placed with them (Steele *et al.* 2003). They also need the skill and application to help those children find ways of talking about their feelings of anger, loss and difference (Howe and Feast 2000). Less certain is how these capacities and commitments are associated with the development of day-to-day practical strategies of behaviour management to help children settle happily and appropriately (Scott 2003). Research findings intended to disentangle and understand at least some of these differing requirements of adoptive parents are still awaited (Rushton and Monck in progress).

In the meantime the central message from experience and research is clear: success in adoptive family life requires professional supporters to become more responsive and competent but it also depends on the capacity of adoptive parents to accept and cope with the normally abnormal demands of family life following the adoption of abused and neglected children. Hence, so long as professionals are able to show a real commitment to a skilful and collaborative approach in supporting adoptive family 'practices', parents should expect to be invited to explore the implications of the empirical research on attachment and openness for their parenting. Arguably, once the practical arrangements are securely in place, the most important thing to be supported in 'adoption support' is the helping relationships formed when parents, professionals and others join together to design strategies that facilitate attachment and communication as well as manage and settle behaviour.

It is the nature and support of these helping relationships that provides the main focus of this book. The 'family practices' perspective certainly places children centre-stage in the process by which family is constructed and experienced. However it does so by recognising that children expect and want to organise their own lives and identities through family and other close relationships (Bell 2002). As a result, as well as avoiding an unnecessary polarisation between 'user' and 'professional' approaches to support, we are also wary of distinguishing between 'parent-centred' and 'child-centred' perspectives. Children have a right to expect safe adults to be available beyond the family to hear their personal concerns and, where necessary, to provide routes of escape from abusive family practices, adoptive as much as any other. Nonetheless a *narrow* 'child-centred' perspective, starting with the assumption that the interests of the child, defined individually, might conflict with those of their new parents, is not a productive point of departure.

Adoption support in the wider context

But why write a book about the support of new and permanent family life for children placed from care that only talks about adoption, and adoption from care within the UK at that? One answer is pragmatic, there is only so much that can be done in a single text. This explains, for example, why all our three case studies (see below) focus on the early weeks of adoptive family life where children have been adopted from care within the UK. Our choice to frame our discussion around what happens in these three case studies means that we have not dealt explicitly and systematically with issues that arise much further on in placement. However, much of what we do say here has general relevance to adoptive family life.

Our pragmatic stance also accounts for the lack of any discussion of the support that birth parents and relatives should receive in their own right when children have been placed for adoption. Any work to help former foster carers settle any ambivalent feelings they may have when children move on remains equally unexplored here.

However, there are other reasons too, why we have chosen to stand our discussion outside the conventional discourses of 'family support' and 'permanent family placement'. The distinctiveness of adoptive family life and its support, reinforced unequivocally in the Adoption and Children Act 2002, has always made it hard to place in the standard academic and practice categories. Despite all the talk of 'multiple family forms' and 'experiments in daily life' the sociology of 'the family' is largely silent on adoption. And comprehensive, helpful texts on 'family support' generally (Canavan, Dolan and Pinkerton 2000; Featherstone 2004) make little connection with the specific literature on adoption. Other commentators approach the question on the assumption that adoptive family life is an alternative to 'family support' work, made available when that work has been unsuccessful or inadequate (Tunstill 2003).

There is a commitment to 'mainstream' adoption support embodied in both adoption legislation (Adoption and Children Act 2002) and the broader government vision for universal parenting support (Department for Education and Skills 2003a). However, neither can be said to actually follow through this commitment with a consideration of what it might mean for adoptive families in practice despite the claim that *Every Child Matters* (Department for Education and Skills 2003a).

Similarly, the unique dynamic and identity of adoptive childhood tends to get obscured when adoption gets seen as one option among several for permanence (Thoburn 2001). Which is not to say that we have any sympathy with the view that other types of family placement cannot provide a real sense of permanence or family belonging. We know that in some circumstances foster care can certainly make children feel 'part of the family' (Schofield 2002). And we know that living with relatives and friends, when birth parents cannot offer the care needed, can provide the stability at least that foster care generally so often fails to achieve (Hunt 2003).

But our interest here is in adoption itself, and the generic emphasis of the literature on both 'family support' and 'permanent family placement' do not yet provide the best context for helping in the specific task of understanding and promoting effective support in this particular family world.

We return at the end of the chapter to the difficulties involved in both providing and receiving effective adoption support. First, however, we briefly map out the details and dimensions of the contemporary community of adoptive families and introduce our three composite case studies. These are not real families taken from practice or field research. However their family composition and experiences are derived directly from our own local evaluation studies.

Adoption today

A safe way of introducing the issues that arise when the nature of adoptive family life is considered is to start with the statistics. What are the characteristics of the contemporary adoptive family, constituted when children are placed from public care? How do the facts and figures help us begin to understand the special dimensions of adoptive childhood and parenting? But it is important also to put some faces on these facts and figures and get a glimpse of adoptive family life as it is often lived. So we combine our discussion of the demographics with three family scenarios of some typical dynamics of adoption. The scenarios, much like the statistics, are illustrative. They are drawn from the accounts of their own family life of the 34 parents in 22 adoptive homes we interviewed for an evaluation of local therapeutic support (Hart *et al.* 2002). We have also collated the reports of a further 46 adoptive parents who contacted us about our research following an advertisement we placed in *Adoption Today*. Finally, the perspectives of adoptive parents, adopted children and adoptive supporters in our own worlds have made their way into the scenarios. To disguise the identities of the real families we interviewed and of those people who are near and dear to us, we have never been explicit about precisely what comes from where. We return time and again to these imagined family worlds throughout the book in order to keep in mind how adoptive family life is actually led.

In the ten years since the implementation of the Children Act 1989 around 25,000 children were adopted from care. The rate has latterly been escalating, as practice falls in line with the requirements of New Labour family policy and the social inclusion agenda. Indeed the target set, of increasing numbers adopted by at least 40 per cent in the five years to March 2005 was on track to being achieved two years early. At present on average ten children are adopted from care every day in England, into eight families. Rather more than this number are placed but not subsequently adopted because around 8 per cent of placements disrupt prior to adoption (Department of Health 2002a).

In care adoption, family, for the most part, is being formed by parents and children who were hitherto strangers. Only about one in eight children get adopted by foster carers who have been looking after them already (Ivaldi 2000). And these strangers get started on their family life together rather late. Hardly any children placed from care get adopted before their first birthday. Most are well into their pre-school years, a few are almost halfway through their childhood. In fact the average age at adoption from care started to rise again in 2002, to four years six months, after it had dropped steadily since the mid 1990s. Of course age at adoption is not the same as age at placement. Hence when the 13 months it takes on average from placement to adoption is taken into account adoptive family life can be said to start somewhat earlier, when children are just over three years old.

And yet averages themselves are questionable. They certainly disguise extremely variable rates of progress for different children, through care to adoptive placement and then on to adoption itself. So for babies placed directly from hospital, perhaps as part of a 'concurrent planning' approach adoptive family life can start a few days after birth (Monck, Reynolds and Wigfall 2003). Meanwhile the six-year-old boy, finally removed permanently from his harmful parents, sometimes with his brother and sister and sometimes not, is just as likely to wait another two and a half years and more before he finally joins his new family (Department for Education and Skills 2003b).

The introduction in April 2003 of the new statutory requirement to consider a permanency plan at the statutory four-month review should now be hastening the process of decision including adoption. But it cannot in itself do much either to ensure children are removed more quickly from home or to secure a speedy placement once the adoption decision is taken. The Ivaldi survey (2000), although now already over three years old, indicates that, following that decision, boys will wait longer than girls and black children longer than white, a difference that increases with age. In any case the legacies of congenital risk, serious medical problems and developmental delay tend to keep those children affected in care longer.

Around one fifth of all adoptive families will include sibling groups (Rushton *et al.* 2001). Those children do not seem to wait longer, following the adoption decision, just because they are in a sibling group. Rather it is their age and other developmental factors that seem to explain any delay. Of course, as we cautioned above, figures taken retrospectively from the point of adoption itself can be somewhat misleading. In the case of delayed placement there is, for example, a suggestion that factors such as ethnicity and size of sibling group are under-estimated if one looks back from the adoption order. If the starting point instead is the group of children who have waited but never been placed it is these factors that often loom largest as is indicated by the early experience of the National Adoption Register (Department of Health 2003a). This experience goes some way to confirming research findings on rates of progress to placement following the agency decision to adopt (Selwyn *et al.* 2003), which show significant numbers of children for whom placements are not found.

Nonetheless, for those who are matched, it is certainly the case that different children arrive in their adoptive homes at different stages of life. Hence from the eight families adopting their ten children somewhere in England today we can expect roughly the following pattern at placement. Only two families would have welcomed infants under a year, in one case a baby less than six months old. Four families, perhaps five, would have taken children who were already one to four years old. Up and running so to speak. For one more family, or maybe two, their new children would already have been of primary school age for a year or longer by the time they arrived. Five of the ten children will be boys and five girls. Nine of them will be white and the tenth will very likely have a mixed ethnic heritage. And in one or two of these eight families the child in question will have been placed with one or more sibling.

The developmental legacy of the late arrival of children in adoptive homes is significant. Original fears about child development in adoption, of risky genetic inheritance and the effects of perceived loss in adolescence, have been increasingly superseded by concerns about the impact of early experience prior to placement. Age is almost universally identified as a risk factor for difficulties and disruptions in adoption but age is just a proxy for experience and reflection on it. So what do we know about the kind of early experience faced by children currently placed in adoptive homes? What would be the typical pattern of pre-placement care received by our ten children adopted today?

These questions are not easily answered. No national statistics are currently produced on the nature of the early experience and placement history of children adopted from care. Local authorities also, it seems (Rushton and Dance 2002), rarely record information in a way that would enable them to describe the characteristics of their local population of adopted children or their placement history.

Nonetheless what we do know is that eight or nine of our ten children will have been 'looked after' on a care order, meaning they will have been significantly harmed in the care of their birth parents, or been at risk of harm because of the quality of that care. This is not surprising when we also know how unsafe and unstable the original family homes are that these children were born into. The picture remains incomplete but the latest research findings paint a bleak scenario. Selwyn *et al.*'s study (2003) is the most comprehensive exposure of the family and parenting context from which children have been removed for adoption in the United Kingdom. Like many recent studies of care adoption (Lowe *et al.* 1999; Quinton *et al.* 1998; Rushton *et al.* 2001) the focus of the Selwyn study is on late-placed children, in this case three years and older. Children relinquished early by their birth parents and their family circumstances are thereby omitted. However, babies are just as likely to be removed as relinquished and smaller scale studies taking a sample either of the whole age range (Harwin, Owen and Forrester 2001) or of younger children alone (Neil 2000) do not substantially contradict the Selwyn account of birth family life. Of course by the time studies like these are published the circumstances of practice will already have changed.

The picture is fairly grim. Harm or the risk of harm, in the nine cases out of ten where it occurs, results from abusive and rejecting parenting in the context of general family hardship and neglect. In almost every case poverty and debt, alongside the debilitating effects of earlier emotional and social deprivation, provide the context for parenting. Nearly two thirds of the birth mothers in the Selwyn study (2003) had themselves been in care or special boarding school. Eighty per cent had no educational qualifications. Mental health problems are the common experience and learning difficulties prevail in a large minority of cases. Family life is characterised by domestic violence, which occurs in almost every case and by drug and alcohol misuse, which occurs in at least a half. As a result as many as six of our ten adopted children will have experienced a combination of abuse of one kind or another and neglect. Of these the Selwyn findings suggest that perhaps three will have been actively rejected in their birth families. This will be particularly so if they are boys. At least one of the six abused and neglected children will have been sexually assaulted. However it would be sensible to assume that one or two more may have been too. This is because a third of birth families include care-takers with a record of Schedule 1 offences.

On the current trend at least five of our ten children will have left these birth family homes before their first birthday, at least two within a month or so of birth (Ivaldi 2000). But even in those cases we now know, from the findings of neuroscience as well as developmental psychology (Siegel 1999; Glaser 1999), that a good deal of developmental damage will already have been done. Children's general health too will have suffered enormously (Hill *et al.* 2002). We say more about the emotional and interpersonal aspects of this damage in Chapter 2 when we explore the implications for the making of fresh attachments in the adoptive family home. When we use the term fresh attachments we recognise that whilst adoptive family life is a fresh start, it is never a clean break. The formation of fresh attachments is always influenced by the legacy of previous relationships.

But it is also important to remember that the physical health and development of adopted children is also affected by the birth family legacy. The Ivaldi survey helps here. It suggests that four of our ten adopted children will have at least one 'special need', where the definition includes 'a developmental or learning difficulty, medical problem or hereditary risk' (2000, p.23). Selwyn *et al.* present an even more challenging picture (2003). Their work suggests that as many as half of our ten children will have at least three significant problems such as learning difficulties, attachment issues and behavioural problems. Only 19 per cent of the children in their study were reported by their adoptive parents to have no significant difficulties.

Learning and health problems are, of course, exacerbated the longer children are left in their neglectful and violent homes. Here the legacy of professional delay in securing child safety and protection is also felt. Selwyn *et al.* (2003) show just how damaging the avoidant practice of the authorities and courts in the post-Children Act 1989 period has been. Hence 43 per cent of the children in their older sample had growth delay on final entry to care, 31 per cent problems with co-ordination and gross motor skills and 54 per cent speech delay and language difficulties. Only 15 per cent had no reported health problem. No fewer than 82 per cent were enuretic and 64 per cent encopretic on admission to care.

These developmental legacies are not played out in adoptive family life straight away. 'Corporate parenting' intervenes (eventually) and the care experience itself may alleviate the impact of early harm and set children off on a better developmental trajectory. A good deal of attention has recently been given to the deleterious effects of instability and transience in local authority care, exemplified in the Department of Health Quality Protects programme (1998a). Progress in areas of social and emotional development is certainly inhibited for children whose care plan is not decided and implemented (Harwin *et al.* 2001) although foster care for younger children can provide a transitional secure base (Dozier *et al.* 2001). However, there are few research studies that systematically explore the potentially beneficial impact of routine temporary foster care, prior to adoption placement.

Our first case study concerns a sibling group placement in which it is likely that several of these legacies are currently being played out. It is to a few moments in the early life of a family divided by two different surnames that we now turn, married couple Lucy and Bill Smith and the children who have been placed with them for adoption: Alan, Brian, Katie and Ellen Jones aged eight, five, four and eighteen months respectively.

Case study: The Smiths and the Joneses

Picture Alan. He's racing against his own personal best around the hall, bashing any kid, especially any little kid, who gets in his way. Every now and then he veers off his route to give his brother Brian, who's been sitting on his own all morning, a belt round the ear. Two scared, unhappy boys coping in their very different ways with their new family life. 'Stop running round now,' shouts Louise, the assistant play-scheme leader. 'Bloody weird kids these two boys', she says, louder than she thinks, to another worker. 'I'll have to talk to their mum. Something's up with both of them, autistic I reckon, or problems at home. We can't have that eight-year-old here any more, he's gonna kill someone.'

Half a mile down the road, at Happy Days nursery, four-year-old Katie's being a kitten. She pads around on all fours and purrs for conversation. Right now she's very sad because the nursery workers won't understand that cats can only drink from a saucer. The first time she refused to drink from a beaker they all thought it charming and put out a little bowl of milk for her on the play mat. But now, three days later, even though she rubs up against them nearly all the time, and even though she purrs loudly for her milk, they ignore Katie Kitten. After three days of this cat act, even the other kids have started to think that something's not quite right, and most run away when she starts to rub against them. So here she is, mostly ignored and scolded, but purring in ecstasy when she gets the odd stroke or pat.

At least her little sister Ellen's been quiet enough. She doesn't really move. She doesn't really cry. Even when she's hungry, even when she's thirsty, and even when her nappy needs changing. Feelings, thoughts and movement all closed down. Funny, thinks Narinda, the nursery worker, you'd reckon that kids with a posh mum like those two would be a bit more up with their developmental milestones.

In a darkened bedroom, lying on top of an unmade bed, prospective adopter Lucy is lying next to Bill, prospective adoptive dad. Her left hand is clenched tight in his right one. She tries to unfold her fingers, but they won't move, and then her whole arm refuses to budge from its position. It wouldn't matter, but she wants to look at her watch. One of them has got to pick up Katie and Ellen at twelve and then the boys at half past.

The alarm goes off. Lucy had set it. But Bill turns it off before it's hardly even bleeped, groans and puts his head under his pillow. He thinks to himself, how time flies when I'm trying to escape from the sibling group Lucy has chosen.

'Oh for god's sake, I'll go and get them then, shall I?' says Lucy. 'You could at least get up and try to clear up the kitchen so we can give them some lunch when I get back.' Bill mumbles something about how it was him who'd got up in the night, three times to calm down Brian's night terrors, and once to change Alan's wet bed. But Lucy is not listening. She's dragged herself up, and with a clenched fist dangling by her side, is busy picking her way over the toys and the pile of wet sheets, pillows and duvets on the landing. Lucy has got more important things than enuresis and night terrors on her mind. Like why the LEA caseworker didn't ring that morning to talk about the boys. She knows she needs some help; her own grasp on statements and learning difficulties feels very emergent. Lucy is also fretting because they've got to find a school for Alan very soon. If he ends up in a dodgy school, she's worried he'll be the only mixed-race kid in a class full of racist white kids. And then there's whether he ought to be still seeing Jason, the therapist. She can feel the panic concentrated in her neck and in her fist. They can't all stay here with me all day come September. It's all right for Bill, he's going back to work next week. Then Lucy really starts telling herself off. Why didn't I get a cleaner? What'll my mum say when she meets her new grandchildren at the weekend? I should have cleared up this mess, got some more cupboards when we bought their beds. I ought to get a book out of the library on how to deal with weird behaviour before my mum comes. I don't really want to be shouting at them in front of my mum and dad.

And on top of all this, her fist still won't unclench, and her arm won't be raised. She's quite worried about how she'll push the buggy like that.

Stepping slowly down the stairs, Lucy tries to keep her eyes a little bit shut. She just can't look at the suitcases and piles of clothes in the kids' bedrooms, and the toys she's just tripped over on the landing. She shuts her eyes tightly when she goes past the sitting room. She knows that some of Brian's shit is still on the walls, with a scrubbing brush and a bucket on the carpet underneath it. 'For Christ's sake, Bill. Get up and have another go at that stain, won't you? When Isabel comes this afternoon she'll take the bloody kids back off us if she sees all this crap.'

Until very recently 19 out of 20 new adoptive families have been headed by married couples like Lucy and Bill (Luckock and Clifton 2003). Indeed conventional normative parenting and household arrangements have prevailed far longer in adoption than in any other family form. Undoubtedly this came about in no small part as a result of agency requirements on the type of parents suitable to be prospective adopters. Income has come from paid employment, and agency data and experience have shown a traditional gendered division of caring and paid labour (Luckock and Clifton 2003). Adoptive fathers have tended to go out to work full-time and adoptive mothers to take the main responsibility for child care, often giving up or reducing paid work on placement of children. The educational achievements of adoptive parents are better than the average and hence the paid work, certainly of fathers, is often professional or managerial in nature. Most adoptive parents live in a house they own themselves, which is already a well-established home. This is partly because they become parents much later than average (Ivaldi 2000).

Of course, despite the traditional social convention, the adoptive family home has been changing in nature too. For some time now, in at least one family out of twenty, children have been placed with a single adoptive parent. The vast majority of these are women. These adoptive homes can differ significantly in other ways too from the married family norm. Locality and ethnicity are important discriminators. In general, single parent adopters are far more likely than married couples to have black and mixed heritage children placed with them (Ivaldi 2000). The status and age of the children placed with single adopters are important too, as many are often fostered first by their adoptive parent and consequently get adopted at a later age (Ivaldi 2000).

Our second case study is about adoptive parent Bella Freeman, her son Jon Freeman and prospective adoptive son Brad Taylor, aged seven and two. It draws on the experiences of parents who already have a biological son or daughter living with them when their adoptive child is placed.

Case study: Bella and Jon Freeman, and Brad Taylor

Number 22 Clayton Road is a messy little house, but it's full of toys and games and has got Jon's paintings plastered all over the walls. Three small bedrooms up the top. One long room on the middle floor, filled with junk mostly at the moment, but Bella is going to make it special for herself now that Brad's come to live with them.

A competent, successful paediatric nurse, right now Bella is off duty. In fact she's off for a while. She's got four months' adoption leave, and then she'll go back part-time. No more shift work. Right this minute, she's eating bread and vegetable soup in her kitchen with seven-year-old Jon and two-year-old Brad, Jon's brother of three weeks. One of the neighbours sent the soup round. Bella knows she's going to need all the friends she's got, and some more in the months and years to come. Shame her neighbour couldn't stop for lunch herself. So that just leaves this three-week-old family, Jon and Bella sitting on the bench behind the table, Brad in his new high chair. Getting to know each other's little ways.

'Mummy, Brad likes to feed himself. Why don't you let him?'

'Mind your own business Jon. Just keep out of it.'

'But he's my new brother, he's mine too.'

'Just shut up won't you?'

'I love my new little brother. He's got the same eyes and hair as me.'

Bella tries to shut out Jon's taunts and keeps her eyes on Brad. They sit there for ages, but she tells herself that it doesn't really matter if Brad doesn't eat. Best not to make it into a battle. It'll be ok. Brad won't have to go to hospital again, as long as she gives him his special diet. Bella had learnt that lesson the hard way. Brad had become floppy and started twitching three days after he had moved in. It had been hard enough for them to keep up with the blood sugar monitoring with everything else that'd been going on. Jon to look after. Stuff to buy. Professionals to liaise with. Allowances to fight for. Bonding to attempt. Then suddenly she'd found herself with Brad, limp in her arms, very pale. Bella had to move fast. Ambulance siren. Doctors, nurses she knew from work, but didn't yet know as Brad's new mum, prodding and poking the new boy. Making him scream with their needles and potions. She'd been worried that they wouldn't be able to control his blood sugars in the hospital and that he would be brain damaged. But things turned out ok. She's thinking, I've got it sussed now, he'll be all right even if he doesn't eat his lunch. And anyway, he'll probably eat if he doesn't think I care whether he does or not. And so what if Jon's being a bit obnoxious? At least he's getting on well with Brad. That's what kids do, test your patience, wind you up and never say thank you. Brad does it more than Jon ever did though.

Bella thinks that she'll be lucky to get through the day without braining one of the kids. But at least Jenny's coming round later. She can always chat to Jenny.

Brad beams at Jon and then spits the soup right into his new mum's eyes. A 'reflex action', Bella smacks Brad hard across the face. She thinks, any normal kid would stop it now. But paradoxically reassured by the look of rage on Bella's face, Brad picks up his bread and butter and rubs it in his own hair. He's angrily trying to get control of at least one part of his out-of-control life. Jon is thrilled by Brad's courage. He thinks how he never dared do anything like that when he was little. And Jon can't believe what Bella has just done. She's never lifted a finger to him in his life.

'Eat your soup Brad.' Bella hardly knows what she's shouting now. She can't bear the children's intimacy, she's livid about being left out. And she's used to being obeyed. But that's not happening today. Brad's screaming and spitting. Bella is shoving and shouting. The doorbell rings and Bella looks away for a second. Brad hurls his bowl at the window. The neighbour's soup is now dripping down the glass. Brad's somehow calmer now.

'I'll go.' Oh god, what a way for a social worker to see us, thinks Bella. What a mess I'm making of all this. But maybe she'll give me a hand. 'Ok Jon, you go, but don't...' 'Don't what?' 'Never mind. Just go on then darling.'

Jon races up the stairs, opens the door and invites Jenny in. What a polite, nice lad he is, thinks Jenny. Great placement. Lucky Brad. Jon leads her down the stairs. He's talking very loudly above the din of Brad's screaming. Bella doesn't move. She sits and stares at the window. 'Mummy's got cross with Brad. She hit him. Brad won't eat the nice soup Louise made for us. I've eaten mine.'

Jenny puts a hand on Bella's shoulder, and smiles down at her eye to eye. 'Oh dear, having a hard time. Cumulative wind up, is it? D'you want to go upstairs and I'll clean up this mess and make us a coffee?' Bella gets up without a word and climbs the stairs to the junk room she's planning to make special. She shuts the door, trying to drown out Brad's screams, puts the telly on very loud, moves the piles of washing from the sofa to the floor, and lies down. Tears wobble on her chin as she tried to watch the news. Bad things are happening in the world. And above the din of a toddler screaming his guts out, this competent paediatric nurse wonders just what fate her social worker's got in store for her.

As our case study illustrates, Bella has made the positive choice to tackle adoptive family life without another adult carer in the house. But for others, as Triseliotis and colleagues have reflected (Triseliotis, Shireman and Hundleby 1997), some nominally single-parent adoptions probably include a second (unmarried) parent. The Lowe *et al.* (1999) study suggested as much. And we know that some of these nominal single parent adoptive families include same-sex couples, who may be lesbian or gay (Hicks 2000; Hicks and McDermott 1999). It is too soon to say to what extent the demography of adoption will be changed by the late and hesitant inclusion in the Adoption and Children Act 2002 of the permission for any couple to seek to adopt. Local adoption agency attitudes are arguably as important in this respect as legal reform and they certainly vary across the country, with some now placing more and more children in households headed by lesbians or gay men.

There is also now a shift more generally towards the legitimisation of the sexual diversity of partnership, parenting and family life (see also Department of Trade and Industry 2003). In these circumstances adoption from care is likely to prove as attractive an option to same-sex as it is to opposite-sex partners who are keen to start or extend a family. And institutionalised forms of discrimination will be opened up more readily to scrutiny and change as a new mixed constituency of adoptive families emerges. Our final case study draws on the experiences of same-sex adoptive couples. Bryony Hall and Rachael Cunningham have had six-year-old Luke Forster and his four-year-old sister Debbie placed with them three weeks ago.

Case study: Bryony Hall, Rachael Cunningham, and Luke and Debbie Forster

Bryony has just been on the phone to Stonewall. A press officer was ringing to see if they'd have their picture taken for a positive feature in the Daily Mail. Trusted journalist. Deals sympathetically with the issues. Bryony said 'no thanks'. She said that they didn't want to be a family of zoo animals for the nation to stare at, particularly before they were official. She won't tell Rachael about the call when she get back from work. Rachael would have said 'Go for it. Let them know that we're out and proud.' But Bryony can't think about all that sexual politics stuff now. She's got a little girl to pick up from nursery. 'Come on Luke, turn the video off and let's go and get Debbie.' Bryony is pleased the nursery's just round the corner. They didn't have a clue which one to choose, so they went for the nearest one. Same approach with the school for Luke. Nearest seemed best. But then they got to hear that he had some sort of educational support plan from his old placement that suggested he move to a special school. Bryony and Rachael didn't really understand why, but they thought they'd better take a look at some special schools if they could find any. Dave, their social worker, offered to come with them to look, but he doesn't have any kids himself and said he didn't know much about schools. So it didn't seem worth them all trekking round them. Bryony went to the nearest special school that catered for children with moderate learning and behavioural difficulties and it seemed nice enough, and had one place in a class of children Luke's age. She's shocked, though, that it's nine miles away and that Luke will have to be transported there by taxi.

Rachael trusted her decision, but Bryony is a bit worried that nobody else has been in on the choice of schools for Luke. His social worker had said he'd got some learning difficulties, but she didn't really know the details, and she hadn't yet managed to get to talk to his old teacher. To Bryony, Luke seems a bright little boy, and anyway, she'd read something in the Guardian about kids with learning difficulties going to ordinary schools now. But then she's never had much to do with other six-year-olds, so what did she know?

'Soon it'll be you I'll be coming to pick up sometimes, Luke. Me and Debbie will get the bus out to your school, you won't always have to go in that taxi,' Bryony's hand is tight in his. 'Be more exciting than staying at home all day with mummy Bryony or mummy Rachael. Are you looking forward to starting school?'

Luke's not thinking about school. He's miserable. He's missing Lindsey and Dave, his foster mum and dad and their nine-year-old daughter Tammy.

He and Debbie loved racing round the garden with her, chasing each other in and out of the paddling pool. Watching telly late on Friday and Saturday night with a big box of sweets on their laps. He couldn't believe his luck ending up there after the terrible time he had with his parents. Hardly ever being fed wasn't so bad, it was the daily beatings and the sexually exploitative relationship he had with his dad that really upset him. Luke wants his cul-de-sac council house back. He doesn't like Bryony and Rachael's big town house. He wants his old corner shop, where he raced along to get his sweets on Saturday mornings. And his old 'not forever family', as Lindsey called it. 'We're here for as long as you need us Luke. 'Til they find you and Debbie a very special new mum and daddy. Then they'll be your forever family.'

If he's very, very good then maybe he can go back to Lindsey and Dave. Once, last week, when he was feeling this massive lump inside him, he knew just what it was and he'd said he was missing Lindsey. Rachael had said not to worry, he'd soon settle down with them and forget all about Lindsey, and she'd seemed a bit cross with him about it, although she'd tried not to show it. So, right now, walking along past the new corner shop he's not allowed to go to on his own, he doesn't tell Bryony how sad he is. He acts cheerful. 'Yeah. That'll be nice, starting my new school,' he says, trying to make himself feel better. 'Can't wait.'

They get to the nursery quickly and Debbie races into Luke's arms. She ignores Bryony, who tries to prise her from Luke. This makes Debbie cling more firmly to her brother. Bryony tries to act normal. 'Hello darling. You had a good morning? Time for lunch now. Home with mummy Bryony and Luke.' Then leaving Debbie in her embrace with Luke she turns to Lesley the nursery worker to ask how Debbie's been on her first morning. 'Not too bad. She's obviously finding it a bit difficult to settle. Cries quite a bit and isn't really playing with the other kids yet. She bit somebody this morning, but we didn't make too much of a fuss about it. The change must be hard for her. Might help if she brings in something special from home, she got a special toy or something?'

'Yes,' says Bryony. 'We got her a new rabbit when she moved.' 'Oh right,' says the worker, who really meant bringing in something older, from wherever it was she lived before. 'That'd be good then.'

They're going back past Luke's new corner shop now. Bryony is letting him push Debbie. Luke's feeling very grown up.

'You can have a new pencil case when you go to school, if you like,' offers Bryony, enjoying the stroll with the children in the sun. 'Thanks. That'd be nice,' says Luke. But he's thinking he'd rather take the furry one he got from Dave and Lindsey for Christmas. He doesn't want a new pencil case, and when he goes to his new school he doesn't want to wear his new uniform. He wants to wear his old one. He loved his old school where Tammy used to look after him at playtime.

That night, when the strange new house is all dark and quiet, and when his strange new mums have gone to bed, Luke will put on his old school uniform over his brand new Spiderman pyjamas. He'll take the photograph of his 'not forever' family out from his secret hiding place. Then, clutching Lindsey, Dave and Tammy tight in his fist, he'll cry himself to sleep and dream of having a proper forever family; one just up the road from his own corner shop.

Luke's grief and sense of displacement remind us that adoption will only be effective if the adoptive family is seen, by adoptive parents and adoption supporters alike, as intrinsically embedded in what we describe in Chapter 2 as a 'wider adoptive kinship network'. By kinship network we mean that set of relationships and affiliations created when a child moves from one family context to a separate and new one. Yet any attempt to map the typical dimensions of contemporary adoptive kinship is currently an almost impossible task. Neither the sociologists of the family nor the social policy analysts have explored in any depth this aspect of adoption and its implications for support. What we do know, from experience as much as research, is that kinship in adoption is marked by fragmentation and diversity. For example, some eight out of ten children placed for adoption have brothers and sisters by the time they are adopted (Ivaldi 2000). Some, like those in our first and last case studies, leave their birth family permanently and get placed together. But many do not and even for Luke, Debbie and the others, new birth siblings may come along once they have left their original home.

In fact the very idea of a birth family home is itself questionable. The dispersed nature of sibling networks is just one aspect of the general tendency of dissolution that characterises birth family relationships in adoption. Hence, whilst it is often possible to start to map the blood kinship of adopted children through their birth mothers the paternal links can be very difficult to sketch out. Lack of knowledge here results from the fact that fathers are often transient figures. National surveys (Ivaldi 2000) show that in only a quarter of cases have birth fathers held parental responsibility for their children. Scrutiny of local files shows that by the time children are adopted as few as one fifth of fathers will still be living in the family home (Luckock and Clifton 2003).

Once efforts are made to track and chart adoptive kinship networks the diversity of the family worlds brought into alignment by adoption of children from care is brought into sharp relief. Differences of 'race' and ethnicity have attracted most attention here (Kirton 2000; Thoburn, Norford and Rashid 2000) but the class and cultural chasm between the birth and the adoptive family is significant too. The fact is that adoption brings together largely young, poorly educated and socially marginalised birth parents (in reality usually mothers) and generally well-educated and socially successful adoptive parents. Achieving a settled adoptive family life requires this diversity of experience, as well as its fragmentation, to be taken into account.

Difficulties in giving and receiving effective support

We said earlier in this chapter that making sense of adoptive family lives as they are lived in practice and developing a vision of effective adoption support is itself a good deal easier said than done. The ambivalence about adoption, which as we shall see more fully in later chapters is embedded in law, policy, professional and adoptive family practice, makes it a tricky area in which to do unequivocal good. Some other risks make for a long list: the weaknesses in the law and policy to give adoptive families strong rights to multi-disciplinary support; insufficient knowledge and experience of adoption workers to practice or supervise effectively; repeated and bureaucratic assessments, competing claims to authority by different professionals; institutional and individual inertia, prioritisation of resources for use elsewhere; unnecessary service duplication and administrative inefficiency.

Many of the above risks apply to children's services more generally, and we pick up on them in other chapters. Our remaining task in this chapter, though, is to explore in a little more depth what we see as three of the main reasons behind the difficulties in giving and receiving effective adoption support. These are: the ambivalent status of adoptive families; the lack of definitive guidance about how adoption is best supported and, finally, the limited adoption competence amongst professional workers.

Regarding the first reason, debates abound about how far adoptive families and their support should be understood within normative frameworks of family life (Barth and Miller 2000; Wegar 2000). Late arrival in placement accentuates further the difference between the 'birth' of the adoptive family, including its conception and gestation, and birth in the 'procreational' family. Neither the normative rituals nor the commonality of experience of early childhood and parenting are available as foundations for family formation. Instead adoptive family life always starts too late for this kind of reassurance.

Hence for some commentators, key here is the role that genetic procreativity plays in the organisation of social life. In these versions of the adoption story, the fact that adoptive families get stigmatised and shunned by others in society looms large (Akhtar and Kramer 2000; Wegar 2000). However, there is also a completely different tale up for the telling. Some see adoptive families as an exemplary form of family headed by parents who have been selected as better than average (Kaniuk 1992). These debates can easily become polarised into splits between idealisation and denigration. And they can become internalised in the minds of adoptive family members themselves, as well as adoption supporters.

Whether processes of denigration, idealisation or something more fragmented and complex is going on, it makes sense for us to see adoptive families as being in some way different from other families. The legacies that children bring to them ensure, often in a very dramatic way, that this so. The routes of adoptive parents to family life too demand that a different birth and family story be told to that of their friends visiting midwives and attending birth preparation classes.

But precisely how different are adoptive families? What form does that difference take and what kind of support might adoptive families need in dealing with it? Whatever the answer to these questions, we certainly know from other studies that family life can be very hard work for those that do not correspond to dominant and normative family forms, however hard they might sometimes try to. Black and mixed race families, those headed by single parents, lesbians and/or gay men, or families where disablement is a regular part of family life certainly all come to mind here.

As people struggle to fit with, or to reject the norms and values of others around them, the fragility of family life can often feel like it needs explicit shoring up. Dealing with prejudice and discrimination, as well as the complexities of identity are part of the daily life of families whose difference is devalued or misunderstood. The experiences of adoptive families accessing support intersect with many such families. Uncertainties about sameness and difference and their consequences are often in the minds of family members. This goes for adoption supporters too, who despite their best intentions, often do not quite understand what the take on adoptive families should be. Decisions about the degree, nature and purpose of external involvement in such contested family lives are then never going to be easy. All the more reason, as we argue later, to ground decisions to intervene in a thorough understanding of what actually goes on in adoptive families.

The second reason why it is often tricky to know what to do is that there is not much research evidence on what constitute the most effective sources of support in adoption. We have already drawn attention to the emergent evidence base from which we have developed many of our own arguments in this book. Later on, we explore the policy and legal context within which new plans for adoption support are being developed. However, parents, children and professionals face some very real dilemmas about how to proceed in a way that works best. Chapters further on in this book explore the evidence underpinning practice responses to different aspects of support service provision.

Our first two reasons for why it is hard to give and to receive effective adoption support contribute to the third. Adoption competence in the context of such ambivalence about adoptive families, and of the fairly thin evidence base about what interventions work best, is a tall order. In Chapter 4 of this book we deal in some detail with the issue of precisely what constitutes adoption competence, and how to go about developing it. At this point suffice it to say that there is much work to be done.

Research suggests that many of the routine professionals who come into contact with adoptive families are likely to be as adoption 'blind' as nursery worker Narinda in the earlier scenario based on Lucy and Bill's family (Hart *et al.* 2002; Howe 2003; McDaniel and Jennings 1997). Although she was puzzled by Katie and Ellen's behaviour and their lack of developmental progress, it did not occur to her that the two girls might not be Lucy's biological children. In line with normative constructions of family composition, she simply assumed that these family members were biologically related. However, Lucy did not explicitly mention to the nursery that her children were newly placed with them. Hence Lucy's apparent ambivalence about the status of her family, and her uncertainty about how 'out' she should be about it, feeds into Narinda's normative constructions.

By contrast, Bryony and Rachael are certainly being more open about their family formation. However, they themselves do not understand the consequences of Luke and Debbie's legacies for their parenting. It is left to Debbie's nursery worker Lesley to demonstrate a sensitive understanding of the consequences of adoption. In possession of such skills as a routine professional, she is certainly something of a rare resource. But this case study shows that knowledge, competence and being adoption sensitive are still not enough; Lesley will have to be more assertive with Bryony and Rachael if her knowledge and sensitivity is to be put to good use in this particular situation.

The lack of adoption competence illustrated here does not simply apply to routine generalist like Narinda and Debbie. Statistically speaking, adoption support workers Isabel, Jenny and Dave are just as likely than not to be fairly unclear how to help these families in a way that makes them feel that they've got somebody who really knows what they are doing alongside them (Parker 1999). In our vignette about Bella's family, Jenny gets off to a good start by both empathising and offering practical support to Bella. But she'll have a lot more work to do over the coming years if Bella is to feel that she's really had some good support in helping Brad to settle.

Whatever Jenny does next, at least she has emotionally engaged with the family, and has offered some useful containment to Bella. As we shall see later in this book, having strategies to deal with difficult behaviour and knowledge of the consequences of abusive and neglectful histories all have a central place in skilled adoption work. But unconscious processes resulting in the avoidance by professionals of the peculiar pain and anxiety that get generated in adoption must also be seen as threats to adoption competence. The classic work of Menzies-Lyth (1988) and more recently Laming's report on the Climbié Inquiry (Laming 2003) powerfully remind us that bureaucratic structures and the pressures of working life often defensively place professionals too far from the experiences of struggling families either to care, or to be of any help to them. Rogers describes the move away from defensive practice as a re-unification of the professional mind with the heart (2001, p.182). Of course proper support must in turn be given to professional workers if they are to cope with intensity of this nature. All to often this is lacking, although there are certainly pockets of excellence around the country. As the Rushton and Dance survey shows (2002), there is a lot of work to be done if adoption competence is to be achieved on a national footing. The chapters that follow in this book go some way towards indicating how adoption competence might be improved both in adoption supporters and in adoptive parents themselves.

Structure of the book

One major step on the road to adoption competence is really understanding and engaging with what goes on in families such as those of Lucy and Bill, Bryony and Rachael, and Bella. In the following chapter we introduce the sociological concepts of family practices and narratives as tools to use in thinking about the meaning and experience of adoptive family life. The legacies of abuse and neglect and the way in which they affect relationships between parents and children in adoptive family life are considered as part of this discussion. So, too, we explore the meaning of adoptive parents' legacies for joint family life in the making. We make the point in Chapter 2 that children and their new parents come to adoptive family life from very different starting points, and with different family histories already underway. What needs supporting then, we argue, is a collaborative process between parents and children of making up for a mutual family past that has been denied to all its members. This same point is elaborated on in later chapters.

In Chapter 3 we outline the contents of contemporary law and policy in relation to adoption support, as well as providing a critique of them. Here, we show how 'ambivalence' about the nature of adoptive family life has had an important role to play in constructing contemporary law and policy. We celebrate the potential for positive shifts to occur as a result of a specific commitment to adoption support from the centre. Nevertheless, we also lament the possibilities for support services to develop within the framework as cautious, bureaucratic and uncreative. In this respect we are particularly concerned that children and parents have been kept in their traditional subordinate place, rather than being included, as they are in other areas of family support, as partners and collaborators in service provision.

Chapter 4 sticks with the potential promises and limitations of the law and policy response, however it hones in on one particular aspect of service provision, namely the role of the Adoption Support Services Advisor (ASSA) and other providers of routine adoption support. We set out in some detail the law and policy guidance in relation to the function of the ASSA and related roles.

Following that, we offer an evidenced-based exploration of the relative merits of different models for support roles of this kind. Here we emphasise the importance of both a therapeutic and a brokerage role for the ASSA.

In Chapter 5 we deal specifically with formal therapeutic interventions and their role in strengthening the capacity of the attachment/care-giving relationship in adoptive families. We explore the relative effectiveness of different therapeutic modes and methods in achieving this central goal. Nevertheless, we do not lose sight of the fact that the provision of formal therapy always happens in a wider context. Key here is our focus on how it can enhance the routine supports of day-to-day family life, rather than displace them. The chapter also returns to a major contention of adoptive family life in its exploration of how difficult it can be for family members to risk therapeutic engagement. This discussion once again brings to the fore in our book the defensive, painful and difficult feelings that are so familiar in adoption and that make the work that has to be done so emotionally exhausting.

Chapter 6 stays with defensiveness and distress, but moves the discussion on further to consider problems of openness in communicating with children about their pasts and its meaning for their lives in the present. We pick up on debates introduced in earlier chapters to think in some detail about what support is needed by families if they are explicitly to co-construct a family script. Here we argue that past legacies and other adoptive kinship relations need to be addressed sensitively, but honestly, if children are to be helped to settle. As part of our discussion of openness in communication, this chapter also considers the purpose of different forms of contact.

Chapter 7 ends the book with a further move outwards from the adoptive family, towards their participation in what we call 'communities of adoptive practice'. Here we draw on a body of literature with its roots in social anthropology as our inspiration to consider ways in which adoptive parents, children, their former carers, adoption supporters and others can actively collaborate in the joint venture of settling children in adoptive families. The chapter argues for a shift towards this kind of work culture in adoption support, and through a discussion about cultivating communities of adoptive practice, suggests practical and specific ways in which such work might be got underway.

For the moment, though, we leave these bigger and broader issues of structure and culture of support provision aside. Our main task in the chapter that follows is to introduce the concept of adoptive families' practices and explain how we think it is helpful in thinking about adoption support.

Chapter 2

Understanding Adoptive Childhood and Family Life

Family Practices and Narratives as the Context for Adoption Support

Introduction

Understanding what is going on in families like those of Lucy and Bill, Bella, Bryony and Rachael, and providing a vision for helping them achieve a good enough family life, is the purpose of our book. In this chapter we begin to develop a fresh way of thinking about adoptive childhood and family life, which we use to inform the proposals we make later for both service development and professional practice. In order to do this we first take a step outside customary explanations of the dynamics of adoption.

The nature and effect of Brad's anger on his attachment to Bella, the implications of Luke's loss of his foster parents and the explanation of the troubled and troublesome behaviour of Alan, Brian, Katie and Ellen, for example, will need consideration. A good deal of what follows sets the scene for doing just this. But we want to begin elsewhere, with the day-to-day experience of adoptive family life in the making, as it is lived, and with theories that convey this most effectively.

New sociological accounts of childhood and family life combine with the contemporary anthropology of kinship to provide us with a point of departure. These perspectives are helpful because they put considerations of 'child development' and 'parenting' in adoption, the usual focus of attention in professional texts like this one, in a family and kinship context. Adoption brings together children and their original kinship network, adoptive parents and their family and social world and social work and other professionals in a process of family re-construction or, as some would say, re-invention (Beck-Gernsheim 2002). We need a way of thinking about this process that captures its daily reality and its distinctiveness – what makes the construction of adoptive family life both familiar, so to speak, and yet so different. The immediacy of adoptive family life and its often uncertain and ambiguous, fraught and contested nature needs recognition.

Hence our starting point is not with theories and research which explain and examine 'family' as if it was largely a given *structure* that people join and 'adjust' or 'adapt' to but with those that see 'family' as a *process*. Adoptive childhood, family life and kinship do not simply involve roles and relationships scripted in advance and measured against an amended lifecycle or life-course template. Instead adoptive family life has the quality of something that is performed, the script developed and re-developed as the real-life drama unfolds. Improvisation tends quickly to take over as daily reality, often exhausting and upsetting, derails any prescribed story lines. We argue that families are *performed* through what is done or practised and through the way these practices are explained or narrated. Thus our first turn is towards sociology, and to a discussion of what we have termed 'adoptive family practices' and 'adoptive family narratives'.

Furthermore, our particular emphasis is on the *distinctive difference* represented by adoption as a family practice and narrative. It is also on the circumstances, involving mechanisms of vulnerability and protection alike, which make the construction of adoptive childhood and family life more or less enjoyable and successful. These mechanisms operate at the socio-cultural level, where children and parents may, for example, continue to experience stigma. Recent government policies may have reasserted the social value of adoptive family life, and reinforced the legitimacy of a diversity of family and parenting arrangements (Department of Health 2000a). However, traditional kinship norms (of blood ties and heterosexual procreation) remain at the heart of contemporary Western culture. And the personal experience of loss in adoption has to be managed in this context.

Difference derived from the particular socio-cultural *status* of adoption is reinforced by the distinctive nature of the psycho-social *relationships* that get formed when a child is placed permanently with new parents. For childhood and family life to be settled and successful adopted children have to be enabled to forge a (secure enough) fresh attachment to their primary carers. And parents have also to recognise and accept the difficult legacies (of genes, temperament and experience) that routinely interrupt and delay 'normal' child development and social relationships. Adopted children and families tend to stick out from the rest for developmental as well as socio-cultural reasons. As a result, any understanding of the dynamics of the family practices and narratives of adoption, especially of adoption from care, must draw on both approaches.

In due course a sociology of contemporary adoptive family life and kinship will, we hope, develop and attempts will no longer need to be made to simply fit adoption into conventional developmental theories of the family lifecycle and the parent–child relationship. In the meantime the approach we take here is pragmatic. We use aspects of the recent sociology of the family in order to emphasise the exploratory, constructed and distinctive nature of adoptive family life and kinship, and to provide a fresh and, we hope, productive frame of reference for some of those developmental theories.

Understanding adoptive childhood and family life: Practices and narratives in a context of difference

In contemporary policy accounts a rather limited psycho-social perspective has been employed almost exclusively to define child development and childhood, parenting and family relationships in child welfare. It now forms the officially sanctioned approach to the understanding and assessment of child and family 'need' (Department of Health 2000b; Ward and Rose 2002). In adoption the dominant psycho-social focus has, if anything, been even narrower. It is as if attachment (together with trauma) has become the beginning and end of the story of family life and relationships, or as Howe and colleagues have asserted, 'the theory that subsumes and integrates all others' (1999, p.10). We think, in these circumstances, that it may be time to step back a little and look first at what might be going on through a different lens. The official Department of Health account of the dimensions of 'parenting capacity', and the academic exploration of 'attachment patterns', might provide fruitful conceptualisations for making sense of adoption. But for Bella and the rest, especially at the moment, family life has a far more diffuse and elusive feel to it. It has to be managed on several different fronts if the struggle to establish any semblance of order is to succeed. We need a way of thinking about family that captures this process of struggle across contexts if practice is to make sense of and engage with the realities of adoptive family life.

The recent sociology of family life (Cheal 2002) speaks of childhood rather than child development, parenthood not parenting capacity, and family life itself as something that is achieved rather than simply socially prescribed or naturally determined. In similar vein social anthropologists point to the constructed nature of kinship itself, where relatedness in and beyond the immediate family is developed across time out of varying combinations of blood ties and shared experience (Carsten 2000). In these respects adoption is just another way of 'doing' childhood, parenthood and kinship in a world where diversity and fluidity characterise family formation and family life. Where it is distinctive, of course, is in the fact that professionals must always be part of the picture, adding 'corporate' parenting into the family and kinship mix. This is the first difference presented by adoption and it means that the construction of adoptive childhood and family life is an especially complex process – more deliberate, explicit and formally negotiated than in almost any other case. From the sociological perspective, then, family life can be seen as a set of practices engaged in by different individuals and in adoption this includes a significant role for professionals.

Family practices

In using the concept of 'family practices', and in extending it to include the idea of 'family narratives', we draw on the analysis of Morgan (1996, 1999) and two key points he makes in respect of the way in which family gets constructed. First the process has to be seen as a practical matter, 'a focus on the everyday' (1999, p.17), and on routines and regularities of family living in a social context. In this way activities and behaviours, e.g. feeding children, deciding on which television programme to watch, going on outings and so on, are the means by which families constitute themselves as well as the means, for example, by which individual children grow healthily and develop interests.

Family is practised in the moment in a stream of encounters and events, the experience of which is a reminder of the kind of family one belongs to. Silva and Smart refer, in this respect, to what they call 'a basic core' of activities, 'the sharing of resources, caring, responsibilities and obligations' (1999, p.7). Family life itself takes on a pattern and shape for the simple reason that people become more practised at managing the day-to-day routines together in ways that accommodate their individual aspirations and collective family interests. This is something that professionals hoping to be helpful need particularly to bear in mind. Family life in the moment is a very *practical* matter and it is practical help that constantly makes a difference.

The example of Bella's family life is instructive here. Jenny, the social worker, will need to give Bella time and space to explore and settle her feelings about 'losing it' with Brad and about her struggle to tune into her new son. But Bella is as likely as most adoptive parents to get extremely annoyed if Jenny cannot also come up with some actual strategies to help her get through mealtimes without confrontation and violence. Making the tea and providing the short break helps enormously too. Over time, and in most cases adoptive family practices, like any family practices, settle into a routine, and adoptive childhood and family life comes to take on a life of its own.

The second main point about 'family practices' is that the process is one of both action and imagination. Parents, children and other family members construct their particular family life by reference to images and expectations of family as they go about their day-to-day lives together and they do so with purpose. A dominant strand of contemporary sociological thinking places particular emphasis on individual agency, the conscious and deliberate stance people occupy as they go about planning their life as if it were a project to be managed successfully. From this perspective it is important to see children themselves as social actors in their own right with sufficient competence and capability, or at least potential for such, to contribute purposefully to the creation of their own family and social worlds. This is the message of research findings from the social studies of childhood (James, Jencks and Prout 1998). The competence children bring to the process of practising family depends a great deal, as we will see, on the quality of the parental care they receive. But children in any case make sense of their experiences at the time in their own terms. Children 'do' their own childhood, alongside other children, even if it is within particular emotional and social constraints. In this way, too, childhood can be seen as a culture in its own right as well as a foundation for adult life as anyone observing in a playground will confirm.

Of course this will sound like so much academic hot air just at the moment in the family lives of Lucy and Bill, Bella, Bryony and Rachael. There is a real danger of romanticising adoptive childhood and forgetting just what a struggle it often is for adoptive parents and children alike to create the conditions under which it becomes a settled experience. It is still most often adoptive mothers who take on the main care-giving responsibility and the research evidence on the pressures put on mothers generally, by expectations that they should create a harmonious as well as productive childhood (Walkerdine and Lucey 1989), applies equally in adoptive family practice too. Adoptive parents can get trapped in the house too, fearful of exposing the socially unacceptable behaviour of their children and their 'failure' to be competent parents. And adoptive childhood is hard work, as well, for the children who are expected to benefit from it.

Meaning and significance, therefore, are given by family members partly through a process of 'explicit monitoring of one's own routine practices against some standard of normality' (Morgan 1999, p.19). Attachment theory explains the emotional basis of these kinds of reflections, where individuals make sense of who they are within the context of specific care-giving or attachment relationships. By contrast the sociological focus is on wider social and cultural perceptions and identifications. Morgan points to the specific influence of professional and other agencies and of academic observers in providing accounts of family practices that contribute to this process. This rings especially true for adoption as a family practice. And arguably the more vulnerable a family is the more likely are professional perspectives to have a role in shaping family practice. Hence, for Bella, because her own parenthood remains conditional, being shared with the 'corporate' parent in the form of Jenny the social worker, she has no choice but to engage with the professional image and expectation of her family.

Bella, Brad and Jon have clearly yet to establish the necessary mutual expectations to make the routine family practice of mealtimes together a settled and enjoyable experience. They are each still making sense of this for themselves. But because adoption, at least at this early stage, is a joint practice with the professionals, Jenny's perceptions remain hugely influential in this process. This happens indirectly as well as directly. The dynamics will be complex but we might safely predict that Bella, already troubled by her loss of control, is going to be particularly vigilant, as Jenny, in what she says and does next, makes clear what the professional reading of events is to be. For at the moment at least it is still the social worker who can decide whether family should be practised at all by Bella, Jon and Brad.

Family narratives and kinship

'Standards of normality' are drawn on by people as they practise and reflect on family with each other and, where necessary, with professionals. These get incorporated in the narrative account that family members develop to explain their family life as they live it out together. As Morgan says, 'family practices are not just any old practices' (1996, p.193) and practice alone does not make perfect in this case. It is through what we call the 'narrative practices' of family life that people fit day-to-day events and experiences into an unfolding and distinctive family story. The family meaning of family practices has to be voiced in order for a sense of belonging to be established and consolidated. Family members in all cases tell the story of their family life to themselves and others as an integral part of the process of family formation. One further way in which adoptive family life differs from that established through procreation, or that re-established through separation and divorce, is that both the family narrative or story and the parenting practices and strategies that it incorporates usually have to be more explicit. From an anthropological perspective Howell (2002) describes this as being 'self-conscious' kinship construction, which neatly encapsulates the active and reflective nature of the process. Family narratives generally serve to enable people to link themselves in time as well as place. The practice of family in the present can be securely anchored in a shared story about continuities with family practices in the past. This provides a story line sufficiently familiar, coherent and reassuring, all being well, for a family future to be contemplated together in optimistic anticipation. Adoptive family narratives have to be worked at more 'self-consciously' than most for two reasons. The first has to do with the painful emotional dynamics of adoption. As Simmonds (2000) reminds us, some adoption stories are easier to tell than others. The second is that the link between past and present in adoption cannot be taken for granted in the familiar way.

The lack of a common history between its members (unless relatives take in a child) produces a paradox at the heart of the adoptive family. On the one hand narrative practice in adoption has to account for the separate histories and experiences of individual children and parents and incorporate them into the new family story. This is what Bella's son Jon is doing when he tries to claim Brad as his new brother, and advise his mother how she should look after him. At the same time this new family is itself being inserted into what has been called an 'adoptive kinship network' (Reitz and Watson 1992; Grotevant and

McRoy 1998). In these circumstances the nature and boundaries of the adoptive identity of both individual children and the family as a whole is constantly being negotiated. This happens in the way people think about themselves individually, how they see their relationships to each other in the immediate family and the wider kinship network and how they account for their own and their family's adoptive status in the outside world. Each individual and each family reaches their own accommodation at some point along a continuum marked out by what Kirk called acknowledgement of difference (1964).

For some parents the traditional aspiration of normalising adoption, 'doing' adoptive family life as if it was no different really from family created by procreation, remains the expectation and objective. Indeed the large majority of people who put themselves forward to adopt still enquire about the availability of babies, in the context of issues of infertility. Most do not see their new family as some addition to the child's original kinship network and the younger the child the less it is often assumed the previous family history has to be accommodated. And indeed it is not every adopted person who wants to maintain a relationship with their family of origin or needs to put significant emphasis on blood or genes as the basis of their identity.

However, for others adoption is not seen so readily as a replication and replacement of the birth family but more as one way of providing legal permanence for care-taking that cannot be provided by birth parents. Substantial numbers of long-term foster carers take on this kind of adoptive parenting role. And very few adopted children feel able to turn their back on the past completely. This is especially so where, as is very often the case, adoption leads to the separation of sibling groups because brothers and sisters are left in the original family or are placed permanently elsewhere. Current debates about 'contact' and 'openness' are partly discussions about reshaping adoptive kinship, affiliation and identity and partly (as we see below), about re-organising emotional roles and relationships and their significance. Adoption support services have to involve support for both aspects of communication and contact within the extended adoptive kinship network.

Meanwhile the idea itself of what constitutes difference is also changing. In the first place the reference points for family life and family narratives have become more diverse. As a result the norm of procreation in the context of heterosexual marriage is losing its overwhelming dominance as the personal and social template for what counts as family. This is precisely why we have started our own account with the idea of family as practice and narrative rather than prescription.

At the same time, although adoptive parenting may be just another way of bringing up children in a world of diverse family forms, the children involved do have different histories and these usually have negative consequences. Whatever the broader trend though, adoptive childhood, parenthood and family life in each case will be a distinctive experience. Sometimes people will want to emphasise the autonomy, independence and normality of their family lives and get on with things pretty much on their own. In other circumstances the differences in the experience of parenting will dominate and the demand will be for specialist help for special problems.

Mutual responsibilities and obligations and a community of adoptive family practice

Family practices are not 'any old practices', as Morgan (1999, p.17) says, and one reason for this is the distinctive mutual obligations family relationships are seen to embody. To a greater or lesser extent duty is being replaced, in family matters as in social life more generally, by the negotiation of responsibilities and commitments (Finch 1989; Finch and Mason 1993). The grand social theorists speak about 'individualisation' (Beck and Beck-Gersheim 1995; Beck-Gersheim 2002; Giddens 1992), and how family life and interpersonal commitment is now based on a contractual ethic, by which it is meant that rights and responsibilities are fairly formally negotiated. They are however, as feminist researchers of everyday life point out, undoubtedly underestimating the extent to which women especially still see themselves and their responsibilities in the context of their relationships with others. And children have much less power and influence in the matter.

An alternative 'ethic of care' (Gilligan 1982; Sevenhuijsen 1998) has been proposed as the basis on which people reach agreements about their responsibilities to each other. Instead of mutual family obligations being based on individual negotiations that draw on fixed moral principles about what is right, the suggestion is that such decisions emerge over time in the context of enduring relationships as specific circumstances arise (Duncan and Edwards 1999; Finch and Mason 1993). Research evidence and personal experience alike show that the mutual commitments of family life are as likely to be based on this ethic of care and connectedness as on any negotiated contract between individuals in which formal rights and responsibilities are traded.

The way in which mutual obligations and commitments in adoptive family practice are established has not yet been researched. We have little empirical evidence, for example, on how decisions are made about the division of child care and paid work or on why some adoptive parents think their responsibilities should include extending support to birth parents whilst most do not. But these decisions have to be taken. We do know, however, that there is usually no shared genealogy, no blood to thicken family duties in the traditional way in adoption. And the connections of family and kin and the social support networks that are often animated by pregnancy, birth and shared early experience are not immediately available in adoption. Adoptive parents have to work particularly hard at re-organising their time and family commitments both in respect of direct care giving and in relation to their wider kinship and social networks. Adoption support should, therefore, include support for this process of re-organisation of responsibilities and obligations.

Adoptive childhood and parenthood: The organisation and re-organisation of social and emotional relationships, behaviour and opportunity

This sociological way of thinking is a good place to start an exploration of adoptive family life for the reasons we have mentioned. In particular it puts individual family members, their intentions, purposes and plans, back in the driving seat – *Heroes of Their Own Lives*, as Linda Gordon (1988) entitled her book on mothers and children in a rather different child-care context.

This imagination gets us a good deal closer to the way people actually live their lives than the lists of developmental dimensions and parenting capacities that can make professional assessments of 'need' so banal and formulaic. It is a welcome relief from the offensive moralism of those who would presume to tell us whether our own choice of family life is suitable or not. The anthropological vision of socially constructed, not biologically determined, kinship is equally emancipating, in which the efforts of people to decide and develop their own identity mix are celebrated not stigmatised. The idea that people should and do organise their own path through life and family relationships and obligations enables us to see adoptive family life and practices as being potentially as good as any other. Better, in fact, than many, not least because they provide compensation where family life first time round has gone wrong, a 'fresh start in life' (Department of Health 2000a, p.3).

But of course adoptive family life, whilst seeming like a fresh start, can never be a clean break from the route already embarked upon by children and parents alike. Adoption certainly provides children and their new parents with an opportunity to re-organise childhood and family life. But it is an opportunity that is always constrained, to a greater or lesser degree, by the enduring legacies of previous experience and the way they get played out in the new family and social context. These intensify the intrinsic conflicts that in any case have to get worked through as parents, children and others negotiate the shared practices, narratives and mutual obligations of family life. It is apparent from the behaviour of Alan, Brian, Katie and Ellen at school and nursery, and of Brad, Luke and Debbie at home, just how much past baggage they are hauling and how obstructively it clutters up their new adoptive lives. These do not seem to be the children of the new sociological imagination, fairly free agents making considered plans and choices about their life. Nonetheless they are clearly children with a purpose who are practising their childhood in patterned ways.

Equally, adoptive parents Lucy and Bill, Bella, Bryony and Rachael have been constrained too, for different reasons, in their choice of family life. How then can these troublesome strategies of the children, in all their preoccupation and disconnection, be explained? What are the implications for adoptive parenting, which is expected to provide a fresh start and new opportunity for vulnerable children at the same time as fulfilling the expectations of their anticipated family story?

Developmental legacies and defensive coping strategies in adoptive childhood

In developing our argument about how we might best understand adoptive childhood and family life we use what has been called the 'organisational perspective' (Toth et al. 1997, p.781) on childhood. This developmental psychological approach is in tune with recent sociological theorising on the way children 'do' their own childhood, how they drive their own development and experience. The research evidence here supports the view that children are enabled to become more or less competent at doing childhood happily and successfully by the extent to which the adults responsible for them create, directly or indirectly, a risky or protective environment for growing up. The environment in this context includes the quality of direct care, the experiences of children in the wider social world and transactions between the two.

Seen as a journey, childhood in each case is embarked upon along a developmental pathway marked out by what have been termed risk and protective factors and mechanisms that modify or exacerbate the effects of adverse experiences encountered en route (Luthar, Cicchetti and Becker 2000). The path beaten to the door of the adoptive family home is usually marked by a negative combination of adverse experiences and of developmental legacies that result. Poor genetic inheritance and developmental adversity in utero combine with continued exposure to risky and harmful care giving and other social environments and experiences. Neglect, maltreatment, transience and instability mark out the adopted child's journey to placement. The experience of the care system itself can exacerbate rather than mitigate the effects of early adversity (Rutter 2000). However, the harmful effects of maltreatment and transience are far more fully documented than are the reparative consequences of good temporary foster care. On the other hand good emotional experiences in foster care will not be a sufficient condition for shifting older children to more resilient pathways if the care planning leaves them uncertain about how long they are staying this time, and how much they should invest themselves in the new relationships. It would be helpful if more research were to be done on these aspects of the care experience (Thomas et al. 1999).

It is important in practice to catalogue the vulnerability of children, which results from their early experiences, and to recognise the protective and ameliorative impact of subsequent foster care and good care planning. By doing so we are reminded of the areas of their development that continue to be marked by impairment, delay and disruption and the work that needs to be done by them and their new adoptive parents to repair or moderate the damage.

Alan Rushton (2003) has made the helpful distinction between the task of 'developmental recovery' in adoptive family life and that of making 'fresh attachments'. For example, Brad's physical health care will need continued attention whether or not he settles into a secure pattern of attachment with Bella, even though the two are of course intrinsically linked (Archer 2003). Alan's extreme over-activity and aggression will need practical management and amelioration as soon as possible if Lucy and Bill are to get beyond their exhaustion and despair in order to get attuned to his emotional needs. But, we suggest, the main legacy of previous experience is in the way children have organised, or have tried to organise, survival and coping strategies in the face of risk and adversity, genetic and environmental. Alarming behaviour such as Alan's, in particular, may be symptomatic of intrusive thoughts and feelings precipitated by neglect and abuse. It will indicate just how persistent are its harmful effects and how child safety remains a central issue in adoptive family life. The sexualised behaviour of some children abused in that way and the risks this poses is a case in point (Farmer and Pollack 1998).

However, our argument here is that the *defensive* quality of much of the behaviour which is used by children to manage anger and upset when situations still feel risky, must above all be recognised. The behaviour of Bill and Lucy's four children is a good example. In various ways Alan, Brian and Katie are managing their situation by keeping themselves as safe as they can in the familiar childhood worlds they have created for themselves. For example, Ellen appears to have closed down altogether as her way of coping. In each case these children are insuring against the risk that any emotional and social engagement with their peers and supervising adults will, once again, be harmful to them.

Attachment and trauma theories are increasingly helpful in explaining the mechanisms by which the emotional legacy of past childhood neglect and maltreatment in the family of origin get played out in current child behaviour in the new adoptive home and beyond (Cassidy and Shaver 1999; Howe *et al.* 1999; Perry *et al.* 1995; Schore 2001). Theories of loss and grief (Bowlby 1980; Brodzinsky, Schechter and Marantz Henig 1992) can also be used to account for child distress at placement and beyond. We look at these two related perspectives next because they help us make better sense of how adopted children like Luke and the others might be trying to organise adoptive family life in the shadow of neglect and loss.

The messages from developmental theory and research can be briefly summarised for our purposes. We would expect securely attached children to arrive in an adoptive home with an internalised sense of emotional security and social competence – they would feel good about themselves and about their relationships with others. Such children would have the capacity to regulate and organise their feelings, thoughts and behaviour, to stay reasonably calm and measured in the face of difficulties. They would fairly quickly make use of supportive people around them if they got upset for any reason but they would then get on with life in a hopeful and happy enough way. Crucially for childhood as experience in its own right, they would also know how to have fun.

All this would be the case because they had been able to rely on a 'secure base' (Bowlby 1988) from which to explore the world. At least one attachment figure would have been physically and emotionally available to them from the start, to contain their scary feelings when things suddenly felt unsafe and to play when things were calm. This may have had a neurological impact in the positive stimulation of optimal brain growth (Perry *et al.* 1995; Siegal 1999).

Parental care-givers facilitate secure attachment because they are sensitive and responsive to the attachment behaviours of their children (Ainsworth *et al.* 1978; Belsky 1999). And they behave in this way because they are able to get in touch with and reflect on the thoughts, feelings and desires both of their children and of themselves in relation to those children and their mental state (Fonagy and Target 1997; Fonagy *et al.* 2002).

It is this reflective function that underpins security and apparently gets passed on from parent to child. Having internalised a sense of security, and an increasing capacity for reflection, any permanent separation from their primary carers would, depending on the way the process was handled, cause children upset through grief at the loss. After a period of protest followed by sadness they would re-organise their affective ties to remaining care-givers (Bowlby 1980). Securely attached children would retain the capacity to reflect coherently on their experience and relationships and they would be able to discuss their feelings of grief with others. In the terms introduced in this chapter, the re-organisation process would involve new family practices and narratives – emotional relationships would have to be rearranged and the family story retold.

For children placed as infants the primary attachment would be with adoptive parents and any (later) grieving will be not for the loss of an existing attachment relationship with original birth parents, but for the loss of the opportunity of having such a relationship and the loss of continuity of the genealogical and cultural links that relationship would have allowed (Brodzinsky *et al.* 1992). The significance of this loss is contested. Despite the lack of empirical research evidence many adults adopted as babies have found helpful the idea that adoption can be seen as creating a 'primal wound' (Verrier 1997), in the way it breaks a 'mystical' bond between a mother and child (p.216). This can be used to account for continued grief and the need to search for lost origins and relationships.

Others would relate the intensity of feelings of loss to the extent to which adoptive childhood itself had facilitated an integrated sense of self (Grotevant 1997; Howe and Feast 2000). A positive evaluation of the adoption experience would follow because the security of attachment achieved by attuned parenting would have overridden any unease felt by differences originating from either genetic incompatibility (physical/temperamental/intelligence), or cultural expectation (blood kinship is real kinship) (Leon 2002).

Of course the story of care adoptions is usually different to the one told here. Most children placed permanently have already formed an emotional relationship with one or more of their original parents, but it is one that has caused them to develop insecurity or even disorganisation in their emotional reactions and behaviour, and in the sense they are forming of self and others. Separation and loss and the grief they cause gets played out in rather different ways in these circumstances. And as we noted earlier, as often as not, the experience is one shared with siblings.

In the absence of sensitive, attuned care-giving from parents who have both the capacity and commitment for reflecting on and responding to their emotional needs, children have to work harder to contain difficult feelings and thoughts when things do not feel safe. They are forced to go on the defensive when the secure base cannot be taken for granted because of parental insensitivity, rejection, neglect or abuse (Howe *et al.* 1999).

Two distinct organisational strategies have been identified in children in their anxiety to settle their scary feelings and thoughts and to get a sufficient sense of security to enable them to get on with childhood development confidently and happily. The first strategy, developed where care-givers are inconsistent and unreliable due to their own preoccupations, is to maximise their emotional and other demands (Sroufe 1996). Feeling insecure, children increase attachment behaviours, such as following and clinging, in the hope that their needs will be recognised and responded to. Constantly preoccupied with getting the proper attention they need from intrusive but erratic care-givers, children alternate in response to their agitation and frustration between anger and despair.

A second strategy, adopted by children where care-givers are dismissing of their emotional needs and functional in their parenting, is to minimise attachment behaviours. Expected rejection is avoided as children learn to become self-reliant and to suppress their feelings. These contrasting approaches to organising attachment in the face of preoccupied or dismissing care-giving, which is insensitive and unresponsive to emotional needs, leave children with internalised feelings of insecurity about themselves and their relationships. For these children, either caught up in or dismissive of their unsettled feelings and anxieties, the loss of the care-giver is not readily grieved in the normal way and any re-organisation of attachment, in favour of new temporary or permanent carers, will be defended against. Those in ambivalent and resistant attachment relationships can find separation of any kind particularly distressing because their efforts are so bound up in the process of keeping parents emotionally connected with them.

In the above circumstances, attachment theory (Bowlby 1980; Fraley and Shaver 1999) predicts that loss will provoke a chronic pattern of grief and mourning with children constantly needing to search out absent parental care-givers and becoming anxious and depressed when they cannot be restored. Practitioners are more likely to see this played out in temporary foster care, where restless children keep saying they want to go home and refuse to participate in their new family life. But Luke and Debbie, recently arrived with new adoptive parents Bryony and Rachael, seem still to be struggling with the fragile emotional connections they have worked hard to establish in transit through care.

By contrast, avoidantly attached children can appear compulsively self-reliant and untouched by grief as they block off emotions for fear that they may become overwhelmed by them. Unexpected angry outbursts are the reminders that this defence is hard to sustain. Something of Brad's experience and strangely relentless approach to the world may be conveyed in this account.

For some children though the odds are so seriously stacked up against their defensive strategies that they are at constant risk of breaking down, if indeed they get established in the first place. Disorganisation and disorientation take over as childhood experience simply becomes too stressful to manage. The emotional unavailability of care-givers to contain normal discomfort and anxiety and to play and have fun, is one thing, but when it is parents themselves who make you scared and alarmed it gets extremely difficult to organise any kind of coherent and integrated coping strategy. In this paradoxical situation children are left with irreconcilable desires – to move both toward and away from the care-giver.

Disorganised children are not always children who have been intentionally abused, scary and intrusive parenting has various faces, and not all abuse causes disorganisation (Lyons-Ruth and Jacobvitz 1999). But the traumatic nature of abuse is magnified if the stress is caused, not regulated, by the care-giver. Children are abandoned to their fear and stress. Actual threats of abandonment, often part and parcel of abuse, are especially traumatising. It is not surprising in this respect that recent research on older placed children who were less likely to establish a fresh attachment in the first year of permanent placement identified those who had been 'preferentially rejected', singled out from siblings in the process, as being most at risk (Dance, Rushton and Quinton 2002). It may also be the case that some abusive parenting traps children in a sense of shame about themselves and that this too contributes to avoidance and disorganisation (Magai 1999). Several practice texts on therapeutic interventions emphasise the importance of diminishing shame as part of the process of reintegration and reorganisation of attachment (Cairns 2002; Hughes 1997, 2003).

Intense and unregulated feelings of fear and abandonment are traumatic because they overwhelm the capacity of children to manage stress. The traumatic impact is especially damaging in infancy where the combination of inadequate positive stimulation and the persistent release of stress hormones has a physiological effect, impairing brain development and functioning (Glaser 1999; Perry *et al.* 1995; Schore 2001). Hyper-arousal and vigilance or disconnection and dissociation are the only ways by which the unresolved stress caused by frightening and abusive parenting can be managed. This is now seen as a neurological response as well as a psychological defence. Children who have been disorientated and traumatised by the parental care-giver who is supposed to make them feel safe and secure therefore labour under what Fonagy calls an 'absence of a core capacity' (2001, p.42) to properly regulate emotions, especially negative feelings. Constantly caught up in these emotions, and with no secure base at hand or in mind, and cognitive development itself impaired, they cannot integrate feelings and thoughts or plan organised behaviour and coping strategies.

Family practices are reactive and it is extremely difficult to think coherently enough to begin to construct a family narrative. It can be more problematic still for children defending themselves (and their parents) against socially stigmatising and devaluing assumptions based, for example, on their class or race (Bernard 2002).

In these circumstances of disorganisation the loss of a traumatising parental care-giver, following removal to care and permanent placement, can be very hard to resolve. Many parents provide traumatic care, or lack the capability to protect their children from it, because their capacity to reflect on child experience and to parent safely and sensitively is impeded by their own unresolved grief and loss. The danger is that their traumatised children will develop the same response. Some children do indeed respond with dissociation, which is the opposite of integrated and reflective self-development because memory, perception and identity are all disrupted (Macfie, Chichetti and Toth 2001). Disorganised infants are particularly vulnerable to dissociative disorders in adolescence if they experience repeated traumas in childhood (Liotti 1999; Ogawa *et al.* 1997).

There is a continuing debate amongst developmental researchers about the relationship between the insecure coping strategies of avoidance and ambivalence and the disorganisation of attachment and dysregulation of emotions and behaviour in children (Vondra and Barnett 1999). There is far less certainty still about the precise dynamics involved in avoidant, ambivalent and unresolved approaches to coping with separation and loss caused by permanent adoptive placement. The standard social work practice texts in particular pay little attention to the effects of trauma and disorganisation (Fahlberg 1994; Jewett 1994).

However, there is a danger in any case that the search for categorical patterns will lead to an academic/clinical process of labelling and pigeonholing children rather than trying to make sense of individual experience in its own terms too. And, of course, adoptive parents and their supportive professionals have the more pressing problem of actually managing the troublesome behaviour of children like Alan, Brian, Katie and Ellen in the meantime, finding a way of simply helping them settle.

Happily, personal experience and academic theory unite in the identification of the coercive and controlling orientation that appears to characterise the behaviour of many children placed from emotionally avoidant, ambivalent and traumatising family backgrounds (Archer 1999a and 1999b; Archer and Burnell 2003). Very young children, like Ellen perhaps, may well arrive in a fairly helpless state, completely overwhelmed by fearful and traumatic experience. As time passes though, it appears that children will have started, in a more or less conscious way, to manipulate their parents in the attempt to gain some control over their frustration or fear (Lyons-Ruth and Jacobvitz 1999). Controlling strategies tend to be of two types – parents are either punished or looked after by their children. It is these solicitous or punitive approaches, more or less moderated by the experience of separation and temporary foster care, that many children bring to their new adoptive home. And it is the experience of parenting in the face of these defensive and controlling approaches by children, and the exhaustion and despair that can result, which causes an increasing number of adoptive parents to find relief and comfort in the practical strategies offered in many contemporary 'attachment therapy' texts (Archer 1999a, 1999b; Keck and Kupecky 2002; Thomas 1997, 2000).

What then are the implications for adoptive parenthood of these conflicted childhood journeys to placement? And what do we expect of adoptive parenting anyway?

Good enough adoptive parenting: securing attachment and orchestrating a successful childhood

One way of thinking about what is expected of adoptive parents is to list the various 'needs' of adopted children and then establish whether the 'parenting capacity' of prospective adopters is such that they will be 'met' in placement. With the extension of the *Framework for the Assessment of Children in Need and their Families* to adoption (Department of Health 2000b, 2003b) this is now the official approach to policy and practice. This presents a partial and rather passive perspective on adoptive family life. A different picture emerges, one consistent with the idea of 'family' as a negotiated and narrated practice, if the active nature of adoptive parenthood is grasped too. Parenting, as we have seen, is about commitment, purpose and struggle in the 'doing' of family and not simply about having the understanding and skill to accomplish specified set tasks. The argument here, as it is throughout this book, is that adoptive parenting shares in common with any parenting the purpose of achieving for children a happy and successful enough childhood and family life through love, care and championing of their interests. It is the circumstances of adoptive childhood and family life that make the process distinctive.

Bynner (2001), following Sen (1992) develops a more active view on the purposes of parenting in relation to social inclusion. The emphasis in this perspective is on the way parenting reinforces the 'capabilities' of children, thereby enabling them to equalise their opportunity for a productive and enjoyable childhood. Instead of seeing children as largely passive bearers of 'needs' the focus shifts to the consideration of what 'resources' they should be enabled to have access to in order to acquire capabilities. Emotional, cultural and material resources are all needed if children are to participate actively in their childhood. This 'equalities' perspective can be used to help clarify political and managerial decisions about policy and provision in adoption support, but it also puts the finger on what is and ought to be going on in adoption. Hence, beyond insuring safety and stability, adoptive parenting is about boosting child capabilities in two main ways – through providing appropriate emotional availability, and by orchestrating child participation in the wider social world.

In the first way, success might be defined by the extent to which children are enabled, through fresh and secure enough parental attachment, to develop a 'reflective self function'. Fonagy and others (Fonagy and Target 1997, Fonagy et al. 2002) have identified this as being a kind of golden thread linking those children who develop the capacity to both protect themselves from the damaging effects of future adversity and become good enough partners and parents themselves. Arguably this is particularly hard to achieve in adoption.

The re-organisation of insecure and disorganised childhood developmental pathways is a significant challenge in some cases as experience and research show (Dance et al. 2002). In light of the evidence of empirical research findings that show high rates of disruption and dissatisfaction in some (late placed) adoptions (Rushton and Dance 2004) pessimism about fresh primary attachment might seem understandable. Relevant here too are the accounts of adopted adults which explain their persisting sense of loss by reference to the idea of a 'primal wound' (Verrier 1997) caused by separation from their birth mother.

Indeed some academic commentators argue that 'resilience' might be a more appropriate expectation and goal, especially for older placed children, and that the aim should be to stabilise and supplement, not replace existing hierarchies of attachment figures (Gilligan 1998, 2000a and b). There are important messages here about building on existing strengths, especially in relation to kinship networks and cultural identities, and on celebrating progress however it comes. But the other evidence we have does confirm that children in adoptive families can and do rearrange their attachment hierarchy in accordance with the availability of attachment figures (Rushton and Mayes 1997) and re-organise their attachment security in line with the new care-giver style (Dozier 2003; Steele *et al.* 2003).

We also know that security in primary attachments predicts harmony in other relationships (Berlin and Cassidy 1999). Changing primary attachment figures and expecting the new adoptive ones to move children towards increased security and self-reflection is a proper objective. The evidence of recent research confirms the experience of many happy adoptive families, that secure enough attachment to new parents can be achieved. The case for optimism can also be defended.

How this is to be done is a matter of continuing debate (O'Connor and Zeanah 2003), and the therapeutic issues are discussed in Chapter 5. What should be clear though is that this is a dynamic, interpersonal process that is certainly to do with the identification and management of the attachment difficulties of children. But it also has a lot to do with the adoptive parents' care-giving capacity. At a time when the emphasis in so much of the 'attachment therapy' practice literature is on parents as therapists and behavioural managers this fact can slip from sight.

There has been a shift from what might be called a loss and identity model developed to account for 'adoption-related' problems for families, parents and children in traditional infant adoptions (Leon 2002; Wegar 2000), to an attachment and trauma perspective on child developmental disorder in care adoption (Archer 1999a, 1999b; Archer and Burnell 2003). Arguably, this perspective results in under-estimating the impact of the attachment histories of adoptive parents on their care-giving practices. More of a focus on parental histories of attachment and loss would allow the relational and inter-subjective nature of persisting placement problems to be illuminated. Inept professional concerns about parenting capability and family dysfunction, offered in ignorance of just how troubling and demanding adopted children can be, may not have helped (Hart *et al.* 2002; Howe 2003). Additionally there may be a danger that the blame commonly felt by adoptive parents at the hands of professionals is simply shifted onto adopted children and their 'disorders'. This is no great help either. Once the placement is made, parents and children alike are in it together when it comes to forming fresh attachments.

The second aspect of adoptive parenting, that of orchestration of the wider social world and experience of children, will seem less contentious. Which is not to say that any great attention has been paid to it in policy and practice, because it has not. The research evidence shows the extent to which adoptive family life compensates for developmental delays in health and learning, as well as overcoming the social and emotional defences, brought by children to the placement (Howe 1998). But it also shows that social work and other professionals, partly due to the dominance in the UK of a 'clinical' mental health and psycho-social support orientation in child-care work, have failed to take

children's rights to equal opportunities in education, health and social participation seriously (Jackson 2001).

In adoption too much has been left to adoptive parents alone. An advocacy
and equalities approach, on the part of supporting professionals, to maximising
opportunity needs now to be emphasised.

Towards a settled adoptive childhood and family life

Family practices in adoption are distinctive for reasons already discussed. They
embody unique demands derived from the deliberate, negotiated nature of
family construction. The realignment of emotional affiliations and kinship
obligations in the context of formal professional surveillance and support
marks adoptive family life out as different, however contested the process turns
out to be in each case. The practice of 'doing' family is more demanding as a
result, and so too is the outcome in that children will have to find their place in a
new adoptive kinship formation. Beyond this, though, it is difficult to say
whether or not any particular pattern of family life becomes consolidated in
care adoption as a distinctive family form.

The traditional approach in family therapy (Carter and McGoldrick 1998)
has been to describe and explain families as systems operating more or less
functionally across a given lifecycle. So too with adoption (Pinderhughes
1996). But the evidence is contradictory and individual experience, which is
where we should start, is of contingency in adoptive family life as it is in any
other. The alternative approach is to focus on the conditions that make for a
settled adoptive childhood and family life because it is generally when people
feel settled that they can go about life together in an ordered and comfortable
way.

Adoptive family practices and adoption support

Our analysis of adoptive childhood and family life as constructive practices in
distinctive circumstances enables a clearer view to emerge of what might constitute support for that process. As we have seen, formal adoption support
provided professionally cannot simply be discussed as if it were something to
be added in, or not, to help adoptive family members cope better with identified needs that might arise in their family life.

Adoptive family life is different because it originates in a formal process of
professional involvement. The adoptive family can only come into existence
through a relationship between children, parents and professionals. As a result
decisions about support in adoption are always at first decisions about how to
change the focus and extent of formal involvement and support and not about
whether support itself should be introduced from scratch. Of course it has not
often felt quite like this, either to parents or professionals. This is because the

processes of vetting, assessing and preparing adoptive parents, and of preparing and placing children, have been largely separated out from those of providing post-placement and particularly post-adoption support (Rushton and Dance 2002).

This discontinuity, in thinking about and organising support for adoption, has left professionals and parents uncertain about how formal involvement in adoptive family life should shift in focus once the adoptive placement is made. Decisions have been made, but all too often they have been made by default (the long-standing family social worker keeping in touch fairly informally) or by custom (the expectation that administrative arrangements for 'letter box' contact will usually be made). And if things go wrong later down the line no one is quite sure what can be done and by whom.

Nonetheless these are always decisions about changing existing involvement even where a new service or resource is to be provided. As we see in the next chapter, the Adoption and Children Act 2002 has the potential to change all this. The new expectation, consistent with the realities of adoptive family formation, is that adoption must be seen as a continuous process that is to be supported rather than as a set of placement and post-placement tasks that are to be completed. What the Act does not do is encourage or facilitate the kind of adoption support practice that is implied by this new commitment to a seamless service. This is the challenge we set ourselves in this book.

The analysis of adoptive family practices developed above has helped us identify those aspects of the adoption process that are most likely to require continued and changing professional involvement and support. It also suggests the type of approach that might most productively be developed. The most distinctive aspect of this approach is that it is seen as a joint 'practice' bringing together parents and professionals, children, relatives and friends as collaborating 'practitioners' of adoptive family life and its support.

In particular, the evidence and indications are that it is three dimensions of adoptive family practice which should provide the focus of the continued engagement of formal professional involvement and support. First, the conditions must be provided for the establishment of an organised, and preferably secure, attachment by the child to at least one adoptive parent. We know that secure emotional relationships, and the more certain sense of self that results, are the main contexts for settled behaviour. We also know, however, that in real life the management, for example, of Alan and Brian's troubling behaviour can hardly wait for some attachment relationship to be formed with Lucy and Bill. The capacity of adoptive parents to contain and manage dysregulated behaviour as well as emotion is routinely challenged in adoption.

Adoption support may work best when the people from outside, who survey the chaos, themselves possess the wherewithal to provide containment and management strategies in turn. Social worker Jenny has started well, we think, because she has conveyed understanding through calm acceptance in the face of the family distress, but this in itself is not likely to be enough to help Bella and her children find practical ways of getting on happily together.

The re-organisation of a further set of relationships, those in the wider kinship network created by adoption, is the second of our core dimensions of adoptive family practice and support. Adopted children organise self in the context of divergent claims on their identity and affiliations. Genealogical history and future parental attachments have both to be accommodated. Original cultural heritage and experience has to be incorporated within a new social context. To a greater or lesser extent this involves the revision of pre-adoptive relationships and the roles they embody, a resettlement of attachments and obligations within the shifting boundaries of an adoptive kinship system. A sufficiently reassuring account of adoptive childhood identity has to be constructed in the process.

Children and their new families find it difficult to tell themselves the story of their joint future unless they have made sense of and put in place their separate pasts. Decisions about the placement of siblings, about 'life-story work' and about 'contact' with the birth family are the main contexts in which these questions about kinship and identity are engaged in professional practice. However professional support across the borderlands of adoptive identity remains uncertain in its commitments and undeveloped in its capabilities. It is certain though that the work needs to be done.

The third dimension puts adoption support in a community context. However, community for us is not simply a community of interest, i.e. adoptive families, but a community of (adoptive) practice. We end the book with an exploration of the potential of this perspective. A primary aim here is to ensure that a really effective collaborative culture of joint working is established across agency and family boundaries to enable adoptive parents especially to feel properly understood and supported. One other aspect of this broader frame of reference is the work that needs to be done to ensure children really do get the life chance benefits that are intended to flow not only from the safety and stability of adoptive family life but also from the opportunities for good health, education and social relationships that are expected to follow. As we have stressed in this chapter, adoptive childhood is organised in the context of adoptive family practices, in and beyond the home, but the destiny of the individual child is not simply bound up in family as such.

Where adoption has succeeded it is partly because a miserable and scary childhood is made happy and reassuring and partly because an effective opportunity has been provided for children to get a life of their own. Adoption support has to inhabit the school, surgery and local park too. And adopted children usually need people additional to their parents who can look out and speak up for them in that wider childhood world, to help make sure they find their place and eventually make their own way with confidence. Adults need to be advocates for children as well as care-givers, educators and the like.

Our primary aim in this book is to emphasise the relational aspects of these three dimensions of adoptive family practice. In doing this we attempt to integrate psycho-social and socio-cultural dynamics of family life. In the meantime, we turn to those frameworks of law, policy and service development and organisation which provide the context for effective practice.

Chapter 3

Adoption Support

The Legal and Organisational Framework for Practice

Introduction

In this chapter we explore the extent to which current law and policy provides the context in which effective adoption support services might be developed and integrated into mainstream practice. By practice we mean the process of constructing family and telling the family story described in the previous chapter. The test of success of 'the introduction of a national framework for adoption support services' (Department of Health 2003c, p.7) is whether it enables the 'practitioners' in adoption, professionals and family members alike, to work effectively together in making family life a success.

But more important even than this is the extent to which services as a whole will be enabled to become adoption-competent, that is, fully understanding of and responsive to the distinctive needs of adoptive childhood, parenting and family life. The contemporary shift of policy in children's services, towards targeting special intervention on children at risk within a context of integrated universal services for all (Hodge 2004), will not necessarily improve understanding and responsiveness. Services are only truly universal in effect if there is equal access to them. And as we know now, equal access for marginal groups is only achieved when the nature of their marginalised status is recognised and policies and practice explicitly designed to confront the dynamics of disadvantage. So it is with adoption. Taking the social inclusion approach that we outlined in the previous chapter, the capabilities and opportunities for adopted children will be compromised unless they really have equal access to resources.

The rhetoric of national policy therefore needs to be translated into the reality of transformed local services that really do secure and prioritise services to support adoptive family life. As we see below, this depends on the imagination local adoption practitioners bring to the task of interpreting the powers and duties now available in the Adoption and Children Act 2002. And transformed services are initially judged by just how practically helpful the support they engender actually is on the ground and from day to day for families like those of Lucy and Bill, Bella, and Bryony and Rachael. For success will be determined by the extent to which adoptive childhood and family life can be enjoyed *en route*, and genuinely supported in the process, as well as by whether it has provided stability and promoted social inclusion and achievement for a group of vulnerable children (Department for Education and Skills 2003a).

So our aim in this chapter is twofold. First, we provide a factual synopsis of the policy and law of adoption support. The intention is to set out in sufficient detail those legal duties and powers that give effect to the policy aspiration to create the new framework of effective adoption support from October 2003. In doing so key elements of the wider reform to adoption services, for example changes to care planning and adoption placement, are only touched upon here.

The chapter is not designed as an overview of the Adoption and Children Act 2002 as a whole. The primary aim, instead, is to explain what approach to adoption support emerges from the way in which policy and law have been constructed. Second, we consider the implications for practice at the local level, in day to day working. Our objective in this respect is social and political rather than legal and procedural. In essence, we ask what will need to happen locally if statutory opportunities are to be grasped with sufficient imagination and purpose to ensure the emergence of an effective new culture of adoptive family support practice. In doing this we try to hold in mind, in particular, the experience of Bella, Jon and Brad. Recall the situation.

Case study: Bella and Jon Freeman, and Brad Taylor

Now bringing up the children alone, Bella feels extremely exposed in her parenting just three weeks after Brad's arrival. She is expecting, and is expected, to help Jon and his new brother thrive as a result of the benefits of adoptive family life. But things already feel out of control. Brad's health needs are demanding enough without his refusal to eat and his aggression. In fact the two are probably connected. Jon, unsettled too by the stress of events, has retreated into dismissive attitudes. There seems to be little informal family and social support around to call upon. And Bella knows she is barely coping. Yet she is still effectively on trial as a parent and the social worker has arrived to see how things are going. This is a scary moment – a real opportunity to get help yet, simultaneously, a serious risk of being judged and blamed for incompetence or worse. Effective adoption support for Bella and the children will depend on the understanding and skill of the social worker (or other professional) who calls. Mutual recognition and trust will enable a really supportive relationship to form, help to be received safely as well as offered in good faith. But Bella, Jon and

Brad, and the key practitioner who shares the task, need other things too. Informed advice on financial benefits and support, a health care and behaviour management plan for Brad that is not simply triggered when things go wrong, time for Bella and Jon to work out together what will help Brad feel a greater sense of security and belonging. All these come immediately to mind. As do practical help in sorting out the house and respite that relieves Bella from constant caring yet does not leave Brad feeling more rejected still. And who else in the neighbourhood and beyond is thinking about this family as it struggles to form and settle into a happy home life?

It is this combination, of opportunity to form a mutually understanding relationship of support and provision of accessible and practically useful services, that we take to be the touchstone for assessing the framework of adoption support services to be developed under the Adoption and Children Act 2002.

The fault-lines of adoption support policy and practice

The Adoption and Children Act 2002 has put adoption support services and practice on a new statutory footing. It might be expected that this would be helpful to parents like Bella. She and her children are now entitled to an assessment of their adoption support needs. For this new adoptive family it will be a central part of the placement process. Following this assessment, the local authority will determine whether to provide services to meet these needs and in doing so will draw on a list of services identified in the regulations. A plan will need to be drawn up (other than for a 'one-off' service) and the plan will need to be reviewed.

A named person will be responsible for seeing if and how services might be made available. However there are significant limitations to the legislation. Despite the policy rhetoric the message in law about both eligibility for services and how they ought to be organised remains an ambiguous one. Where the aims seem clear they are conveyed in rather dispiriting bureaucratic terms. As a result the successful establishment of an effective local culture of adoption support still looks uncertain.

The danger is, we think, that Bella will continue to feel rather like a traditional social work client albeit with a few more consumer rights. No substantial transformation of the context of adoptive family life and support will automatically emerge from what has been proposed. This is partly because adoption support has to compete for scarce resources with other national and local child-care demands. Eligibility as of right for services, as distinct from eligibility for assessment, would indeed be costly. So too would be a system that gave priority to those people affected by adoption. There are understandable, if perhaps regrettable, economic and political reasons why the legislation gives mixed messages.

But it is also the case, we suggest here, that family policy has an intrinsic problem when it comes to considering both the status and claims for services and support of families such as Bella's and the way in which those services are provided once claims are established. These two related dilemmas emerge as fault-lines when the policy aspirations conveyed in the Act are examined. They create tension in law and official guidance and this has to be managed at the local level when policy is implemented. We begin by examining these tensions.

The adoptive family in law and policy: a special claim for support?

In the first place there is the question of how to understand the status and claims for services of the adoptive family. In particular, should the law treat the adoptive family as if it were exactly the same as any other family? The case that it should is made in the following terms. Adoption provides a substitute family in law for children like Brad and gives full parental responsibility to adoptive parents like Bella. In so doing it is intended to replicate the (birth) family norm in society. It follows that Bella, like any other parent, should expect and be expected to get on with bringing up her children as she wishes. The 'fresh start' approach to adoptive family life embraced by New Labour fits this vision perfectly because it emphasises the fact that the adoptive family is a *substitute* for the original birth family. There is no hint of shared parenting or supplementary family care in modern adoption policy discourse. Adoption is unequivocally an alternative family life for children like Brad.

Underlining this very traditional approach is the fact that new rights are given to prospective adoptive parents in the Act. For example, they can now appeal to an independent review panel if agency decisions are disputed in relation to their suitability to adopt at an Adoption Panel. And prospective adopters now acquire parental responsibility on placement, formally giving them a place at any decision-making table. It might also be argued that the decision to end the legal discrimination against same-sex and unmarried adopters, which will of course have positive implications for Bryony and Rachael's family, reinforces this emphasis on normalising parental rights in adoption. For the intention was to ensure in all new families that parental responsibility would be acquired through adoption by both parents. In any case the status of adoptive parenting in law is, and remains in the Adoption and Children Act 2002, the same as that of the birth parenting (heterosexual at least) it replaces once the adoption order is made. This explains why adoptive families have had the same basic claim on services and support as any other family.

In line with the traditional cultural assumptions of British social policy, eligibility for formal support with, or surveillance of, family life should be determined by the particular needs of a child. Any child can have their needs assessed. Children's legislation provides for this to happen both generally and in relation to specific child development circumstances. Hence the Children Act 1989 sets out the overall local authority duty to assess need and determine eligibility. Particular agency responses to special developmental needs of various kinds are determined in other legislation, especially Education Acts. Adopted children have equal eligibility for services in accordance with any needs they may have, general or specialist. Adoptive parents thereby have equal access to support services.

In this account the case for normalising adoptive family life for parents like Bella can therefore be made. If Brad has special educational or health needs they will be assessed and services provided just as they would if he was still with his birth family. Bella and Jon can get support as a result. The fact of adoption might, therefore, appear to be irrelevant.

Yet, as we have seen, adoption does make a difference. It is not simply the legal means of providing a 'fresh start' for independent family life. Adoptive families are quite distinct. Their claims on services are distinctive as a result. Recognition has to be given in law to this fact.

As we discussed earlier, this distinctiveness of adoption is partly because it attracts a stigma, still representing a difference too far even in the new world of diversity in family practice (Wegar 2000). But the difference of adoption also lies nowadays in the new role expected of adoptive family life. Adoptive family life continues to replace and replicate in law the substituted birth family ideal. But it is now increasingly required also to compensate explicitly for previous family and parenting failures. The abandoned, neglected and traumatised children of contemporary 'care' adoption are expected to receive reparative parenting as well as a stable, replacement family status. Bella herself is in little doubt of this fact, which is why she feels so desperate in her failure to get Brad to eat and so exposed by the visit of Jenny, the social worker.

To some extent, of course, all parenting has a socially prescribed function. And this is increasingly so as family policy, under highly interventionist governments such as New Labour, expects family life to provide the conditions for 'social inclusion' and child achievement (Department for Education and Skills 2003a). Birth parents will get a knock on the door from a Sure Start visitor in the same way as will their adoptive family neighbours. However adoptive parenting is now 'social parenting' almost par excellence and this raises questions about the conditions under which adoptive family life should be established and maintained. The consequence is that family policy must legislate for the difference of adoption and adoptive parenting, paying attention to those conditions, whilst at the same time confirming the normality of its status.

The Adoption and Children Act 2002, and the framework of adoption support services it creates, is best seen, we argue here, as an attempt to do just this. Hence adoption support, rather like the adoptive family, is to be 'mainstreamed' (Department of Health 2002b, p.4). But a new range of adoption-specific support services is to be provided in each local area. People affected by adoption will be expected to have the same eligibility for mainstream services as anyone else, but they will get an extra right to assessment for co-ordinated 'adoption support' too. In this chapter we explore the implications of the attempt made to manage the tension.

The adoptive family in service delivery: how much professional direction and control?

We turn next to the second fault-line in adoption policy that needs to be identified if the legal framework and procedures advised for adoption support are to be understood. This adds to complexity and risk in policy-making and practice. The question here is about which way services should be provided once the status and claims of the adoptive family have been determined. Precisely what approach should be taken to constructing adoption support?

This second policy dilemma follows from the first, and the best way of understanding it is to return to the contrast between the family created by procreation and the family born out of adoption. Thus the average birth parent can get on with their parenting as they wish, and can call as required on formal services, as needs dictate. They will only have their parental autonomy curtailed by professional surveillance if they harm their children or put their well-being at risk. And the services themselves will be designed with the lifecycle of the procreational family in mind. By contrast, because of the role expected of them, adoptive parents like Bella have to earn autonomy in parenting. In adoption the independent status of the family follows extensive professional surveillance and support, it does not precede it. The right to exercise parental responsibility fully comes later down the line and only after agencies and courts are persuaded.

It is in these circumstances that Bella and her children encounter support services and make their own claim on them. Adoptive parents, in particular, enter the mainstream world of children's services in quite a different way from their neighbours. Not only do they arrive in the playground late, so to speak, but they have also taken a quite different route through the system of service support to get there. Very few other parents will have to bring a social worker with them, as it were, as they find a place for the child in their own informal social networks. They also need help in finding a way into formal services for their new family. The risks and opportunities for ensuring support is effective, in these unusual circumstances, are apparent.

There is of course potential here for the professional surveillance and case management aspects of the care planning process, in adoption approval, matching and placement, to transform smoothly. It could become a genuinely enabling yet attentive role as the adoptive family takes its place alongside all the others. But experience shows there are obvious risks too. Chief amongst these is the difficulty services operating in a care planning and case management mode have in steering a middle course between two possible approaches. The first of these approaches is capturing, and holding too long, onto professional control and its bureaucracy; the second is avoiding responsibility altogether.

The test of the Act is the extent to which it facilitates an approach to support, linking and co-ordinating informal and formal sources of help, that is collaborative in nature, neither controlling or rejecting. In the case of Brad's tricky start, will social worker Jenny feel enabled by the 'adoption support' agenda to get alongside Bella to help her through and learn from the initial crisis and manage it all rather better? She can hardly, in these circumstances, bail out altogether under cover of respecting Bella's rights to get on with her own family life. After all, she still retains her 'corporate parenting' role, and the pressures to be assertive within it on behalf of child safety and achievement have become immense. But one role has to give way to the other in the end. So Jenny will need to gain confidence, in taking this journey with the family, from a local service culture that must be designed to support this helping relationship, rather than trapping it in bureaucratic procedure and defensive professional control.

It is this dual commitment that defines the second fault-line in adoption support policy. As demands increase on the local authority to guarantee stability, permanence and achievement for children the tendency is for the traditional 'corporate parenting' mode of practice to prevail. The conventional care planning and case management stance is carried over into the wider world of adoption support. Yet the commitment to family autonomy in adoption, and the costs of continued corporate care and case management, pull in the other direction. Arguably the extension of an apparently bureaucratic keywork model of practice across children's services (Department for Education and Skills 2003a) makes this more generally an issue in the family life of vulnerable children. However, the distinctive status of the adoptive family means that the problem is intensified in that case.

Central policy caution and local practice imagination

So exactly how, in practice, does policy accommodate these dilemmas? As we see in the rest of this chapter it is indeed the traditional bureaucratic vision that has largely determined how the balance should be struck. Adoptive parents certainly improve their legal status by acquiring parental responsibility on placement. This moderates the exercise of professional control and should improve collaborative practices in family formation. They, with others affected by adoption, also have increased opportunities for access to adoption-specific support.

However, these opportunities remain restricted. Bella and her children continue to inhabit the ambiguous borderlands marked out by the enhanced access of 'looked after' children and their (foster) parents to services and the chances that have to be taken by other families where needs arise. And, crucially for our argument in this book, the *way* in which adoption support is provided remains disappointingly familiar. At a time when imagination and energy are being brought to service reform in some other areas of child and family policy and practice, the direction of travel in adoption support is mapped out cautiously and in very conventional terms.

Legal and policy changes have provided some opportunities for Bella and other parents like her, and for professionals like Jenny who are looking for new approaches to support and its co-ordination. But it will be down to local imagination, as well as personal and political commitment, to make the services that develop feel really helpful in day-to-day family life.

In the next sections we explore in some detail how these dilemmas of adoption policy are accommodated in the legislative framework created by the Adoption and Children Act 2002. We do this first by separating out what are in effect the two contrasting ways in which law and policy seek to construct a new system of adoption support.

The Adoption and Children Act 2002 and a twin-track approach to adoption support

The Adoption and Children Act 2002 provides the legislative underpinning for what might be seen as a twin-track approach to adoption support. The first approach is an attempt to improve support *through service development and re-organisation*. This is sometimes referred to as institutional capacity building (Cars *et al.* 2002). We think this is a fairly helpful term because it makes us consider exactly what capacity or capability we might expect an effective service system to have. As we will see, the official view is conventional, narrowly focusing on professional and bureaucratic service delivery arrangements.

Recent research (Rushton and Dance 2002), itself taking a conventional perspective, confirmed the general recognition that agencies had an inconsistent approach to providing services designed to address adoption-specific needs. As a result provision was patchy and undeveloped. Much attention, therefore, is given in the Act, its Regulations and Guidance (as well as in National Standards) to adoption-specific service development. Hence duties and powers are placed on local authorities to plan and arrange for the provision of a variety of specified 'adoption support services' within their area including financial support.

Regulations and Guidance make clear that these specific services must be seen as taking their place within a wider system of support. This incorporates the full range of mainstream services for all children, families and adults. A large proportion of these services is provided by other statutory agencies for health and education. Hence the additional emphasis in the Act on mainstreaming adoption support in an inter-professional service context. As a result the aim is that a national framework of adoption support services, specified in law, must be integrated in each locality with existing services. This is intended to offer consistent as well as effective services wherever people live. However, in practice it does seem that it will fall to local authorities to determine the precise level and focus of adoption support within their own areas. These requirements and expectations should be seen as the service development aspects of the legislation.

The second approach involves duties and powers that *facilitate individual entitlement and access* to those services. The Act prescribes arrangements for determining eligibility for specified adoption support services in individual circumstances of need. In so doing it confirms, by giving to people affected by adoption a right to claim an assessment of need and eligibility for those services, that adoptive family life is distinctive. But as we have said the intention is that these prescribed facilities should be offered alongside (or even from) mainstream child and family services. This is in line with the primary belief that adoptive families should expect to get an equal deal from those services, universal and specialist.

Regulations and Guidance describe how such support should be provided. These obligations to establish individually planned 'packages' of adoption support constitute a rather different focus in the legislation for facilitating the overall intention, which is to co-ordinate as well as improve the quality of adoption support. Co-ordination at the individual level of access is supposed to complement service level co-ordination within the inter-professional system as a whole.

The lynchpin connecting the two is the Adoption Support Services Advisor (ASSA), a complex role involving both strategic development of service as well as signposting to individual inquirers. This is a statutory role marked out at the heart of the strategy to link people entitled to specific support with the new framework of services established to provide such support. Because both the service development duties and powers in the Act and those to do with access are relatively weak, the ASSA role is a crucial one. As a result of their positional power in the local authority, and because the notion of mainstreaming itself is actually ambiguous, it will fall substantially to this new breed of advisors to make the adoption support system work. And the way they conceive the role and go about the tasks expected will have an enormous influence on the service culture established in each local area. The next chapter is devoted to a detailed account and analysis of the role and its potential in these respects.

Service development: The duty to arrange for the provision of adoption support services

The Adoption and Children Act 2002 places, for the first time, a clear duty on local social services authorities to make and participate in arrangements to provide adoption support services, including financial support. The 1976 Adoption Act required local authorities to provide an adoption service and the 1983 Adoption Regulations provided a first step along the line to a statutory framework for adoption support within this service. The 2002 Act regulations are made as an amendment to the 1976 Act. Phase 2 of the support regulations integrates and implements these in the Act. The 2002 Act then, largely in Guidance and Regulations (Department of Health 2003b, 2003d), specifies the focus and dimensions of the adoption support arrangements that have now to be provided within that local service.

Unquestionably, therefore, the Act has opened the door to a new era in the development of adoption support services. Nonetheless, the law now requires the establishment of a standardised national framework of assessment for adoption support services, although, as we said above, the degree to which service provision itself is being standardised on a national basis is far less clear. And it certainly provides only limited impetus for the development of really responsive local services that might sustain a culture of adoption support in each area.

The legal duty to arrange for the provision of services may now be clear but it is also limited. Limited too are the finances made available to fund developments. The argument from central government has been that putting into operation the newly established framework takes some time, which is why it has been phased in. The decision to implement the new duties in this phased way was seen to be the appropriate response to evidence that many local authorities were starting from a low base of provision. Inspection and research certainly confirmed this (Department of Health 2001a; Lowe *et al.* 1999; Rushton and Dance 2002), and the draft Regulations made this explicit (Department of Health 2003c).

The draft Regulations declared that a stepping stone rather than an insurmountable barrier was being provided for local authorities starting from 'a low base' of provision. However, as became apparent during the passage of the Bill in Parliament, an equal concern of government was to contain expectations generally about the extent to which already hard-pressed local authority funds could be devoted to adoption, as opposed to other kinds of 'family' support. The ring-fenced injection of £70m to fund the implementation between 2003 and 2006 provided a sweetener. The real responsibility for driving through changes then has been neatly delegated to various local political and professional communities.

The legislative underpinning for adoption support consists of the following core duties and powers:

- the definition of 'adoption support services' that must be provided locally
- a duty on local authorities to arrange the provision of those services in a planned and co-ordinated way (as it is in the 1989 Act)
- the legal recognition and registration of adoption support agencies, enabling them to provide services on commission to local authorities along with existing voluntary adoption agencies.

We look at the meaning and effect of each of these in turn by posing questions about the implications of the law for service development.

What are 'adoption support services' and how are they expected to enhance existing adoption support?

The Act attempts to deal with the ambiguous claims for services of the adoptive family in two ways. It prescribes a list of adoption-specific services that each local authority must provide and it also, in official Guidance (Department of Health 2003b), expects that these services contribute to the process of mainstreaming adoption support as a whole. The strategy itself makes good sense. The duty to provide specified services means that those people affected by adoption can expect to find standard sources of adoption support in their area. Gaps will be filled in local services because the law now requires that they must. In this way the 'key elements' (Department of Health 2003b, para 13) of a national framework of services, specific to those people affected by adoption, will be established. In line with recent policy concern the emphasis on consistency in the provision of these services should establish national standards in service provision.

Much less clear though is exactly how this framework in itself will actually enhance the quality of support generally to adoptive families like Bella's. This is partly because of the way the Act specifies how local authorities are expected to provide adoption support services, and we look at this below. But the question also arises because of the nature of the prescribed list itself.

Adoption support services include:

- financial support
- support groups for adoptive parents and adoptive children
- support for contact arrangements between adoptive children and their birth relatives or with other people with whom they share significant relationships

- therapeutic services for children
- services to ensure the success of the adoptive placement or adoption including training for adoptive parents and 'respite care'
- counselling, advice and information

Assistance in cash can be given to enable a specific service to be used, for example, travel expenses to facilitate contact or participation in a group.

It is immediately apparent that the list, financial support aside, describes a limited range of what might be called direct professional support and intervention. For the most part this is the kind of support traditionally provided by social services and Child and Adolescent Mental Health Services (CAMHS). This is because the primary beneficiaries will be children who have been placed for adoption and their new adoptive parents and families. A strategy of risk reduction rather than service innovation ultimately informs renewed policy interest in adoption support. Adoption support is intended, at least in the first instance, to be 'particularly targeted on meeting the needs of adoptive families created when children are adopted from care' (Department of Health 2003b, para 14). This is unsurprising in the circumstances. As increasing numbers of children like Brad leave public care for new families the risk of placement disruption and adoption breakdown increases.

However, when parents and children in late placements receive routine social case work and standard mental health interventions the evidence on the stability and experience of family life raises real concerns. Research has confirmed that often routine social work and CAMHS practices in adoption are of limited effect or worse (Hart *et al.* 2002; Parker 1999; Selwyn *et al.* 2003). The main concern in policy is to ensure, filling gaps in provision aside, that 'when the 2002 Act is implemented in full…support arrangements will flow smoothly for adopters from the initial enquiry through the adoption order and beyond' (Department of Health 2003b, para 18). Yet the adoption support services prescribed in the framework are largely the kind, as Guidance says, that 'will already be in place to meet the child's needs' (2003b, para 14).

The danger here is that the rush to establish such services as therapy for children, groups for adoptive parents and support for contact, runs the risk of institutionalising traditional practices. As we discuss in subsequent chapters, the evidence is that it is some of these practices, and the conventional clinical and case management perspectives that inform them, that ought now to be questioned.

It is not clear either how a support framework derived from a conventional case management approach, suitable for 'corporate parenting', provides the means by which adoptive families earn autonomy and get equally effective help from mainstream services. It is important, as the government said at the time, that 'adoption support services must not be seen in isolation' (Department of Health 2002b, p.4).

However, a successful strategy for 'mainstreaming adoption support' demands a good deal more than raising the 'profile' of adopted children and families 'as potential users of existing services' (2002b, p.4). The needs of adoptive families and others have certainly been 'overlooked' (2002b, p.5) by existing services, especially after the adoption was finalised. However, the central problem is rather one of making sure the mainstream and specialist services, already widely used by adoptive families, really understand the different challenges faced by Bella, Jon, Brad and the rest. The evidence is that mainstream services have hardly got to grips at all with the dynamics of adoptive childhood and family life. As a result parents and children have felt either ignored or misunderstood and alienated, as the influential study by Nigel Lowe and his colleagues showed (Lowe *et al.* 1999).

In fact the seeds of an effective mainstreaming strategy are to be found in the Act, but only in relation to financial support rather than service provision. We say more about this in the next section. For adoption support generally, though, the conventional way in which the framework of required services is specified leaves very uncertain the main question. For this is about how the local service culture, especially as expressed in routine daily practice in schools, clinics and offices, will itself become adoption competent.

Planned and co-ordinated: what are local agency responsibilities for developing effective adoption support services and mainstreaming adoption support?

The 2002 Act requires that local authorities take a planned and co-ordinated approach in meeting their duty to arrange adoption support services. This might have provided a means by which the mainstreaming agenda could be given effect. In fact the model of co-ordination in the Act itself is as conventional as the approach taken to constructing the framework of adoption support. This seems especially surprising given the more ambitious contemporary shift in policy towards fully integrated children's services and inter-professional practices (Department for Education and Skills 2003a). The specific duties placed on the local authority are set out below:

- to make and participate in arrangements for the provision of adoption support services.

- to ensure services are provided in conjunction with the local authority's other social services and with registered adoption societies in their area, so that help may be given in a co-ordinated manner without duplication, omission or delay.

- to prepare and publish a plan for the provision of services maintained.

Understandably, given the route taken through public care by the majority of children who get adopted, the 2002 Act retains the lead responsibility for arranging adoption support services in the hands of the social services authority. And the duties placed in this respect relate only to the specified list of services set out earlier. The implimentation of the Children Act 2004 may well provide the impetus for a fuller integration of services in adoption support as elsewhere. However, as it stands, the law itself only requires that the social services functions, and those of voluntary adoption agencies, are co-ordinated. The wider aspiration of mainstreaming adoption support and building local service capacity across health and education as well as social work is given no additional statutory force in the Act. Further regulations or even legislation will be needed to strengthen this policy commitment.

Instead, co-ordinating and mainstreaming the development of adoption support services is driven by performance management systems connected, for example, to the National Adoption Standards (Department of Health 2001b) and by policy exhortation. Hence each local authority is expected to plan therapeutic services for adopted children within the context of the local CAMHS strategy with the NHS and other agencies, making full use of joint funding arrangements where appropriate. As it stands this is a weak statutory mandate for co-ordinating services and building their capacity to provide a responsive and integrated approach to adoption support in the round.

More than this, it also embodies a very conventional professional and bureaucratic approach to service development and to day-to-day practice culture. The legal mandate is likely to be strengthened and service structures may get better integrated where Children's Trusts are established. This may provide the opportunity for a related shift in the culture of practice. But, for now, the Act sustains the age-old divide between 'service provision' by professionals and 'service use' by clients or consumers.

This is partly due to the individual care planning approach to assessing eligibility for services at the heart of the legislation. As we see below, in the discussion of the duties and powers relating to eligibility and access, this approach can trap people like Bella and the rest in a 'service user' role. At the service system level, however, it is the emphasis on the 'corporate' nature of joint working and partnership that confirms the restricted vision underpinning the commitment to planning and co-ordination. There is no talk here of different 'stakeholder' groups, as there has been elsewhere in the new era of integrated children's services (Department for Education and Employment 1999). For example, nothing is said about people affected by adoption being 'engaged in the planning of service developments' (Department for Education and Skills 2003c, p.38) as is now the aspiration for families with disabled children who have been born to them. No mention is made of adoptive parents and others being enabled to play a central role in the 'design and delivery' of their own services. Contrast this, for example, with the position of parents with young children living in Sure Start areas or service users generally under the Social Care and Health Act 2000. Curiously, adoptive status seems to marginalise those affected in relation to the new participation rights of other vulnerable groups. Arguably, this is a good example of discrimation against minority groups.

Only in the case of financial support does a slightly different picture emerge. Here the policy of integration and mainstreaming is far more effectively advanced in law. Unlike the co-ordination of local agency services, the mainstreaming of financial support has been underpinned by new legal duties. Under the Act itself financial support, in the form of one-off and continuous payments, can be made where it is shown that such payments 'help secure a suitable adoption where a child cannot be readily adopted because of a financial obstacle' (Department of Health 2003b, para 99). And in recognition of this special claim on additional financial support by adoptive families, changes in the Finance Act 2003 ensured that such payments were to be disregarded for the purposes of income-related benefits and tax credits. Additionally a right to Statutory Adoption Pay and Leave and Statutory Paternity Pay and Leave was introduced in the Employment Act 2002, commencing in April 2003. This too conveyed the recognition that adopters and their children, where relationships were not already established, should have a right to retrieve, in effect, support consistent with that received by procreational families at birth.

Contrast this, for example, with the silence in the Adoption and Children Act 2002 about any corresponding right to health visiting or community nursing advice on placement of an older child. It seems that the need to co-ordinate support in adoption has been taken more seriously in the Treasury than it has been at the Department of Health. In this respect, at least, it could be said that financial overall support is being more effectively mainstreamed than is local service delivery. Adoptive parents are enabled to enter the mainstream world of parenting whilst also having their specific claims of distinctiveness recognised. It is just this balance that is missing in the way the planning and co-ordination duties have been placed on local agencies by the Act.

Arguably, too, co-ordination could be further compromised by an additional power in the Act that enables local authorities to separate out their duty to arrange services from their role in providing directly themselves. This is the third question to be asked about how the emergent adoption support framework will function at the local level.

Commissioning adoption support: what shape will the adoption support service system take locally?

The Act allows local authorities to commission adoption support services as well as, or instead of, providing them directly themselves. If services are contracted out it must be either to registered adoption societies or to the new breed of adoption support agencies defined in the Act. The Guidance makes it clear that the development of a local mixed economy of specialist services should be seen as a positive opportunity for enhancing services. Local authorities 'are encouraged to work with existing non-statutory providers of high quality adoption support services, especially voluntary adoption agencies, to take advantage of the expertise that they have in this area and avoid duplication of service provision' (Department of Health 2003b, para 22).

It is also possible for consortia of authorities to devise a tailored plan for a wider geographical area. Proposals to move to regional support services for specific therapeutic interventions have already been made, in lieu of any accurate evidence about the exact nature and extent of need for specialist support at the local level (Rushton and Dance 2002). Given the fact that it has been almost invariably voluntary agencies (for example, Coram Family and the Post Adoption Centre) and mutual aid organisations (for example, Adoption UK) that have provided any dynamism and innovation in adoption support prior to the Act, this encouragement is well judged.

However, it is important to make a distinction between a model of commissioning that is driven by market values and methods in local services and one which is informed by a network approach to organising and managing services (Hill and Hupe 2002). The argument here is that the first, based on consumerist principles, is a good deal less likely to stimulate a local culture of supportive practice than the latter, based on collaboration. This is not to say that many adoptive parents themselves have not for some time been voting with their feet at the point when they come to feel that their needs and requests for effective help locally are not met with an adequate response.

A case can even be made here for the facilitation of a network and market in expert services, funded on commission by the local authority. Services might be purchased through service level agreements on behalf of a group of parents or children and/or by direct payments made on an individual basis. Law and guidance encourages this strategy inasmuch as it tends to define adoption support services as professionally provided interventions of one sort or another. Indeed the demand for funds to purchase external expertise in exceptional circumstances has been driven as much by pressure from parents as it has by service entrepreneurs and policy makers.

However, it is difficult to see how the occasional benefit in the individual situation should be elevated as a guiding principle for service development in general. The aim of the Act, to build a local inter-professional capacity for the provision of responsive adoption support services, is not served by the wider recent policy turn back to consumerist and market models.

One danger here is that co-ordinated networks of local professional competence in, and commitment to, adoption will be less likely to emerge and consolidate. For when it comes to joint working, networks and markets tend to make uneasy bed-fellows, as Hill and Hupe (2002) explain. This is not to say that carefully managed commissioning arrangements are impossible to conceive and implement. Good examples can be found and have been supported by research evidence.

An early model was provided by the 'complementary contact' established between the independent, Post Adoption Centre (PAC) and East Sussex County Council (Burnell and Briggs 1996, 1997). Here specialist advice and therapeutic support informed by the expertise of the PAC was made available locally to both family members and professionals involved in adoption and adoption support, at certain key points of the decision-making and service provision process. The project itself was steered by a joint group consisting of agency managers and adoption professionals and representatives of local adoption service user-groups. There is evidence that such an approach can make a positive impact on the culture of a local service (Luckock 1997, 2000). Nonetheless, as we discuss in Chapter 5, specialist consultation and formal intervention is best understood as an enhancement to rather than a replacement of routine adoption support.

Equally important, though, is the need to think afresh about the idea of 'expertise'. For expertise is just as much something that is produced by practitioners, parents and children engaged together in the search for supportive solutions as it is something owned and delivered professionally from the clinic or office. Hence, still less does the market model of commissioning meet the test set for adoption support by the 'family practices' perspective developed in this book. Any distinctive local culture of adoption support would arguably fail to emerge. Just such a culture, of collaboration by parents, professionals and children in the careful nurturing of adoptive family life, is essential if the aspirations of the Act are to be realised in the day-to-day experiences of adoptive family practice. The service as a whole must be adoption competent. In these circumstances it is especially important that the service mix and the means by which it is purchased are carefully constructed. In the final chapter of this book we explore one approach to the development of a culture of collaborative support, by making use of the idea that effective adoption support is more likely to be achieved when a 'community of practice' is explicitly cultivated (Wenger, McDermott and Snyder 2002).

Eligibility and access: The duty to assess need for adoption support services and facilitate access

If co-ordination of the general service framework for adoption support is weakly underpinned in legislation greater responsibility falls on planning and co-ordination in each particular situation when needs arise. The opportunity also arises in face-to-face practice engagements for the establishment of the kind of collaborative culture of working we are arguing in favour of here. After all, policy is made as well as implemented through the way in which the actual day-to-day encounters at the front door of services are played out.

We turn now to the second aspect of the twin-track strategy for adoption support. Here we explore the extent to which the duties of assessment in the Act, and the powers enabling local authorities to facilitate entitlement and access to adoption support services, really do provide keys to help open the door to effective support in mainstream services as a whole. We consider too whether the approach to assessment and co-ordination on the ground might enable a culture of collaborative adoptive family support practice to be built up in day-to-day practice.

There are two main questions to be posed here. First, do the duties and powers in respect of assessing need and planning services guarantee eligibility and access to support sufficient to meet the needs of adoptive families? And second, is the way in which that assessment and planning is done appropriate given those needs?

Case study: Bella and Jon Freeman, and Brad Taylor

Take the case of Bella, Brad and Jon once more. It may well be that this new family would benefit from some of the adoption support services now available in their area. Extra money to sort out the house would obviously help. An introduction for Bella to other adoptive parents who meet in the monthly support group in town, and babysitting for Brad and Jon when she is there, might be useful. Perhaps the adoption therapist employed by the local independent adoption support agency would be able to offer time to Bella, maybe Jon too, so that she can think and talk through any impact of partner Jeremy's departure on present difficulties at home. And so on. But can social worker Jenny deliver the goods if she and Bella agree they might be helpful? And in any case how would this sort of support, available only because she is adopting Brad, help with the bigger problems she anticipates in getting family life into a settled pattern? How will Jenny's promised adoption support services help Bella make the health visitor understand that Brad's current health care plan is not working now he has moved from the familiar foster home, and assist in getting the hospital to agree to an earlier clinic appointment? And who will help her explain to his school that Jon's deteriorating behaviour in class is probably connected to Brad's arrival and ensure that he too gets some time with the special needs assistant? How, in real life, will the 'profile' of Bella's adoptive family and its particular needs be raised in these busy mainstream services, which have more than enough to do already?

We think about Bella and her family again as we explore what the law and policy prescribes. First, though, we summarise the main duties placed on local authorities in relation to the task of linking people affected by adoption to the framework of support services that must be developed in the area.

Local authority duties to facilitate access to adoption support services

At the request of:

(a) a child who may be adopted, their parents and guardians

(b) a person wishing to adopt a child

(c) an adopted person, their parents, natural parents and former guardians

(d) any other person described in Regulations,

or in the following circumstances:

(a) when considering adoption for a 'looked after child'

(b) when considering a match for a child

(c) at the 4 week review of adoption placement,

each local authority must, in order to facilitate access to the new support services:

- carry out an assessment (or review) of the needs for adoption support services

- decide whether to provide (or continue providing) services to meet assessed needs

- prepare a plan for the provision of those services and review that plan

- notify the local Primary Care Trust and Local Education Authority if there may be a need for the provision of their services.

In order to undertake these duties effectively each local authority may:

- request the help of local voluntary adoption or adoption support agencies in assessing need and any other local authority who can assist in assessing, deciding about and planning services
- link the assessment of need for adoption support to any other assessment of needs being undertaken.

The concern to reduce risk of placement breakdown in the escalating number of new adoptions of children from public care, whilst minimising pressure on local authority budgets, has created a hierarchy of eligibility within the wider adoptive kinship network. In the first phase of implementation, from October 2003, the Regulations were particularly targeted on meeting the needs of adoptive families created when children were placed from care. They covered both new adoptions and existing adoptions where the adopted child was less than 18 years old.

Bella has certainly had her family needs put firmly at the forefront. By contrast the right to an assessment for adoption support services for a birth parent (or relative of the adoptive child or any other person with whom the adoptive child had an important relationship) was restricted to claims for assistance to facilitate (existing) contact arrangements. We discuss the nature of effective support for communication and contact between birth and adoptive families in detail in Chapter 6. It took persistent lobbying by the British Association for Adoption and Fostering (BAAF) and others to persuade the government to recognise the need to offer the equal opportunity of specific support to birth relatives if contact was to succeed in some cases. This was unsurprising given the fact that, under the New Labour 'fresh start' approach to adoption, contact tends to be seen as a potential risk to placement rather than as a proper source of continuity and stability in adoptive family life (Bridge and Swindells 2003).

Managing eligibility and access: who has the right to get what in adoption support?

Whilst the Adoption and Children Act 2002 ensures that adoptive status gives Bella and her family a right to an *assessment* of their needs for adoption support services it does not guarantee that they will actually be *eligible* to receive them. Still less will it secure any right to priority for assessment or provision of the extra mainstream service help they might need.

Jenny, on behalf of the local authority, must establish what Brad and Bella's needs now are for additional support from the specified services. In fact she, or a colleague, will have already made this assessment, as the list of duties above indicates. This would have been done first when the decision was taken that Brad should be adopted and again when he was matched with Bella. It is now time, three weeks into placement, for earlier judgements about needs and services to be reviewed. However there is no requirement in law that the local authority must prioritise any needs Bella may have over those of other adoptive families, especially where resources are scarce. The decision might be that Bella and Jon would benefit from time with the independent adoption therapist but that another adoptive family had a prior claim because their situation is more pressing. And maybe the budget for financial support for home improvement, to maximise space and thereby help Brad settle, is spent for now.

By providing a right to assessment of needs for adoption support services but not automatic entitlement to those services the law tries to manage the tension between two policy objectives. It recognises the special claims of adoptive families to enhanced support whilst at the same time heeding the fears of local authorities that these claims might overwhelm resources available to fund the services demanded.

This is an improvement on what went before. Local authorities must formally assess and make decisions on who should get what additional help. And they were given extra funds from April 2003 to fill gaps in and develop their adoption support services to enable more people to be included. However, Bella, Brad and Jon still have no right to appeal (as opposed to simply complain) about a decision that goes against them. Bella may choose to call on the local ASSA but, as we see later, whilst the ASSA might be able to trouble-shoot a better deal in an individual case she or he has no authority to guarantee any service will always be provided.

Furthermore, Bella and the family have fewer formal claims still when it comes to getting the health visitor, hospital and school to give priority to their needs as a new adoptive family. Jenny the social worker can link the adoption support services assessment she must do under the Act with any assessment that health and education colleagues are undertaking in accordance with the legislation they work to. She must also notify education and health if she thinks Brad, or Jon, has a need for their services. She may be a good advocate, as might the local authority ASSA who can be called in the formal broker role under the Act.

Health and education plans may already be in place, for Brad at least, because he remains a 'looked after' child until he is actually adopted. Care planning arrangements and 'corporate parenting' demand that the mainstream services collaborate with social work in making sure they are sensitive to need. The Children Acts 1989 and 2004, and other legislation, demands that this is so. And the local Children's Trust, as and when it has developed the capacity to co-ordinate and fund services across the board, may prioritise the needs for integrated services of adoptive families once children like Brad cease to remain 'looked after'.

Yet Brad's adoptive status, and the distinctive needs that come with it, are not themselves recognised in law as giving him and his family any special claim on mainstream service support. In this way eligibility and access in adoption to effective family support remains only partially provided for in legislation. Bella's adoptive family could certainly become anonymous, its particular needs ignored or misunderstood, if the local service culture is not itself informed and responsive.

Assessment and planning in practice: the worst of both worlds?

In a situation like this, where Bella as an adoptive parent can look forward to few formal rights to services, it is the quality of the professional practice available to help her get access that takes on particular importance. Of course the ASSA role is crucial here, as we have suggested. And we discuss in detail how it might be best deployed in the next chapter. But for now it is the nature and focus of professional practice per se, in assessing need and planning proposed services, that is our concern. Government policy in this respect is extremely upbeat. For example, official Guidance goes so far as to suggest that people like Bella will become 'armed' with the information that emerges in any assessment under the Act (Department of Health 2003b, para 51). They will be enabled as a result to refer themselves directly to services or to make use of the professional help on offer in gaining access.

This could well become a reality. In many cases a speedy and flexible response to a request for support, combined with good information and advice, will suffice. This makes absolute sense where people who ask for some support know exactly what they need, but understand less how to go about getting it. Additional financial support is the prime example. The Act certainly allows for a light touch and minimal bureaucracy where this kind of assessment and planning is concerned. And where one-off advice and sign-posting will not suffice, in more demanding and complex situations such as that faced by Bella and Jenny, a formal professional approach is not necessarily a bad thing. Formal plans do at least enable service providers who have signed up to them to be called to some account later down the line if they fail to deliver.

At least Bella, if she can convince Jenny and her managers of her pressing need, will get written confirmation of exactly what help she is going to get, who is responsible for providing it and when the arrangements will be checked and revised. This was not the experience of the large majority of adoptive parents prior to the implementation of the Act. The planning and review requirements now laid down in law make sense for this reason, even if Jenny (and the local authority ASSA who oversees it all) ultimately have limited authority over the extent to which mainstream services can be held to account.

But Bella and others could also be disarmed. For this is a professional process that faces back to a 'corporate parenting' mode of care planning rather than forward to an approach grounded in facilitating increased recognition and autonomy for adoptive family life. This underlying incongruity is accentuated by risks of bureaucracy and poor sensitivity. This is because the standard Assessment Framework model (Department of Health 2000b) is required to be the main means of making sense of adoptive family life. The criticism of the Framework, that it is intrinsically bureaucratic and insensitive in reaching an in-depth understanding of family dynamics, applies generally in children's social services (Cleaver, Walker and Meadows 2004). There is no evidence that the change to this broader model of 'needs' assessment has produced a notable improvement in services.

The risks are enhanced in the case of adoptive family dynamics. These are even less well described in theory and empirical research, as we saw in Chapter 2, let alone grasped and understood with confidence and authority by most professional practitioners. It is not at all clear that the amended version of the Framework, proposed for use specifically in adoption support, will address the core problem. As we explained in the earlier discussion and analysis adoptive family life is not best understood by taking a conventional, normative developmental, systemic or life-cycle approach and adding in special 'adoption tasks' that must be overcome if success is to be achieved.

Bureaucratic procedures, unless they are sensitively managed by adoption-competent practitioners, tend to reinforce the sense of exposure parents like Bella feel when they are faced with the need to ask for support. Anxiety and ambivalence dominate, as we have said, as struggling and often desperate parents have to present themselves for official scrutiny once more as a condition of getting access to support. The way this is handled is of the utmost significance. Indeed the evidence of research (Hart *et al.* 2002; Lowe *et al.* 1999) and experience is unequivocal. The primary test of effectiveness in arrangements for adoption support is the capacity of practitioners at the front door of the system to recognise and contain that anxiety and ambivalence and to allow people to feel safe enough to explore their real fears.

The Assessment Framework formula for family life Jenny carries in her professional head might be of use in the official process of recording details of Brad's compromised development, and Jon's unease, informing the case a social worker must make for additional support. But Bella is not likely to feel that this is her story too unless her feelings, say of shame, humiliation, fear and growing anger, are grasped first and reflected back to her. Nor, therefore, are things at home and beyond really going to change for Brad and Jon. And of course it is just these feelings and their impact that have got lost from sight in the contemporary administrative discourse of 'needs-led services' (Ward and Rose 2002), 'risk minimisation' (Hodge 2003), and 'integrated children's system' approaches to services (Department of Health 2002c).

So unless care and imagination are brought to the task locally it is possible that Bella and the family could get the worst of both worlds of adoption support, on the one hand given no formal rights to eligibility for adoption support services, or priority claims on mainstream services, and on the other having to endure potentially alienating bureaucratic procedures that prove a depressing reminder that they are, after all, still clients of the corporate state.

In conclusion: getting the balance right?

The limitations of the legislation of adoption support are best understood as being the outcome of the intrinsically tricky balancing act we have described in this chapter. The adoptive family, we have argued, is caught in the borderlands between the world of 'corporate parenting' and the earned autonomy of normative family life. The distinctiveness of the adoptive family, and its demands on systems of support, requires that law and policy find the best resolution of the tensions in the ambiguous status of this different and potentially marginalised family. As we have seen, legislation gets it only partly right. The duties on agencies for service development and individual eligibility are too weak whilst the reliance on bureaucratic fixes is too great. Yet at the heart of the framework, where specific services for those affected by adoption might be united with shifts in the responsiveness of mainstream services, there is a real space for effective practice at the local level.

Bella will not just have to rely on her social worker Jenny being better than average, genuinely understanding in helping her face her scary feelings and practically effective at getting things done in the confusing service world. She can now also call on her ASSA, and the statutory role and positional power that person has been given. This will help her to promote the claims of her family to really useful help now that things have started to get seriously difficult at home. In the next chapter we explore in detail exactly how the ASSA might make a difference.

Chapter 4

'Someone There for Us'

The Adoption Support Services Adviser in Context

Introduction: Adoption Support Services Advisers and other helpers

This chapter explores potential ways for the role of the Adoption Support Services Adviser (ASSA), along with related roles such as key and family support workers, to develop within the law and policy guidance outlined in the previous chapter. The ASSA is there to provide help to anybody affected by adoption, at any stage of the adoption process. However, given the remit of this book, we focus mostly on their role in helping adoptive families, and in supporting other formal helpers involved with them. The guidance makes it clear that some families will not need much, if any, formal support. But, this chapter is about adoptive families like those of Lucy and Bill, Bryony and Rachael, and Bella. Each of these families is likely to need a lot of support, and the local ASSA, in collaboration with other practitioners, should play an important role in both providing and facilitating it, throughout the adoption process.

Chapter 4 is organised as follows: first we outline precisely how the law and policy guidance frame the role, its responsibilities and its place within local organisational contexts. Second, we consider the support needs of adoptive families, along with the functions and the relationships that are best established to fulfil them. Finally we consider both the difficulties and the opportunities that the development of the ASSA and other support roles offer in fulfilling the needs of families. In doing this, we map out five different models of the ways in which support roles in adoption can develop. These models are broker, systems healer, social supporter, educator and therapeutic-broker.

Broadly speaking, the first two roles – broker and systems healer – are about doing things to the service system, i.e. the capacity-building ASSA to which we referred in the previous chapter and the reactive trouble-shooter for individual families. The other three roles – social supporter, educator and therapeutic-broker – are each about relationships, i.e. particular modes of support provision to individuals and families. Each role as we discuss it here is an ideal type. Of course, in practice elements of the different models can be combined, and we discuss our ideas about how this might best happen.

To give the reader a working understanding of how we will be using terms throughout this chapter, in relation to the ASSA role, we have provided brief overviews of our ideal type support models in Table 4.1.

Table 4.1 Models of adoption support	
Role	**Characteristics**
Broker	• Fulfils a strictly care management role with individual families. • Operates as a mediator between different services, and to some extent as an advocate/trouble-shooter. • Puts together packages of support for individual families and/or provides them with relevant information to access services directly themselves.
Systems healer	• Provides advocacy for 'communities of adoptive practice'. • Has little or no involvement with individual families. • Ensures appropriate systems and organisational structures are in place to help adoptive families.
Social supporter	• Provides long-term direct help to individuals. • May have statutory professional support role, or non-professional support role.
Therapeutic-broker	• Works directly with parents and/or children. • Undertakes intensive emotional labour, often underpinned by a professional training, key task. • Holds in mind the difficulties faced by adoptive families. • Contains the family – explicitly avoids involving other workers where possible. • Provides advocacy within the service system for children and parents.
Educator	• Has explicit pedagogic function. • Teaches others – members of adoptive families, or professionals – about the consequences of adoption and how to deal with them.

Further on in the chapter, lessons learned from other contexts, in particular services to disabled children and adults with mental health problems, are drawn on to consider further the development of the five support models outlined in Table 4.1 for the roles of ASSAs and other helpers. We make the case for combining elements of the different models to ensure that, within any given service system, adoptive families have access to workers who are adoption-competent. However, we argue that to be effective in whatever the ASSA does locally, the therapeutic-broker model must be at the heart of her or his practice. Central to this role is really understanding and appreciating what adoptive family practice means.

We now set out the role of the ASSA and related helpers, as stated in law and policy guidance. We then go on to consider the different ways in which the role of the ASSA and other adoption support roles might be put into practice.

The ASSA and other helpers in the law and policy guidance

Someone there: to do what?

In accordance with legislation, every local authority with social services responsibilities is required to appoint a person who is identified by the title 'ASSA'. Whilst an actual ASSA must be appointed, many functions of the role can be delegated and dispersed. The Adoption and Children Act 2002 makes it possible for most adoption support services to be delegated to other statutory disciplines or agencies, or contracted out, for example, to voluntary groups. However, three key support functions for which the ASSA has responsibility – the provision of counselling, advice and information about support through the tax and benefits system – cannot be contracted out. Therefore, if ASSAs are to have no other role in local support provision, they must at the very least be seen to fulfil these three functions.

For many years now adoptive parents in particular have complained at the lack of adoption-specific support services. Some comfort can then be taken in the fact that under the Act, every local authority must appoint somebody whose role it is to come into work, possibly even five days a week, and address, at least in some way, the needs of people affected by adoption. If the ASSA undertakes this task with an understanding of the difficulties inherent in giving and receiving adoption support which we outlined in Chapter 1, there is much to be optimistic about.

Regarding what is stated in the Regulations and Guidance about how the ASSA role should be executed, let us start with the precise wording of the Regulations:

The function of the adoption support services adviser shall be to give advice and information, to

Persons who may be affected by the adoption or proposed adoption of a child, as to –

(i) services that may be appropriate to those persons; and

(ii) how those services may be made available to them.

(Department of Health 2003d, Regulation 4 (2))

At first sight, ASSAs are little more than glorified and, we hope, well-informed signposters, sympathetically pointing people affected by adoption towards services ASSAs think might be helpful.

But, of course, even this very limited role takes for granted that there is sufficient capacity in local service systems for ASSAs to have somewhere to point. This dilemma provides a good explanation for the lack of ambition seemingly encompassed within the role. We know that in developing policy guidance the government is working from a very low base line of provision and expertise across the country (Rushton and Dance 2002). Pragmatism is a key feature of the way in which the role has been envisaged. Adoption services are patchy, with the operation of a postcode lottery of available services (Rushton and Dance 2002). Little wonder then that the role specified in the regulations seems unambitious to anyone wanting to profoundly improve adoption services.

Significantly, the accompanying guidance to the regulations proposes that the ASSA should address the patchy nature of provision and includes strategic capacity building within the remit. Though nothing is said of the means by which the ASSA her or himself will rise above the general capacity deficit: she or he is to have a 'proactive role in promoting and maintaining the necessary agreements at a strategic level across agencies' (Department of Health 2003b, para 36).

Some national visibility is also proposed. ASSAs are encouraged by the guidance to work inter-professionally with each other across geographical boundaries by developing ASSA networks. This practice will:

...also provide a mechanism for helping to support smooth transitions. [ASSAs] will provide a route in for social workers where looked after children are placed for adoption across local authority boundaries or where an adoptive family with a current adoption support plan moves to another local authority area. (Department of Health 2003, para 40)

A pessimistic reading is that ASSAs might end up being scapegoated for the failure of different authorities to reach agreement over payments for support services. A more optimistic reading sees them making effective regional and national connections to the benefit of local families and the local service system.

With regard to how much direct support ASSAs might give in individual cases, the regulations are confusing. They do not explicitly distinguish between the roles of the children's social worker, the family support worker and the appointed ASSA. Also, despite the references directly to the ASSA in relation to individual families in the regulations, the guidance specifies a more proactive role for the ASSA in healing the troubles of the system, both local and nationwide, than it does for those of individual children and their families. However, this Systems Healer role might have a knock-on effect. Furthermore, at least *some* role in helping individual families is envisaged.

The confusion about this in the Regulations and Guidance has partially come about as a result of government policy makers trying to balance different priorities for developing the role of the ASSA and related helpers. To some extent, efforts have been made to please everybody: healing the system, providing a visible entry to the service world, and working intensively with individual families have all been emphasised somewhere as important jobs to be done under the broad banner of the ASSA role. The guidance makes an attempt to bring together the Systems Healer role with one that addresses the needs of individual families, making the ASSA a kind of super-advocate:

> [The ASSA should have] a pro-active, brokerage role in ensuring that the best possible arrangements are in place to support each particular adoption placement, and a role in responding quickly and constructively to problems that arise with these arrangements. (Department of Health 2003b, para 36)

However, when it comes down to work with individual families, once again pragmatism seems to be the order of the day. Distinctions are made in the guidance between the role of ASSAs in large authorities and in smaller ones. In large authorities they are full-time posts, and would 'not personally be responsible for delivering adoption support services beyond advice and information, the hands on tasks being undertaken by adoption support workers or link workers'; in smaller authorities 'the level of demand for the adviser may mean that they can provide more hands-on-support' (Department of Health 2003b, para 39).

We wonder if the division of labour in this way, according to whether an authority is large or small, is somewhat over-simplistic and inappropriate. However, it is when it comes to assessment and day-to-day service co-ordination at an individual level, that the envisaged role of the ASSA is most confusing. Let us first consider assessment. The guidance suggests that requests for assessment or services will usually be routed through the ASSA. However, 'this does not preclude it coming by other routes such as the child's social worker, the link worker for the family or referral from another agency' (Department of Health 2003b, para 50).

Thinking about what might happen in practice, one soon realises that the ASSA is only likely to serve as a conduit for established adoptive families seeking an entry into the service world. That is to say those who have had little or no contact with adoption workers, possibly for many years, and who may have become aware of the ASSA as a first port of call, for example by seeing an advertisement in the local paper. Thinking back to our three families, it is unlikely that in putting together their support plan, or even subsequently, any of them would have any automatic involvement with their local ASSA. This is because, as new families, their family support worker or other practitioner would have put their plan together before the ASSA had a chance to get involved. In thinking about assessment then, the Regulations and Guidance do not make clear the distinctions between what should happen for newly formed families and those established prior to the Act.

Moving on to consider service co-ordination, no mention at all is made of a role for the ASSA:

> One of the workers already involved in delivering services in the plan will be responsible for overseeing the delivery of the plan, and will be the first point of contact for the service recipient. This may be the child's social worker, the adoptive parents' link worker, the birth parents' independent support worker, or any other worker delivering services in the plan who will be able to fulfil the coordination and monitoring role. This will provide a sound foundation for the provision of the services. (Department of Health 2003b, para 77)

As well as not mentioning the ASSA as a potential co-ordinator of services, adoptive parents are not acknowledged as people who might fulfil a co-ordination role with respect to their own family. Thinking back to our case studies, given the strain they are under at the moment it might seem quite unlikely that any of the parents in our three families would wish to take on this function themselves at present. However, they might, since doing this task might help give some of them more of a feeling of being in control of their family. Also, as we know from accounts of parents of disabled children, the failure of professionals to respond to the needs of such families means that the role may fall to the parent by default anyway (Close 1999). Better, maybe, to be formally prepared for it.

This omission flies in the face of developments in other areas, for example in services to disabled children (Department for Education and Skills 2003c). In one pilot study, parents were trained alongside professionals to be the co-ordinators of their own families (Tait, Beattie and Dejnega 2002). Given the way in which adoptive parents and others affected by adoption have played a key role in developing adoption services, not to include them as potential co-ordinators is a regrettable omission. Furthermore, it falls foul of the broad moves towards participatory and collaborative approaches of current health and social care policy (Department of Health 1999a; Department of Health 2000c; Sang 2002).

Whilst the regulations give the ASSA the opportunity to have a direct support role, it is clear from the guidance that, depending on the context, dual structures are envisaged. The message is that in most authorities, the ASSA will not undertake much direct work, such as social support or therapy, with families. Rather, the emphasis has been placed on her or his role as:

- a first port of call (for established adoptive families not in contact with local services at least)

- an information and advice provider (primarily for service users)

- a Systems Healer in her or his role as network facilitator for professionals, and super-advocate for anyone involved in adoption.

What is missing however, is a discussion of the ASSA's potential role as a therapist, social supporter or educator. The implication in the guidance is that the first two of these three roles are somehow delegated to other professional helpers such as family support workers, although how such delegation might occur and what, organisationally, the relationship between ASSAs and key or family support workers might be is up for grabs. The third role, that of educator, is entirely missing from the discussion in the guidance on the role of the ASSA. Given the major emphasis now in government policy on the importance of learning, both within public sector organisations, and for users of those services, it is surprising that no mention is made of the ASSA's educative role (National Health Service 2002). The guidance recognises the role of the ASSA in building capacity locally. However, the question remains as to how this 'capacity' is to acquire appropriate skills in adoption work.

Someone there: who?

In order to do justice to the needs of adoptive families, adoption workers need appropriate skills to do their job. The regulations acknowledge this skills need since they actually lay down what the ASSA must be capable of.

> The local authority shall not appoint a person as an adoption support services adviser unless satisfied that his knowledge and experience of –
>
> (a) the process of adoption; and
>
> (b) the effect of the adoption of a child on persons likely to be affected by the adoption,
>
> is sufficient for the purposes of the work that he is to perform. (Department of Health 2003d, Regulation 4(3))

The ASSA is required to be adoption *competent*, with knowledge and experience of its process and effects commensurate with the actual work that they will undertake. Implicit here is an understanding of the fragility and differences that are embedded within adoptive family life that we discussed in the first two chapters of this book. However, depending on the precise local interpretation of the ASSA role, the application of this competence may vary. For example, an ASSA working principally as a broker will need different skills to one incorporating a therapeutic function into their role.

No specific professional qualifications for the ASSA are referred to. Thus in theory, ASSAs could be adoptive parents, birth parents, adopted persons, social workers, therapists, teachers or any other individual who proved her or his competence in relation to the work she or he was to perform. This flexibility in constituting the role has the potential to lead to some very creative job descriptions and selection criteria.

The flexibility in the perceived background of the ASSA is, however, not followed through to the vision in the guidance for the keyworker co-ordinating the plan. As with the keyworker role envisaged by government for families with disabled children (Department for Education and Skills 2003c), the guidance suggests that it makes most sense for the adoption keyworker to be one of the professionals working most closely with the family. This could, for example be a Special Educational Needs Co-ordinator (SENCO) or a Child and Adolescent Mental Health Services (CAMHS) therapist. It is not automatically a social work role.

The proposed competence of the ASSA does not specifically include knowledge and/or experiences of services to meet the needs of those affected by adoption. Given the ASSA's major role as a systems healer outlined in the guidance, this is surprising. Furthermore, whilst adoption competence is stressed, no generic skills, such as multi-disciplinary teamworking, benefits knowledge, administrative capabilities, are highlighted as necessary for the role. One might argue that such issues are beyond the remit of Regulations and Guidance. However, these are important omissions since even a cursory glance at the literature shows that the effectiveness of roles such as that of the ASSA can hardly be taken for granted (Mukherjee, Beresford and Sloper 1999; Roaf 2002; Simpson, Miller and Bowers 2003a, 2003b).

In order to make life better for people affected by adoption, ASSAs must be up to the job. For example, the provision of information and advice about financial support is a key component of the ASSA role. This is to be welcomed since we have known for some time now that securing financial help for adoptive families is an important component of successful placements (Barth and Berry 1988). Because of this, ASSAs and other adoption workers should prioritise helping parents claim their entitlements, including adoption and Disability Living Allowance (DLA). However, working at a time when Welfare Rights Work has been gradually eroded from mainstream social work practice (Adams

2002), social worker ASSAs or family support workers may not have such skills. Manthorpe and Bradley draw attention to a series of research reports which identify that social workers are not trained and not interested in benefits (2002, p.279). Here, we are reminded of Hill's allegation that social workers often turn a deaf ear to material need (2000, p.132). Parents like Lucy and Bill, having cut their working hours considerably to care for the children, will need someone to help them through the complex benefits system to claim their entitlements. In-depth knowledge of how to claim financial support is then essential for the ASSA role.

Assisting with finances is, however, just one of the capabilities needed by prospective ASSAs. It is worth specifying precisely what we consider to be the optimum collection of skills for this role. Elaborating on the person-specification in the regulations, Tables 4.2 and 4.3 outline our interpretation of the skill and competence ideally required by ASSAs.

Table 4.2 Knowledge base for adoption competence

Knowledge base needed	Evidenced by
Local service system	Experience of working within, or being a user of, relevant local services (or demonstrating capacity to acquire this knowledge)
Effects of previous neglect and trauma Attachment theory 'Contact' issues in adoption	Relevant professional qualification Attendance at relevant training courses Self-learning
Formal adoption process	Work-related or personal experience
Statementing process	Work-related or personal experience

Towards the end of this chapter we will see how our different support models encompass potential skills of the ASSA. For the moment, it is enough to say that getting all these capabilities in one person is highly unlikely. Little wonder then that the guidance envisages dual structures (hence our emphasis on ASSA roles, in addition to a specific ASSA practitioner), as well as a relatively senior position for appointed ASSAs. It suggests that the role is formally vested in the second tier of council management, i.e. Head of Children's Services or Assistant Director for Children and Families: 'In larger authorities in particular, day to day delegation would occur as appropriate, thus giving the necessary direct

Table 4.3 Skills base for adoption competence

Skills needed	Evidenced by
Therapeutic	Relevant professional qualification *or* Membership of UKCP or BAC *or* Successful experience of adoption, fostering or working in a therapeutic community
Effective co-working with parents and children	Experience of co-working with parents and children
Effective working within multi-disciplinary team	Experience of multi-disciplinary team working
Effective inter-agency negotiator	Experience of having undertaken this
Effective IT and general administration	Experience of effectively administrating and IT literacy
Advocacy/welfare rights with clients	Experience of being an advocate *and/or* undertaking welfare rights work (or demonstrating the capacity to acquire these skills)
Advice on parenting and/or teaching skills	Relevant professional qualification *or* Experience of working in advice capacity to parents and/or teachers *or* Experience of adoption, fostering or therapeutic community working
Pedagogic	Experience of training and/or teaching adults

access to the Director of Social Services and the necessary influence across agencies' (Department of Health 2003b, para 39).

The envisaged seniority of this role is certainly to be welcomed, both because of the wide skills base that ASSAs would ideally possess, and to ensure that the ASSA has the necessary positional power to underpin the key role of advocating for adoptive communities of interest, and negotiating with other workers and other agencies.

Understanding what families need

So far in this chapter we have offered a working understanding of how the roles of ASSAs and related helpers are described in the Regulations and Guidance. But what does all this really mean to individual families and those who support them? We made some general points about the needs of adoptive families in the previous chapter. However, taking the adoptive family practice approach we outlined in Chapter 2, in this section we take a more detailed look at the everyday life of just one of our three adoptive families and explore what needs to happen to make it better for them.

Imagine that Lucy and Bill want some help with their family. It is one with fairly significant support needs. What kind of help might this family, with its complex combination of legacies and current difficulties, need? And what sort of a helper, at which part of the adoption process, would best enable them to get it? Table 4.4 shows the issues that are likely to be identified by Lucy and Bill soon after placement. The right-hand column suggests the realm of expertise within which addressing these needs belongs.

In a perfect world, most of these problems would have been anticipated by their family support worker and a plan made to address them even before the children moved in. Given what we know, however, about the current state of capacity and capabilities in adoption support, this is unlikely to have happened in most local authorities, although it is more likely in some voluntary agencies (J. Kaniuk, personal communication 2003).

Thinking now about processes and people, how might the help that Lucy and Bill need be given to them? In Parker's review (1999), adopters were clear on some rather basic factors, which might constitute the most valuable form of 'support' for them:

> Broadly speaking they were: its availability, a warm and trustworthy relationship, reliability (especially in doing what was promised when it was promised); the opportunity for unhurried discussion (not least the opportunity to share 'the good things'); informed guidance and advice about day-to-day problems and ... the sense of committed allegiance. (Parker 1999, p.90)

Table 4.4 Difficulties faced by Lucy, Bill and their children and the expertise needed to address them

Issues	Primary sphere of expertise
• How best to stop Brian smearing faeces and hitting out at others? • What must be done to help Alan, at the age of 8, attach? • Is Ellen traumatised and how can she recover from it? • How can the children be helped to have fun and enjoy childhood?	Therapeutic
• Which schools/nurseries should they go to and what extra support can they have? • Do Katie and Brian need a statement and if so, how do they get one? • Given the children's emotional and behavioural difficulties, how might they best learn at school?	Educational/ Therapeutic
• Are Lucy and Bill entitled to help with the housework and if so, who will arrange it? Who will do it? • What works best to help Lucy and Bill get through each day at the moment? • How do they find a babysitter for these children?	Social support
• How should Lucy and Bill go about integrating the children into their circle of friends and family? • How can Lucy and Bill keep their relationship intact? • Should the children see, write to or phone up their birth parents and former foster carers, and if so, when, where and why? What would be the implications of keeping up this communication and contact for daily family life?	Social support/ Therapeutic
Research evidence regarding the efficacy of grommets is unclear. • Should the children have them to help with their hearing difficulties? • If the medical evidence suggests they should, will the operations be too traumatic for them given the separations they have already endured?	Medical/ Therapeutic
• Are Lucy and Bill entitled to any specific benefits, and if so who is going to help them fill out the forms?	Welfare rights

A single 'hands on helper' who knows what she or he is doing is at the heart of this support vision (Gordon 2003). However, in addressing their difficulties, Lucy and Bill's family might well end up with many different professional helpers willing to lend a hand. The proposed ASSA role and structure of other (possibly delegated) helpers does nothing to sort out the potential for too many helpers to be involved in complex cases. It will be up to local workers and inter-agency groups to ensure that systems are streamlined.

This will be no easy task. Hart and Thomas (2000) showed that shortly after placement, in a family with three children, there were no less than 20 professional helpers involved as a result of the children's adoptive status. Add to these professional contacts relations with former foster carers, birth parents, new extended family and friends, and the list of new people in the children's lives become even longer. Clearly, in cases like this, parents, on behalf of their children, may well need some help co-ordinating involvement. As we explored above, the Regulations and Guidance provide some ideas about who might do this – in cases like Lucy and Bill's it is likely to be the family support worker – but not much on how they might go about it.

However, there is a step to be taken before the co-ordination role begins. Just because practitioners are available to help does not mean that they are helpful. Broadly speaking, the literature on the effectiveness of the role of the keyworker in the mental health and children's services context is awash with debates about lack of role clarity, unnecessary duplication of service delivery, professional infighting and the time professionals waste on using clients as metaphorical tennis balls (Roaf 2002; Simpson *et al.* 2003a and 2003b). Problems with keyworker management, burnout, training and adequacy of resources have also been raised.

Regarding indicators of effectiveness, developing a continuing therapeutic rapport with clients, adequate training and managerial supervision, as well as the need to develop responsive services, are highlighted as fundamental components of good practice (Bland 1997; Downing and Hatfield 1999; Simpson, Miller and Bowers 2003a).

A recent government publication endorsed the practice of one parent of a disabled child. She gave counters to those professionals she deemed to be worth working with. Those professionals could push their counters through her door so that she would know that it was worth opening to them (Department for Education and Skills 2003c). Exercising such control as a parent might seem extraordinary in the world of adoption.

Another issue related to this concerns the involvement of lots of new people in the lives of children with attachment difficulties like Alan, Brian, Katie and Ellen. They already have new parents, friends and extended family to get to know. Swamping them with professionals is unlikely to constitute good practice. The benefits of their involvement must clearly outweigh the attachment difficulties that might get exacerbated in the children, and the extra burden that professional involvement can place on parents. However, cutting down the number of professionals is not easy. As we can see from Table 4.4, a range of expertise is needed to address the needs of Lucy and Bill's family. Balancing the need for different expertise with keeping the number of people involved to a minimum is clearly no easy task.

Because of this dilemma, for an individual practitioner to be effective in supporting adoptive families with complex needs, they will need inter-disciplinary expertise. In this they are not dissimilar to practitioners working effectively with families with disabled children. Several sources clearly show that parents of children with special needs and other difficulties generally want a hands on co-ordinated keyworker approach to their needs by someone who knows what they are doing (Anon 1989; Audit Commission 1994; Cigno and Gore 1999; Close 1999; Mukherjee *et al.* 1999), and that provision of this type of service can help parents to cope better with their difficulties (Mukherjee *et al.* 1999; Tait *et al.* 2002).

In this way, a good worker would be someone who can get on with much of the work him or herself, and yet point people in exactly the right direction if others must be involved. In the case of Lucy and Bill's family, somebody who could fulfil their therapeutic needs, as well as co-ordinate the provision of other services, and help them access community and educational support would be ideal. Table 4.5 presents a summary of components from research in mental health and services to children with difficulties, which have been shown to be helpful in case management. These components can usefully be drawn on to help us think about the development of support roles in adoption.

Whilst in individual cases some components of this list would be more important than others, the table illustrates that inter-disciplinary skills are needed. Given the current arrangements for adoption support, and those implied by the Regulations and Guidance, these inter-disciplinary skills must stretch to family support workers.

Research also shows that for keyworkers to be effective, multi-disciplinary teamwork must take place in the context of a shared philosophy of care. Studies show that where this is lacking teams do not often function well, and yet regrettably such a lack is often a feature of multi-disciplinary teams (Miller, Freeman and Ross 2001; Norman and Peck 1999; Simpson *et al.* 2003a and 2003b). As Eraut argues, the problem is that multiple professions imply multiple perspectives and multiple practices and issues of differing power and status and different allegiances constrain co-operation (2002, p.11).

Making provision for strong inter-disciplinary roles in the law was an evidence-based aspect of the draft consultation that has become weakened in the actual Regulations and Guidance. It is only in smaller authorities that the role of 'broker' and 'hands-on helper' clearly come within the remit of the ASSA. In the final chapter of this book we return to this issue of shared working, and present our vision of how it might best proceed in the adoption

Table 4.5 Components of effective case management and keyworking

Small caseloads	Therapeutic relationship key
Clinical role for case manager	Psycho-social interventions used
Integrated team approach	Experienced team leader
Good supervision and training	Assertive outreach
Long-term regular and proactive relationship with parents and children	Working for children and parents, rather than the agency
Support in daily living	Focus on personal resources/strengths
24-hour or extended access	Most contact in the community
Liaison and improvement of communication between family members and other professionals/services involved with the family	Provision of information about, and help with access to facilities, opportunities, benefits and entitlements, with respect to all relevant statutory and voluntary agencies
Co-ordination of the delivery of services and the involvement of other professional workers	Participation in decisions made by statutory services concerning service provision to the family, acting as an advocate on behalf of parents and children

Source: from Mukherjee *et al.* 1999 and Simpson *et al.* 2003a.

context. We see the lack of a 'hands-on' support role as, envisaged for the ASSA by the Regulations and Guidance (Department of Health 2003b and 2003c), as a potential difficulty. Certainly when it comes to understanding what adoptive families need, practitioners must work with their hearts in connection with their minds. The Climbié Report makes clear that actual contact with clients in a caring role needs to occur if this connection is to happen (Laming 2003). Below we spell out the different models we see developing for the ASSA, and suggest where we think emphasis should be best placed.

Models of support provision: The ASSA and beyond

Our final purpose in this chapter is to explore in more detail how different ASSA functions might best be combined. In this section then, we first explore in some detail the support model ideal types introduced at the beginning of this chapter in relation to the work of the ASSA and the needs of Lucy and Bill's family. We then go on to consider how they might be combined if the ASSA is to work effectively with families like those of Lucy and Bill.

The Broker ASSA

The guidance, if not the regulations, clearly endorses the ASSA role developing primarily in the brokerage tradition. Here she or he is a kind of travel agent of the adoption world who knows her or his product very well, and who is able to put together a good deal for those who come forward expressing a wish to avail themselves of services. In the statutory sector, this is a popular model of keyworking (Burns 1997; Simpson *et al.* 2003a and 2003b).

Implicit here is the idea that supply of adoption support services, and indeed ASSAs, meets demand. For the ASSA, it is simply a question of sorting out which services are suitable for the particular individual who has presented themselves as being in need of a service. As we make clear throughout this book, we know that the social relations of help-seeking and help-giving in adoption support are far more complex than this. As such, these kinds of rational, consumerist models of care delivery are not necessarily the most helpful ways of thinking about support provision.

The fears, aspirations and personal motivations of service users and providers need to be understood within the complex interpersonal dynamics of adoption support provision (Hart *et al.* 2002). For example, having been through an intensive and intrusive assessment process by social services, where they had to prove their fitness to parent, Lucy and Bill are unlikely to simply nip down to their local ASSA for signposting to services. They are too busy working at being seen to cope by the professional who is already involved with their family. In this sense, the role of the ASSA in the legislation does not appear to take account of the difficulties that practitioners have in understanding adoptive family practices, their dynamics and difficulties, and the aspiration to make things better.

Nevertheless, developing the ASSA role in the brokerage tradition would certainly dovetail it closely to dominant forms of organisation in social work of roles of this type. There is some comfort in such familiarity. But the problems that have been encountered in other care management contexts with over-bureaucratisation, and the difficulty of practising individualised care with clients in these situations, apply equally well to the adoption context (Bjorkman and Hansson 2000). There are great dangers in the 'purchase' of services being so far removed from their 'consumption', not least of which is that the professional heart can get too quickly detached from the professional mind (Rogers 2001).

How might a Broker ASSA best respond to the difficulties experienced by Lucy and Bill's family? Given the issues we raised when we considered their likely support needs, this family could use some help in sorting out what services have to offer them. However, if, as is suggested in the guidance, the support plan is completed prior to the children moving in, and if Lucy and Bill are living in a large authority, the local ASSA is unlikely to have anything to do with them. Isobel, their family support worker, would most probably undertake co-ordination of the plan. In this sense the Broker ASSA's role with individual families would be delegated (either formally as part of an inter-agency plan, or simply by default) to somebody who had more direct contact with them.

But what if Lucy and Bill heard about their ASSA and wanted to approach her or him in a snatched moment whilst their children were all out at nursery or school? Their free time would need to correspond with the ASSA's advertised surgery time; if it did not, at least one of them would have to have gone to the evening surgery. Let us leave aside the fact that in going to the ASSA Lucy and Bill might themselves end up being responsible for unnecessarily duplicating services and roles, a criticism that has more often been levied at professionals and professional systems than at service users themselves. For parents who have not been properly briefed by their front-line workers, the ASSA is there to fall back on. If Isobel had not made them aware of wider services, a Broker ASSA could certainly signpost Lucy and Bill to local services set up under the Adoption and Children Act 2002, networks such as Adoption UK and useful texts on adoption. Assuming she or he had the necessary skills, she or he could also act as an information facilitator, individualising the overwhelming knowledge base to the specific needs of Lucy and Bill.

However, if family support workers or other front-line workers do their jobs properly, this level of involvement from the ASSA with individual families formed after the passing of the Adoption and Children Act 2002 is unlikely to be necessary. Local authorities should have standard user-friendly information packs which go out to adoptive parents on, or prior to, approval. Support workers should make a point of looking through the pack with the adoptive parents and where appropriate the children themselves, answering any questions they might have. For new adopters, the support worker is better placed than the ASSA to help parents find their way through it.

Appropriately trained, one job that the Broker ASSA might not have too much difficulty in undertaking is that of arranging financial support. However, particularly during the initial assessment, even this role would require in-depth knowledge of the family's circumstances. Once again, in Lucy and Bill's case, this role is probably best delegated to the family support worker.

And what would the relative stranger ASSA make of the big problems, for example the faeces smearing, attachment difficulties and the crisis in Lucy and Bill's relationship? To be effective, a Broker ASSA would have to rely on Lucy and Bill understanding what their difficulties are, and their being able and/or willing to communicate them to a stranger, most probably over the phone or within an office environment. Given Lucy and Bill's vulnerability, trust in this stranger ASSA, particularly as a statutory authority figure, might well not be forthcoming. And this might well apply even if the ASSA presents to them as more wise and knowledgeable than their support worker.

The need for brokers to develop a continuous trusting relationship with clients is pertinent here (Kanter 1989; Watkins 2001). ASSAs in large authorities in particular are unlikely to establish sufficient rapport to be anything more than superficial helpers to individual families. And without Lucy and Bill's trust and self-awareness of their own needs, the Broker ASSA is unlikely to undertake any in-depth social or therapeutic work (Howe 1996). Because of these reasons, Broker ASSAs may best be used by parents (and indeed other workers) as a kind of super advocate, in situations where the efforts of front-line workers have proved insufficient. For example, were Lucy and Bill to be having difficulty getting speech therapy for Ellen, given her or his relative authority, a Broker ASSA is more likely than a family support worker to work the system to Ellen's advantage. The danger here, though, is that the ASSA will do little more than present an extra layer of bureaucracy to be cut through.

Systems Healer ASSA

As we explained above, systems healer is an ASSA role specified in the guidance, if not in the regulations. The role here is of a relatively high-powered, strategic advocate, moving and shaking systems and influencing people within them, so that needs are better met. The acknowledged failure of service systems to children and families to act in a joined up way, and to meet the needs of adoptive families means that despite the best efforts of other helpers, Systems Healer ASSAs are likely to be kept very busy.

Thinking back to Lucy and Bill's family and the difficulties they are having, how might the local availability of a Systems Healer ASSA make their lives better? First, depending on local organisational structures, the Systems Healer ASSA might actually supervise Isobel, the front-line worker supporting Lucy and Bill. Her or his indirect influence may then be evidenced in Isobel's increased confidence and abilities. Second, and possibly a more likely scenario, is that of the Systems Healer ASSA offering consultations to others working with adoptive families. Lucy and Bill's children might benefit if, for example, their nursery workers or teacher were to attend. This type of inter-professional consultation practice is now becoming a feature of child and adolescent work, and has received positive endorsement (Hart, Wilding and Watson 2002).

Obviously the potential for Systems Healer ASSAs to heal depends to a large extent on the local organisational context, as well as the skills of the ASSA. The local organisational context is important because the capacity of Systems Healer ASSAs depends crucially on how much authority they are given, or are able to seize for themselves, to really affect what services get provided to people affected by adoption.

The guidance suggests a fairly senior role for the ASSA with social services. However, even with a seat on inter-agency planning groups, and a relatively senior role in a local authority, Systems Healer ASSAs cannot move mountains. Managers in other agencies, for example education, over whose budgets Systems Healer ASSAs might have influence, but not control, may have quite different priorities. The local ASSA might recognise the need for a specialist educationalist to offer consultations with teachers about the effects on trauma and neglect on the learning process, and about individual children in their classes. However, the weak requirements on other agencies to meet the needs of people affected by adoption will do nothing to help this particular Systems Healer ASSA persuade the education department to provide, or contribute to, such a post. It remains to be seen whether the move towards incorporating health, education and social services within the Children's Trust may enable a greater degree of influence to be exerted by Systems Healer ASSAs. In the meantime an effective Systems Healer ASSA will need to have firmly in mind a model of collaborative practice. We explore one way of conceptualising such collaboration in Chapter 7 when we consider the development of 'communities of adoptive practice'.

Social Support ASSA

The Social Support ASSA model is a far cry from brokerage or systems healing, since it offers a continuing supportive relationship with a practitioner to the individual service user. Such a continuing relationship is key to the components of successful keyworking which we outlined in Table 4.5. In its purest form, it involves no other service provision. However, like the therapeutic model, in can be combined with a broker function. In adoption, this hands-on role is likely to be one that in smaller authorities ASSAs themselves may undertake, or which they may delegate to others in larger ones. In such contexts, delegation is likely to be to family support workers, who already have historically played a significant role in this regard, at least up until the adoption order.

What do we know about how family support workers have fared in fulfilling their social support role? A recent overview of the research evidence regarding the role of the support social worker with permanent families demonstrates the limitations of the social support model of case management in this context (Parker 1999, p.89). Drawing on two studies in particular (Quinton et al. 1998; Thoburn, Wilding and Watson 2000), Parker concludes that family support workers were seen by parents as best able to provide support in the form of reassurance. That the social worker was kind and supportive, in the most general sense of the word, is undisputed. Hence a family placement worker would go some way towards addressing the needs of Lucy and Bill's family as identified in Table 4.4. She or he would most probably be empathic and emotionally available to them. However, the study found that rates of satisfaction for more active types of support, such as dealing with children's difficult behaviour, finding out information about the child, completing administrative tasks and meeting the material needs of families were considerably lower (around 40%) (Parker 1999, p.94). For a social support worker to be effective with Lucy and Bill's family, she or he would certainly need all these skills and more.

Our Table 4.3 identifies these issues of informed guidance and advocacy as important to effectively supporting families. Parker's finding that most families were supported by the family support worker alone, suggests that 60 per cent of families in their study were largely struggling with these particular issues with no outside assistance. Results from our own research study are consistent with findings from other recent research on the subject (Lowe *et al.* 1999; Parker 1999; Quinton *et al.* 1998). What frustrates parents and professionals alike is the weak capacity and capability of the social work service for the placed child. The kind of confident, knowledgeable authority figures identified as needed by adopters in Tables 4.2 and 4.3 were certainly few and far between.

Furthermore, in our study, parents routinely complained about poor availability, inconsistency and unreliability. They were unsure as to what they could expect from their support worker, with basic issues such as frequency, length of visits and when they might taper off, unclear. For example, one mother spoke of her feelings that she was 'dumped' by the support worker after the children had been in placement for a year, without ever having really understood what help she was entitled to. If the Adoption and Children Act 2002 is put into practice properly, the adoption support plan will make such confusion a thing of the past. It should make transparent precisely what support individual families will be getting from whom, and why. It will also make clear when, as well as for how long, they will be getting it.

None of the families in our study had written information on the role of the support worker, nor a contract outlining what they personally might expect in the form of support. Indeed there was a general acceptance, almost a sense of resignation, that the service would be second-rate, even though several parents provided positive accounts of individual practitioners. Our requests for good practice example from Adoption UK members also drew in some positive experiences from parents. That is, the worker was appreciated for reassurance, for being non-judgemental, for availability, for putting parents in touch with appropriate specialist services and for advocacy should those services not be readily available, e.g. 'she always made sure if we were entitled to something she would get it for us'. Things went wrong if the worker was unreliable or left parents with the impression that they did not trust them, and then the feeling became mutual. In general the impression formed here is of a service which combined the linking and the general support functions adequately but which tended to do neither in a particularly skilled or assertive way. Certainly few parents thought they could usefully call on the family support worker for the kind of advice and therapy that caused them to seek out therapy from specialist services.

There are clearly some problems in delegating the hands-on tasks of the ASSA to family support workers, without a considerable increase in professional training. Here, therapeutic expertise, along with greater administrative efficiency and an authoritative advice role, is key. However, before we think about other professional models of ASSA support, let us first consider the considerable evidence to support claims that ASSAs working in the social support tradition could develop in a completely non-professional direction, from the bottom up, rather than from the top down.

Challenges to models which emphasise the professional orientation of ASSA-type roles, particularly those that in smaller authorities will be delegated to other workers, have actually come from effectiveness research on the role of non-professionals in the human services (Durlak 1979; Faust and Zlotnick 1995; Harchik *et al.* 1989; Hattie, Sharpley and Rogers 1984). Changes in perceptions around professional authority, the shift towards services becoming accountable to their users and the growth of voluntary organisations as well as the drive towards greater cost-effectiveness in service provision have all contributed to the opening up of new possibilities for practice by non-professionals. Milne argues that 'the evidence for their relative contribution is actually quite stunning for the self-important professionals groups' (Milne 1999, p.34). For example, a Sainsbury Centre Review (Murray *et al.* 1997) showed that non-professional mental health support workers were more involved in social and emotional support than other members of the Community Mental Health Team. They were better able to help patients establish and sustain social networks, be available out of hours for crisis support, and help patients communicate with family members. This is reflected in the Workforce Action Team's recommendations (since taken up by government) to introduce 'support, time and recovery workers' in community mental health services (Workforce Action Team 2001 and 2002). Others have argued that working with current or ex-service users decreases clients' feelings of stigmatisation (Dozier *et al.* 2002).

Thinking specifically about adoption, what would a non-professional hands-on helper, for example an experienced foster carer or adoptive parent, offer Lucy and Bill? Understanding, availability and knowledge of the system all come to mind, as do connections within the world of adoptive families in order that services develop within supportive communities. Represented in the role of ASSAs and other helpers working in the social support tradition should then be those with experience of having been an adopted parent or foster carer.

Of course the issue of what Handy (1985) calls 'position power' presents a sticking point here. The ability to command authority from other workers, as well as from service users, must be part of the ASSA's profile. Whether or not service users would be at a disadvantage here is worth considering.

Therapeutic-broker ASSA

Just like the Social Support ASSA, the Therapeutic-broker ASSA works directly and longitudinally with parents and/or children. Bachrach has referred to cases in which this direct role is put into practice in combination with a broker-age role in metaphorical terms as putting together the functions of the travel agent and the travelling companion (1993). As Downing and Hatfield suggest, 'for service users whose mental health difficulties are substantial, this relation-ship may be crucial in the accurate identification of needs and take-up of ser-vices' (1999, p.842). Here, the notion is that other services may be incorpo-rated into the care plan. And the idea is that the Therapeutic-broker ASSA knows the client well enough to understand what they need.

But what then is the difference between the Social Support and Therapeu-tic model? There are two elements of the model to emphasise here. The first is that some have viewed the therapeutic relationship more along the continuum towards a 'treatment' relationship than that implied by the social support model. To avoid what we see as the unnecessary biomedical connotations of 'treatment', we prefer the concept of 'a more directive helping relationship' (Kanter 1989; Watkins 2001) in which the therapist, as Dozier puts it, 'offers a gentle challenge' (Dozier 2003, p.254). Using the travel agent metaphor once again, the Therapeutic-broker ASSA would be a travelling companion on a par-ticularly difficult journey, one who knew the route and had already struggled along it. They would be an informed guide, rather than simply a co-traveller.

Clearly in less complex cases a social support model is sufficient, with the worker not being expected to offer interventions. However, as we saw above, research suggests that the social support provided by family support workers was sometimes not sufficiently powerful, particularly in complex cases, and thus a worker with a greater array of skills is needed. One such approach is what has been termed the 'clinical case management model'. This is similar to our concept of the Therapeutic-broker ASSA.

With the growth of the self-help movement, in recent years there has been tensions about whether the language and practice of this 'clinical treatment' relationship over-pathologises clients (Milne 1999). We prefer the term thera-peutic, rather than clinical. This is because the concept of therapy steers us away from the discourse exemplified by the biomedical terms now in common use to describe the helping relationship. Such a discourse implicitly shores up profes-sional grandiosity, obscuring the actual realities of practitioner insecurities and dilemmas around practice decision-making in what is certainly an uncertain science (White and Stancombe 2003).

In the mental health field, a feature of this biomedical dominance has been the way in which 'clinical' case management and brokerage models overlooked how service users themselves participated in their own recoveries. These models also ignore the importance of informal networks in the recovery process (Faulkner and Layzell 2000).

In the light of shifting boundaries between users and professionals, proponents of the clinical case management model claim that it now incorporates many elements of the humanistic strengths model. This offers a philosophy of keyworking that is community orientated, with maximum effort designed to reorientate service users into their communities (Simpson *et al.* 2003a).

In services to disabled children, as we have seen earlier in this chapter, one pilot project took the strengths model almost to its logical extreme by providing the opportunity for parents to be the keyworker for their own children (Tait *et al.* 2002). Whilst this was a very successful model in the pilot, questions could be raised about the fact that the parents were not paid for this work. Arguably, shifting this kind of position onto unpaid parents can be seen as the state failing in its responsibilities to provide appropriate professional support. In relation to our families, if there was somebody competent enough to do the job properly, would Lucy and Bill really want the burden of self-treatment and co-ordination of their own services? They might be better freed up to spend more time engaging with their children, rather than with professional helpers.

We do then see the worth of families having access to somebody with a therapeutically orientated support role external to their family. This could be part of the ASSA role, although in large authorities they will need a very small caseload. In the next chapter we go on to say a lot more about the nature and organisation of therapeutic work in adoption.

The second way in which the Therapeutic-broker ASSA differs from a social supporter is in how they use their knowledge of psychological processes to contain what is going on. A key ability of the Therapeutic-broker ASSA is to hold in mind the many difficulties potentially faced by adoptive families, to care about them and yet not to be overwhelmed by them. To avoid a professional free-for-all, Therapeutic-broker ASSAs explicitly try to address families' problems themselves rather than getting other services involved. However, their broker function would enable the ASSA to have a proactive role in accessing or working with other services too, if absolutely necessary.

To be effective, the intensive emotional labour of the therapist is likely to be underpinned by a professional training, which has specifically addressed the needs of those involved in adoption. However, this is not necessarily so. Whilst in the service sector much currency is given to formal therapeutic training, given their first-hand experience of parenting, and the tacit knowledge acquired through it, non-professionals with first-hand experience of adoptive care-giving may be effective at improving relations between parents and children. Being an adoptive parent or foster carer is, as has been shown in other contexts, likely to work in favour of developing a good therapeutic alliance (Dozier *et al.* 2002). A number of studies have highlighted the therapeutic alliance as the single most important factor in securing positive therapeutic outcomes (Orlinsky, Grawe and Parks 1994). Add to this equation the lack of overwhelming evidence for the effectiveness of adoption therapists, and the jury surely still has to be out on whether or not professional therapists are always necessary to do a good job.

Educator ASSA

In conceptualising the Educator ASSA a more proactive pedagogic role is envisaged for her or him than that specified in the Regulations and Guidance, i.e. giving out advice and information to adoptive families. Educator ASSAs are key to ensuring that local authorities take the training and education needs of all those involved in adoption seriously.

As we saw earlier in this chapter, adequate training was highlighted both in the context of mental health and services for children with disabilities as fundamental to the success of roles similar to that of the ASSA and related helpers. In the adoption context, too, we cannot stress it enough. Similarly the Regulations and Guidance accompanying the Act emphasise the need for training.

Given the ASSA's seniority and necessary expertise, they should have a key role in ensuring that the capacity built locally in adoption support is underpinned by a sound knowledge and skills base. They should do this both in relation to individuals (being a warm expert for parents, and providing consultation to other formal helpers), and to the service system (organising training courses in collaboration with others and so on.)

Specialist agencies such as Family Futures, the Post Adoption Centre, Parents for Children and After Adoption provide training packages for practitioners and parents. In each case professionals and parents are equally eligible to take part on the course, and often a subsidised rate is offered for parent participants. However, teachers and other professionals such as nurses can get left out of the equation. There is certainly scope to expand multi-disciplinary training courses such as these to other stakeholders. A key challenge will be for ASSAs to stimulate learning and teaching in the local context based on these sorts of models.

Combining support models within service systems

Our final point in this chapter returns to the suggestions we made at the beginning of it. To effectively meet the needs of adoptive families, the support models we have identified need to be represented within a team with a shared philosophy of care. This team needs to be symbolically (and possibly structurally) led by a local ASSA who commands respect, and who has influence across service sectors. Team members may not all formally belong to the same organisation, although it would probably be better if they did. Given the move towards the integration of different agencies in children's services, the future of keyworking looks set to develop in this way.

Without institutional clout, however, the age-old problem remains of what actually provides the impetus to make formal helpers take up an effective team position in adoption support. In the absence of clear managerial directives, and with competing priorities, unless a priority is covered by the latest policy directive it may not actually count as a priority.

How adoption support workers are structurally located in terms of their ability to act on behalf of families can, however, be seen in a different way. For example, the advantages that come from the formal authority conferred by professional status, and belonging to the same organisation, may be outweighed by the lack of independence with which professional keyworkers are able to work when systemically located within the statutory sector. Mukherjee *et al.* (1999) consider acting on behalf of the family, rather than the agency, as a key component of the keyworker role. Their study draws attention to the difficulties keyworkers working within the statutory sector can get into, for example, when being asked to represent a family at forums such as the Educational Tribunal for Special Needs. In this situation, their solution was for the keyworker to stress to all concerned that she or he was acting in the keyworker role, which included acting as an advocate for the family, rather than acting as a social worker. However, some may be more convinced of the keyworker's ability to act on behalf of families if their roles are developed outside the statutory sector. This may be especially necessary in adoption, because the law does not make provision for an independent appeals structure with specific regard to the provision of support.

Given the framework provided by the Regulations and Guidance, it is likely that in most authorities the ASSA will perform a Systems Healer and Broker role. As we have shown in this chapter, it is unlikely that simply fulfilling these roles will be sufficient to provide effective support to local families. We propose the following: in order to avoid practice which is defensively dissociative, in every authority, even in large ones, the ASSA should hold their own practice caseload of individual families, working as a Therapeutic-broker in the strengths tradition as discussed earlier in this chapter.

The ASSA's caseload should be made up of families who are likely to present with the most difficulties, therefore large sibling groups and histories of sexual and physical abuse together with developmental delay should feature in it. Even in a large authority an ASSA should ideally be engaged in direct work with at least two such families. In this way the ASSA, both in heart and in mind, will be kept in touch with the experiences of those he or she is trying to support.

This model of care management is relatively unfamiliar in the local authority context. Here, managerialism provides the dominant organisational structure (Farrell and Morris 2003; Schofield 2001). However, in health, the history of managerialism is not so clear cut. Although it has made significant inroads, powerful resistance has come from practitioners, who have been keen to both manage and practice (Farrell and Morris 2003). Hence managerialism has been shown to be more contestable in this part of the public sector than has been the case in social services. The concept of clinical governance provides a powerful challenge to managerialism. Strikingly, the concept of clinical governance has no equivalent in social services.

And what of models of support for other helpers? The lead here might best be taken from work in voluntary agencies. Key to it is the importance of enduring human relationships. This is illustrated by reference to Parker's study (1999), and can be collaborated by evaluations of specialist foster care (Walker, Hill and Triseliotis 2002). In Parker's work, the role of the support worker in Voluntary Adoption Agencies (VAAs) emerges in a more positive light than that of their role in local authorities.

It is in the VAA context that we can most clearly see the emergence of a therapeutic-broker system to keyworking. Parker reports that in cases where children were placed by a VAA, family support workers played a much greater role in supporting the family than did those where placement was made by a local authority (1999, p.84). This is unsurprising since VAAs in this field such as Parents for Children, Coram Family and the Catholic Children Society have a tradition of working with hard to place children, and in some cases with children considered 'unadoptable' (Irving 2003). These agencies understand that families will need more support than has traditionally been offered in adoption, and they have built up capacity by building their work around the practice of enhanced forms of social support (Irving 2003).

In some agencies, models employed come close to therapeutic-brokerage with for example, adoption-competent clinical psychologists as well as play therapists included in the support team. From our own discussion with parents and practitioners in the field it appears that VAAs are playing a greater role than most local authorities in providing welfare rights assistance and educational advocacy, both of which are important in adoption, and which form part of the strengths model in mental health which we outlined above.

Others agencies such as Family Futures and the Post Adoption Centre have developed their therapeutic case management/strengths model practice with even greater intensity of contact, providing a quasi therapeutic community approach (Archer and Burnell 2003). Thus models of keyworking employed by some agencies within the adoption field are emerging which resemble the therapeutic-broker/strengths model combination identified in mental health.

Our own view regarding the ASSA and related roles is that given the current state of capacity built in adoption support across the UK, pragmatism must prevail in the development of the role and its supporting structure. Just as with other service arenas, in different parts of the country, adoption service capacity varies. Whether the National Service Framework for Children's

Services will do its prescribed job of ending the general 'postcode lottery' that exists in access to services, including that of adoption support, remains to be seen.

However, it is unlikely that in the short term the level of inter-disciplinary working needed to fulfil the role of ASSA and her or his delegates as we envisage will be achieved. All these skills and knowledge bases are unlikely to be found in any one person, whether professional or parent. Many practitioners are now becoming adoption-*sensitive*, however, we have some way to go before inter-disciplinary adoption-*competent* practitioners are embedded throughout mainstream services and voluntary organisations. Clearly resources need to be pooled, and much inter-disciplinary learning on the job, as well as formal training, needs to occur.

As we have seen from our own recent research study, and from reports of work in other areas, much can be achieved in adoption support when those with different perspectives share them and learn from others (Archer and Burnell 2003; Hart *et al.* 2002). However, perhaps this is most easily facilitated when roles are embedded within a multi-disciplinary team context where members are physically present with each other, rather than operating as a virtual team with different bases in different agencies. In the case of adoption support, social work, therapeutic, education, welfare rights and service user perspectives need to be incorporated within a team context, both at the supervisory and operational level. In this way, individuals who are competent in one discipline can learn from others in the multi-disciplinary team and develop their own inter-disciplinarity. The ASSA is ideally placed to take a lead on this.

Developing practitioners as therapeutic-brokers will require far greater capacity building than simply employing glorified signposters. This chapter has demonstrated that in the first instance, desperate adoptive parents like Lucy and Bill, and their children where appropriate, need hands-on help from adoption-competent, inter-disciplinary keyworkers. Of course, some families may need to draw on other, more specialist therapeutic support. However, when to make the decision to do so, and precisely what kind of therapy might be helpful, are questions that need careful consideration. Hence the following chapter explores in some detail precisely what the role of formal specialist therapy should be in adoption support. It outlines an integrative model of therapeutic support that facilitates the development of positive attachments between adoptive parents and their children. Following that, the chapter goes on to consider the evidence base regarding therapeutic interventions.

Chapter 5

Facilitating 'Good Enough' Adoptive Parenting Through Formal Therapeutic Interventions

Introduction

The idea of formal therapeutic interventions led by clinicians has increasingly taken centre stage in debates about adoption support (Scott and Lindsey 2003). For some time now research has demonstrated that 'routine' arrangements for support, that is those provided directly by social workers and other front-line staff, often have limited impact in helping adoptive families manage or resolve parenting and child-care difficulties (Parker 1999). The variability of the skill and expertise of front-line workers has led increasingly to calls for wider availability of 'specialist interventions', particularly in situations of severe family difficulty (Rushton 2003; Rushton and Dance 2002). This has been as much a demand of adoptive parents as it has of academic commentators as they have sought, with increasing desperation, someone who both understands their predicament and knows what to do to help (Benton 2000).

The Adoption and Children Act 2002 includes 'therapeutic services for children' in its prescribed framework of services. This provides further impetus for the development of adoption-specific specialist interventions, although if taken too literally the emphasis on therapeutic services *for children* (rather than *families* or *adoptive parents*) could lead to some very restrictive service development (see below). As we have seen in Chapter 3, therapeutic services are expected, if not actually legally required, to be provided through local collaborations between mental health (CAMHS) and other children's services. Specialist interventions, based mainly in the clinic and centre, are to be developed alongside routine approaches practised from day to day in the office, school and home.

Attention has now turned to the question of exactly which interventions might best be provided to ensure appropriate therapeutic support in adoption and how they should be organised. In recent years attachment theory has become the dominant perspective. This has substituted for traditional psychotherapeutic and psychiatric approaches to diagnosing and treating specific 'disorders' in children, a more overarching approach to explaining and responding to problems. Instead of being seen as just one aspect amongst several of child development and family functioning, the attach-ment/care-giving relationship is considered of foundational importance in the cause and remedy of many, if not most, emotional and behavioural difficulties (Howe 1998). However not everyone is persuaded by the encompassing claims made for attachment theory (Rushton 2003), and there is no consensus yet, in the world of attachment therapy itself, about methods of intervention (O'Connor and Zeanah 2003). In the meantime, there is still very little sound empirical evidence on the effectiveness of applying any one method of theoret-ical framework for understanding adoption and its problems. The same can be said of the choice of intervention method (Barth and Miller 2000).

In this chapter we approach these issues, of the role, focus and method of formal therapeutic support, from the day-to-day 'adoptive family practice' per-spective developed in this book. Trials of effectiveness of specific interventions are crucial in informing decisions about what might work best and why (Rushton and Monck, in progress). For this reason we review what is known about the impact of different therapeutic methods currently propounded. However, it is the distinctive context in which adoptive parents and children engage with therapy, and the implications this has for the focus and provision of therapeutic interventions, that concerns us too. Achieving therapeutic effec-tiveness is not simply a matter of amending successful conventional methods to make them adoption-sensitive, although this is an essential prerequisite. It is also a matter of making sure that any therapeutic intervention itself, and the way different family members are involved in it, is really helpful to the main objective. This is to enable children and parents to find their own way together towards a settled and satisfying adoptive family life.

In this respect we develop arguments made in Chapters 1 and 2, about the primacy in adoptive family practice of the task of establishing secure enough fresh attachments. Here we are at one with the attachment theorists and thera-pists in seeing the parent–child relationship as the foundational context for all other therapeutic endeavours in adoption. It may well be that some child problems originate somewhere beyond attachment experience alone, such as in genetic or congenital inheritance or in those ambiguities of ethnic, class or kinship identity discussed later, in Chapter 6. However, in adoptive family life more than any other, this distinctive and vulnerable relationship is always the one in which emotional and behavioural problems are both managed and given meaning.

It is essential to remember that these are two rather different processes. On the one hand, so far as is possible, these problems need to abate if family life is to become settled. Therapeutic interventions should aim to change behaviour. On the other hand some behaviours need to be normalised too if a realistic vision of family life, an acceptable adoptive family script, is to be established. Therapeutic interventions also need, sometimes, to change expectations.

The focus in this chapter is on formal therapy, whatever its particular orientation, as an enhancement of the routine supports of day-to-day family life, not a displacement of them. This perspective is consistent with the idea, from the 'family practices' approach, that professional support should be seen less as an external expert intervention and more as the importation of an informed and skilled resource. As ecological approaches to therapeutic interventions argue, too often the gap between daily experience and formal therapeutic support is made wider than it need be (Livingston Smith and Howard 1999; Stormshak and Dishion 2002). Issues of cost and geography figure here. But the wider culture of therapeutic practice needs attention too. Instead of sustaining mechanisms of referral and response that add to feelings of distance, and the anxiety and anger this often provokes, those working in the clinic and centre need to consider different approaches. These need to be ones that help them understand better and engage with the daily experience of parents and children and their immediate supporters (Barratt 2002).

The proposals made in the previous chapter for the development of the adoption support services adviser (ASSA) and keyworker roles will help to bridge the gap that can emerge between routine support and specialist and intensive therapy. Ways in which a more communal approach might be taken to support practice in adoption are discussed in more detail in Chapter 7.

This chapter refocuses the contemporary debate about the objectives of formal therapy. In doing so our overall aim is to ensure that practical principles, derived from the reported experience of getting therapeutic support in adoption, are kept to the fore (Hart et al. 2002). Thus therapists should work from the start in ways that reassure parents and children they really are 'there for us'. This principle is well supported by the general literature on the effect of the therapeutic alliance on outcomes. Establishing and maintaining a good relationship between therapist(s) and client(s) is fundamental to successful therapy (Eaton, Abeles and Gutfreund 1993; Elkin 1999).

Therapists need to show they are on the side of the family in its struggles by hearing and appreciating just how difficult it all can be. In line with the spirit of clinical governance, there is now more onus on therapists to demonstrate how they actually make things better as a result of becoming involved, not complicate them more. Amongst others, Nickman and Lewis (1994) argue that in adoption the positive impact of therapeutic 'help' cannot be taken for granted (see also Delaney and Kunstal 1993). This also helps remind us that the ultimate goal of therapeutic support is not simply about modelling (and marketing) a particular method of intervention in itself, however well evidenced its effectiveness. It has as much to do with the way therapy generally ought to be recruited in each locality to support family practice.

The chapter begins with a consideration of what conditions are needed to make therapeutic engagements really supportive. It then moves on to propose a therapeutic strategy in adoption by identifying four core objectives. We then review what is known about the effectiveness of the *modes* and *methods* through which they are best achieved. By modes we mean whether therapy is undertaken exclusively with children, whether it involves the whole family, or whether it is undertaken primarily with parents. By methods we refer to the therapeutic orientation of the work, for example whether it is psychotherapeutic or behavioural. We consider the implications of employing particular modes and methods for the achievement of the central goal – the strengthening of the capacity of the attachment/care-giving relationship to contain, manage and resolve problems in adoptive family life as they arise.

Building on our discussion in the previous chapter, we first return to the experience of Lucy and Bill's family. This is in order to recall the kind of difficulties that need to be overcome if parents and children are to benefit from the formal therapy typically offered in an attempt to help things settle.

Case study: The Smiths and the Joneses

Two months into placement and Alan continues with the therapy he was receiving whilst in foster care. Because of the length of the local CAMHS waiting list, social services had contracted out therapeutic support to foster children to a pool of private therapists. Lucy drives him the 15 miles to the office in which he's always seen Jason the therapist, taking the two little ones with her. Alan's had four sessions now since he's been living in his new family. Lucy herself has spent about 20 minutes alone with the therapist Jason, in his consulting room. During that time, Jason did mention something to her about what he'd done and was now planning to do with Alan, but she didn't take it in, too busy worrying about how Bill was coping home alone with three kids and what Alan was up to waiting for her in the car. Something written down might have helped perhaps. Lucy knows she's had too much to take in over the past two months, and she hasn't got another meeting planned to talk to Jason face-to-face for three weeks. Social services had offered to send a taxi for Alan, but Lucy felt that as his mum she should take him.

Whilst he's in with Jason, Lucy, Katie and Ellen wait in the car outside; there isn't a waiting room. Katie, still being a cat, keeps herself busy by purring, rubbing against the window and scratching at the car seat. The cover's already in shreds from her weeks of cat scratching. The noise grates, but Lucy just turns up the radio and leaves her to it. Perhaps she's a bit like that mum who sent her kid off on a holiday with someone they hardly knew. Lucy had really slagged her off at the time, but now she knows they've got something in common. And right now she'd do anything to really get rid of her kids. Send them anywhere in fact. Vaguely she also remembers that Jason said she could phone him for a chat, and she feels guilty that she's not really had the energy to initiate a call. She remembers how the one meeting they did have left her feeling uncomfortable and totally out of her depth. But never mind all these excuses. It's finally dawned on Lucy that she is actually very unclear about the specific aims and objectives of Alan's therapy, and that she feels very unhappy about this. In fact Lucy and Bill don't know much about therapy at all, nor do they feel good about it. Counting themselves as more than averagely sane, neither of them have ever been directly involved with it. One of Bill's brothers had a dose of therapy for alcohol addiction, but nobody in the family ever talked about what went on, and Bill certainly didn't mention the problem to Isabel, the social worker, when she was doing their preparation. Too embarrassed and ashamed. Preferred to pretend it hadn't happened in his family. And now Lucy hasn't asked Alan anything about his therapy. Lucy thinks that asking about it might be too intrusive for him. Bill's hardly registered that Alan goes. Lucy imagines that Alan moans on about how much he dislikes his new family. But actually, his new family has been hardly mentioned by either Alan or Jason. Alan himself is happy enough when Jason lets him play on his own. He gets uncomfortable and confused when he feels Jason is trying to make him talk about things he'd rather forget. Mostly though, he's focusing on the burger and chips he gets afterwards from Lucy as treat for going to therapy and behaving in the car.

Getting Alan to therapy is a real trial for Lucy and disruptive to daily routines. And of most concern to her now is that she knows that she and the other kids will suffer even more from his difficult behaviour when they get back home. Sitting in the car Lucy's in two minds as to whether or not he should continue. She thinks that probably on the one hand the therapy provides a space for him to talk about difficult things with another mixed race person, a bloke he's known for some time now. On the other it seems to stir things up, not settle them. And one thing Lucy really hates is that she's left feeling out of the loop herself. She frets over the little contribution she feels she has to make to Alan's mental health. She doesn't know how to influence what might happen. Bill meanwhile has simply cut off from the whole process of getting outside help, and never engages with her when she tries to discuss it. More generally too, things in the family are not looking good. When Alan goes in to see his therapist Lucy sometimes wishes she could just dump all the kids in the car and go into Jason's room herself for a good sob about how awful it all is. But Lucy is determined to do something about the desperate state they're all in. She's going to ask Isabel for her advice on how therapy might help them. These thoughts are interrupted as Alan comes out, his 50 minutes up, and they make the journey home.

Making therapy really helpful

Social worker Isabel will need to be able to do three things within the therapeutic-broker role if she is to going to be effective in helping Lucy and Bill decide whether, and then how, formal therapy might help them in their predicament. She will first need to reflect on her own skills to determine where the limits of her expertise lie in helping the family herself. Second, she will need the skill, time and commitment to support them in the process of keeping Jason involved, or in getting any further therapist involved, if she herself cannot delivery the necessary help. Third, Isabel needs to be sufficiently knowledgeable to inform and advise them about what therapy is locally available and how it might help if Lucy and Bill decide to make use of it.

These tasks include helping them define what they need. It also means supporting the negotiation and management of arrangements so that therapy assists rather than complicates their own efforts to get family life more settled. Isabel should, of course, be able to count on the support of the ASSA, and other colleagues in and beyond her local inter-professional world, in doing this work. In some situations of course, it can be therapists themselves who act as brokers to other professionals, for example, social workers and teachers. Our case scenario offers only one view of how things might proceed, although we know from research and experience that it is certainly not an uncommon one.

The engagement process, bringing therapy to a better informed family, is crucial. It is important to consider it carefully because we know, from qualitative studies (Hart *et al.* 2002; Wuest 2000) and personal accounts (Adoption Today 2003a), that the experience of negotiating the involvement of formal therapeutic services can escalate anxiety. This is a poor basis on which to make decisions about introducing further new faces into the already complex daily business of family life.

Anxiety and ambivalence is intrinsic to the process of asking for extra help when things feel out of control and customary coping strategies cease to have effect. Stress is further amplified by confusion and uncertainty about exactly what therapeutic support is on offer and how it might help (or not). In adoption this experience is often particularly acutely felt because the stakes can seem so high. Not only do adoptive parents like Lucy and Bill have to confront their current failure to create the family life they anticipated but they also have to do so under the public gaze of those professionals they had to persuade to let them try.

In these circumstances therapy can get used defensively, by parents and professionals alike. This is especially so when desperation sets in and the viability of the family life, as well as of any particular parenting strategy, feels in question. People can respond in contrasting ways. One approach is to cling on to existing coping strategies and avoid and resist offers of therapeutic help. Lucy and Bill could try to persuade themselves and Isabel that things are not that bad and that their original vision of adoptive family life, along with the methods of parenting they are employing in order to maintain it, will ultimately succeed. To do otherwise would be to admit defeat (in relation to both hopes and strategies) and concede control of the fragile family destiny to outsiders. An alternative response to feelings of desperation and fear is for parents to grasp at any offer that comes along, and demand the immediate provision of still more, so unbearable is the experience of not coping. Rather than holding on to all the responsibility themselves for making things work better they in effect hand it back to the professionals, who might be said to have caused the problems anyway by placing these particular children with them. Individual psychotherapy in particular can get used in this way, to 'fix' the child who is causing the problems.

Social workers like Isabel can provoke and exacerbate these intrinsic defensive tendencies. They can do this by failing to recognise, respect and contain, through their own helping relationship, parental anxiety and fear. They can also forget how important it is for parents (and children) to feel a real sense of involvement and say in any therapeutic strategy suggested. The development of a 'therapeutic alliance' at this first level of support is essential if the introduction of specialist therapy is to contribute to restoring rather than undermining the attachment/care-giving relationship, through which any intervention must operate. If the alliance between Isabel and Lucy and Bill is one of trust and mutual respect, considered and sensible rather than desperate and risky, realistic decisions are more likely to be made about whether, when and how to recruit additional help. The primary task for the front-line support worker is to enable parents (and children) to feel safe enough to share and face their real fears and disappointments. This provides a context in which to decide the right balance of parental and professional responsibility in managing and resolving the problems that have provoked them (Kaniuk 1992).

For example, Lucy, who is the primary care-giver for the children, might be tempted to imagine that Alan's troubled and troubling behaviour will eventually be resolved and family life and school settle down normally once his own therapy is complete. Rather than help sustain this unrealistic, if understandable, hope or expectation Isabel will need to win Lucy's trust sufficiently to enable her to recognise and accept a different reality. This is that Alan will almost certainly retain to some extent his impulsive and reckless streak (for reasons Isabel should feel informed enough to explain). Crucial too is the need for Lucy to recognise that it is her relationship with her new son that will be critical to settling him well enough, not the one he has with his therapist. This is not to say that Lucy should withdraw Alan from his therapy (and, as we have seen, he will have his own view to be properly considered). Instead she should be encouraged to get much more directly involved in the process of ensuring what the therapist is doing explicitly supports her parenting strategy.

Of course Bill's place in all this also needs consideration. How does Isabel persuade him that he should do more of what Pam Smith refers to as 'emotional labour' in parenting these children (Smith 1992)? It is generally known that in families where men and women co-parent, this work most often falls to, or is taken up by, women (Featherstone 2004). However, research evidence certainly points to the value of democratisation of such family responsibilities (Bakermans-Kranenburg, van Ijzendoorn and Juffer 2003).

To our knowledge no specific research has been conducted on gendered emotional labour in adoption. However, it is likely that given the children's legacies in families like those of Lucy and Bill, the work to be done makes the burden on Lucy a substantial one. However, Isabel may not find it easy to convince Lucy to concede some responsibility and Bill to further engage. One reason for this Featherstone (2004) argues, lies in the gendered nature of professional practice itself. She suggests that women helping professionals often lack confidence in working with fathers, as well as in doing couples work. As a result, they can unwittingly contribute to the exclusion of fathers from family support work. Engaging both parents then, in a therapeutic alliance will take some doing.

Assessment and decision-making

This basic therapeutic alliance must be the basis for sound assessment of the problems that are raising the question about the possible need for additional, and specialist, therapeutic support. It should also be the basis for well-judged decisions about what type of therapy might help.

The social work assessment here involves making sense of two aspects of the problem in question. Lucy, Bill and Isabel will need to make an analysis of the dimensions and circumstances of the children's difficult behaviours, drawing in the perspective from others involved, such as teachers. Tools to help with this will have to include the amended assessment framework developed specifically to incorporate this wider view.

Together the three of them, led by Isabel, should generate an informed hypothesis that tries to explain what might be causing and sustaining each of the children's difficulties. They should also carefully reflect on the meaning the problem has in the family and/or the school; why it is so difficult to cope with. Some behaviours are obviously disturbing whatever the context. If children continue to whirl destructively around at school and at home, any parent would be expected to become alarmed, especially if despite their best efforts things failed to change.

Nonetheless, the particular impact this demonstration of distress and aggression has on Lucy and Bill will depend on what they expected their children's behaviour to be like and how far the reality differs. Alarm and a sense of inadequacy or failure is likely to increase in line with the size of the gap between what was hoped for and what actually happens. Parents should certainly expect the process of assessment to demonstrate the ability of their support worker to help them understand the likely causes of any problems children present. However they should also anticipate that the worker will want them in turn to think through carefully exactly why they are responding in the way they are, why they are more or less troubled and distressed themselves.

There are reasons why this kind of assessment for referral for additional therapy might not always take place in practice. First-line support workers in adoption have typically developed some specialist knowledge and skills in the field of permanence planning and substitute family care. As a result, they are more likely than many social workers to feel some confidence in their own judgements, even if this is to a degree misplaced (Parker 1999; Rushton, Treseder and Quinton 1993). Conventional agency cultures and structures continue to undermine this capability. We have already discussed in Chapter 3 the risks to confident, responsible and reassuring practice inherent in the current official emphasis, found also in the Adoption and Children Act 2002, on narrow, bureaucratic methods of 'needs assessment' in children's services. These may be intended to be child and family focused but there is no evidence yet that they will do much more than simply make assessments of eligibility for services somewhat more standardised and transparent (Cleaver *et al.* 2004).

A second potential constraint on the kind of confident and enabling assessment for therapy we have in mind here comes from conventional 'clinical' approaches to referral and response. The problem lies in the unspoken assumption that it is the clinicians alone who possess the expertise necessary to understand and resolve the problems presented. For example Scott and Lindsey (2003) allow only passive roles for parents and support social workers in their clinician-centred model of assessment. Social workers are welcome to attend because they will be helped in understanding the child's difficulties, learn about the intervention and be enabled to co-ordinate proposed multi-agency services as a result. Parents will have their parenting 'evaluated' and be helped to understand their children better and manage the difficulties they present through specific strategies. Various interventions will be 'prescribed' (2003, p.226) in line with research evidence on their general effectiveness.

Whilst it is unquestionable that therapeutic expertise should be recognised and respected we think this clinician-centred model of assessment and decision-making for therapeutic support, especially as it stands, poses significant difficulties. There are practical problems to bear in mind. For example, it can take a very long time for an assessment to be done, let alone therapy to commence, if the local system of referral and response invests ownership and control of legitimate knowledge and expertise solely in the clinic or specialist centre. The length of CAMHS waiting lists and other barriers to access have been identified as a substantial problem for some time (Audit Commission 1999; Glover *et al.* 2002; Richardson and Joughin 2000).

Reder and Duncan extend the analysis of delayed decision making by identifying the dynamics and dangers of 'assessment paralysis' (1999). Here judgements, decisions and action are all suspended whilst anxious and unconfident first-level workers constantly defer to specialist 'clinicians' for a definitive opinion on the nature of the worrying problem. In the Reder and Duncan case the issues were to do with mental health and dangerous parenting but the same tendencies of avoidance, delay and increasing alienation between desperate parents and immobilised workers can be detected in the field of adoption support. The process of enabling and supporting first-line workers themselves to work on a thorough preliminary assessment, alongside parents (and children), as to whether or not a referral for therapy is necessary can be undermined by the clinic-centred model. And as we know that simply sharing worries formally with a skilled worker, who can listen properly and offer options for help, can in itself be greatly reassuring, this is cause for concern (Parker 1999). However, the growing practice of CAMHS professionals providing consultations to other workers such as teachers and social workers clearly has the potential to help local service systems develop the capacity to retain more of the therapeutic work at the first-line (Hart *et al.* 2002).

A further danger in approaches that give the lead role to clinicians and the professional work team is that they are just as likely to disrupt and exclude important routine supports underpinning day-to-day family practice as they are to enhance them. Family, friends and other more proximal supporters do not always feature in the clinical field of vision. Yet it is in the context of these enduring relationships, and with their help, that any changes in child behaviour and parenting that might result from therapy will be accommodated and sustained. Sometimes missing also in the clinic-centred model is any sense that parents and children are actively trying to beat their own routes too, through the complexities and troubles that are besetting their messy family lives. The idea that therapy ought to be a joint process is hardly new (Alexander and Dore 1999), and some therapists, especially those whose practice is guided by attachment theory, are keen to locate their own work in the collaborative tradition (Hart and Thomas 2000; Hughes 1997). But all too often information and control is simply retained in the specialist therapeutic role, whether in the form of appointment systems that are heedless of the daily realities and demands of family life or of professional methods that confuse or alarm both parents and other workers such as teachers and social workers. This can leave people feeling as if they are being put through a standard process rather than getting their unique personal situation really understood and helped (Hart *et al.* 2002).

Perhaps unsurprisingly people sometimes vote with their feet and start to shop around, and not always because they are defensively avoiding the proper challenge of an effective therapeutic encounter. This in turn can lead to calls for a consumer culture in adoption therapy. In line with the market assumptions of US welfare services some therapists in that country have proposed that adoptive parents take advice from other adopters, interview prospective service providers and then move on again if the first ones chosen fail to deliver. Hence Keck and Kupecky advise, 'If a programme is helpful...stay put. Otherwise look elsewhere. It is not your job to make therapists happy' (2002, p.163). And indeed it is not. No one should be left with the sense that they will have to take it (as and when, and where, it becomes available) or leave it. Parents (and children too) should obviously enquire about reputations and have a say over who to see and for how long. But gaining and retaining a sense of autonomy in seeking and declining support does not require that people be simply turned into 'consumers'. Instead it is that quality of recognition and 'mutual respect' (Sennett 2003) between family and therapeutic worlds that, once secured, builds trust and a common interest in making sure the therapy fits the family and not the other way round. Facilitating this recognition and respect is the primary task for the keyworker as broker of formal therapeutic support, if such support proves to be necessary. And the organisation and culture of therapy services, however engaged, should be established on exactly the same basis.

Towards an effective and inclusive therapeutic strategy in adoption support

When social worker Isabel has helped Lucy and Bill establish sufficient order and a pattern to family life, by providing the practical and other support outlined in the last chapter, they may still have to sit down and consider if additional therapy is necessary. The focus, as we have said, should be on strengthening the capacity of the attachment/care-giving relationship. This will enable particular emotional and behavioural problems, whatever their origins, to be better self-managed and their meaning in the adoptive family script to be explored. It should also ensure that additional therapeutic support is strictly limited. Alan and the other children are already likely to be feeling bewildered as well as unsettled by the sheer number of adult relationships, professional and kin, they are expected to cope with, in the transition to their new family. The same goes for Lucy and Bill. Practically, too, the complexity and effort of fitting in a trail of appointments and attendances is as likely to be exhausting and disruptive as it is helpful. The principle of the least detrimental alternative should apply when decisions are made about adding formal therapy into family practice. If improving relationship capacity is to be the main aim of therapy, what particular therapeutic objectives might be set in order to achieve it? What modes of intervention might be consistent with this aim and these objectives?

We look in detail at the evidence of effectiveness of child-focused, parent-focused and parent–child and family-focused methods of practice in the second half of the chapter. First though, we list below four objectives that we think might be expected to be held in mind by therapists who claim to be adoption-competent in their work, whatever their method of practice or theoretical background. We are not suggesting that these objectives be used as a 'cook book' guide to adoption therapy. However, as a general rule, we suggest that if a proposed therapeutic intervention can be seen to fulfil none of our four objectives, it is unlikely to be worth pursuing in the adoption context.

Core objectives in therapeutic support of adoptive parenting and family life are:

1. *Promoting emotion regulation and reflective thinking*
    These are foundational conditions for enabling troubled children to settle and make use of the family relationships provided by adoption. Soothing anxieties and calming impulsive behaviour to allow children a safe enough space for thinking about themselves in relation to others and building secure fresh attachments is the main task here. Containing and sensitive care-giving is the central means of achieving it. Adoptive parents who are secure and autonomous in their own emotional relationships may still find this a challenging task. Those with unresolved feelings and thoughts about their own childhood and adult relationships will need particular support in facing these issues too if they are to be able to get in touch and cope with child experience and thereby make themselves fully available as a secure parental base (Dozier 2003; Fonagy *et al.* 2002; Steele *et al.* 2003).

2. *Enhancing behaviour management skills*
    Disturbed child behaviour and emotion, both internalised and externalised, needs to be managed effectively if family life is to become settled, relaxing and enjoyable. Parenting works best when strategies and skills of careful behaviour management and supervision are combined with emotional availability and a capacity for reflection (O'Connor *et al.* 2003). It is important to chose the right kind of response to difficult behaviours and emotions presented by children. Sometimes comfort is needed and at other times discipline (Hill *et al.* 2003). Given the often difficult, inexplicable and severe behaviours of many adopted children, strategies and skills often need to be learned and tried out with the guidance of skilled practitioners, including experienced adoptive parents themselves.

3. *Opening family communication*

   Things work best in adoption when confusion and ambivalence about the past and future of family life can be spoken about increasingly openly (Feast and Howe 2002). Open communication is necessary if an acceptable adoptive family story is to be jointly scripted and parents and children are to be enabled to take charge of their family destiny together. Clearing the way for this process of communication should be a key objective of therapy. It often remains marginal as an aim because so much attention is given to deleting behavioural problems and maximising child development outcomes. However, establishing a family story everyone can feel comfortable with is just as important a goal to be supported.

4. *Facilitating social participation*

   Adoption affects the way children and parents alike find their niche in the wider social context of family and community life. Children can feel victimised in their difference in their social relationships beyond the home and their troubling behaviour can accentuate the problem (Engels, Dekovic and Meeus 2002; Thomas *et al.* 1999). Parents have to find ways of securing their place in the larger community of local parenting. In both cases therapeutic support can help in the development of effective social strategies. It can be especially useful when it actively involves other people from the various social worlds in question, such as the school (Twemlow, Fonagy and Sacco 2002).

This list of objectives is consistent with a relational rather than a narrowly individual perspective on emotional and behavioural problems in families. The distinctive, vulnerable and fragile nature of adoptive family life means that relationships between family members need to be consistently held in mind, and worked with, rather than undermined by formal therapeutic input. Our objectives also give prominence to the narrative quality of the adoptive family experience as well as to issues of social and psychological development and well-being in themselves.

As we said in Chapter 2, a successful adoptive family life is one where the family script becomes shared and owned over time by all the family members as well as one that maximises the potential for the optimal development of the children. This *relational-narrative* approach is anchored in psychosocial, rather than purely psychiatric or psychotherapeutic perspectives. It also has a strong foothold in attachment theory.

With regard to attachment theory as the overarching guide to practice, as we said earlier, caution is sensible. Especially, as we see later, when the evidence for the effectiveness of various attachment therapies used in adoption still begs empirical proof. However the theory of attachment is well supported by the findings of empirical research (Cassidy and Shaver 1999) and it has an added attraction, in its capacity to span conventional theoretical and clinical boundaries. For example, it can be used to build bridges with the ideas of psychoanalysis (Fonagy 2001; Main and Solomon 1986), the systemic orientation of family therapy (Byng-Hall 1999; Hill et al. 2003) and the behavioural orientation of psychiatric and other approaches (Bifulco 2002; Scott 2003). It is this therapeutically integrative stance that underpins the identification of our four core therapeutic objectives. An attachment orientation should not exclude the use of therapy based upon psychiatric or other approaches. A full range of methods should be drawn on, especially where there is good evidence of their effectiveness in helping difficult behaviour abate.

But we are not proposing the kind of 'pick and mix', therapeutically eclectic approach that has increased in popularity either (Dryden 1992). Our integrative approach never loses sight of the key task: that of using the best methods to help parents and children manage and accommodate the distinctive demands of adoption in a way that strengthens the emotional tie between them as they build a satisfactory substitute family life for themselves.

Modes and methods of therapeutic intervention in adoption support

Having explored the main aim and core therapeutic objectives of practice we turn now to a discussion of the modes and methods of intervention currently used. The most important questions here concern which family members might best directly be involved in therapy, how the therapeutic alliance ought to be structured and what the effect will be in each case in achieving the goals set. No one mode of practice has yet become established. Indeed the very idea that adoptive family life might require a distinctive therapeutic strategy, rather than simply remaining anonymous within the generality of families and their troubles encountered in the clinic, has only recently been grasped in many areas (McDaniel and Jennings 1997). This poses problems for any review of effectiveness.

With adoption and its discontents being largely subsumed in general therapeutic practice and research, very few adoption-specific findings are available to inform decisions on what might work best in this particular case. A recent review by Rushton concludes that reliable research findings are urgently needed (2003), especially in respect of families facing severe child and parenting difficulties. One suggestion is that existing methods which have proven effectiveness be adapted and used in adoption (Barth and Miller 2000). Our own brief review here draws on what is known generally about the therapeutic value of different modes and methods as well as on the very limited information available on adoption-specific interventions.

Child-focused approaches

Earlier in this chapter we stated our main therapeutic objective as helping parents and children manage and accommodate the distinctive demands of adoption in a way that strengthens the emotional tie between them. Can child-focused therapies assist in this work? Before we consider this question specifically let us consider the general evidence for child-focused therapeutic interventions.

In their attempts to make an informed decision about the worth of formal therapy, Lucy, Bill and Isabel may find it helpful to know the following about modes of therapeutic help: isolating children, and treating them, rather than actively involving their parents in therapy, seems to be less effective than other ways of working (van de Wiel *et al.* 2002; Weiss *et al.* 1999; Weiss, Catron and Harris 2000). The evidence here comes from meta-studies of therapeutic efficacy and effectiveness in large cohorts from the general population of children with emotional and behavioural difficulties.

Regarding the comparative effectiveness of child-focused methods themselves, far more research has been done on the effectiveness of cognitive behavioural therapies in treating symptoms than on other therapies. However, the comparative studies that have been undertaken show cognitive behaviour therapy (CBT) to have the best (but even then only a small to moderate) effect when working solely with children, regardless of the problem which needs addressing (Bennett and Gibbons 2000; van de Wiel *et al.* 2002). What researchers define as 'unfocused supportive therapies', which may be psychotherapeutic or client-centred in their orientation, appear to come down the ladder on effectiveness (Cohen and Mannarino 1998; James and Mennen 2001). Weiss *et al.* (1999) also found that traditional child psychotherapy was no more effective than academic tutoring in helping children with emotional and behavioural difficulties.

But should Lucy, Isabel and Bill take these research findings conducted with large cohorts of children wholesale and apply them in their own particular context? For one thing, many comparative experiments have left the question begging about how far they are representative of, and can be applied to, the complex dynamics of real life therapy. In general terms, therapists do not necessarily practise either pure CBT or pure psychotherapy (Ryle 1990). Looking closely at accounts of practice in adoption specifically, it is clear that therapeutic practice with children is informed by a combination of traditions (Hughes 1997, 2003; Keck and Kupecky 2002; Levy and Orlans 1998; Scott and Lindsey 2003).

Also, as we have seen earlier in this book, adoptive families are quite distinctive, and their therapeutic needs should be considered in relation to the four objectives we outlined earlier in this chapter. If child-focused interventions designed for the general population are to be useful to Lucy and Bill's family, they will have to show their worth in relation to these objectives.

Cognitive behaviour therapy is moderately effective in child-focused work, but then only in relation to treating symptoms (Jones and Rampchandarni 1999). Given that our overall aim is to strengthen the emotional ties between parents and children, how might reducing symptoms through CBT help? Lucy and Bill could send their children to a CBT therapist in the hope of achieving small shifts in their behaviour. It could be argued that if the children's behaviour was successfully altered, this might have an impact on Lucy and Bill's ability to improve their own interaction with them. We know from research that such a shift in the quality of familial relationships is likely to make our first core objective, promoting emotion regulation and reflective thinking, more accessible (Bakermans-Kranenburg *et al.* 2003). However, we also know from the research evidence that this is best achieved by involving parents themselves in the process of CBT.

Also, how helpful CBT can be in adoption is likely to depend on the severity of the children's attachment difficulties. There is very little available research on this. In our own qualiative study one therapist described how those children he treats do not respond well to traditional CBT methods. This is because many of them do not have consequential thinking; 'So nice star charts tend to be eaten for breakfast' (Hart *et al.* 2002, p.147). Therapeutic methods that engage both the heart and the mind need to be drawn on. Other practice accounts endorse this position (Hart and Thomas 2000; Hughes 1997, 2003; Keck and Kupecky 2002).

Thus evidence points to adopted children with attachment difficulties often needing something other than direct, exclusive CBT to help them settle. How then do the other major approaches fare in this regard? There are two main orientations to direct work with adopted children, which make up the other major genre, i.e. the psychotherapeutic. The first follows the tradition of publishing case studies of classic object relations work with children using play and talk (Edwards 2000; Hodges 1984; Hunter 2001; Kenrick 2000). The second promotes or explores the effectiveness of holding therapies. We will deal with the classic psychotherapeutic genre first. However it should be noted at this point that a strict demarcation between intra-psychic and attachment approaches is somewhat artificial since many object relations therapists use the attachment concept of the secure base (Fonagy 2001; Hopkins 2000).

Studies in the classic tradition give us much insight into children's inner worlds, 'the what' of their experience, as Kenrick puts it (2000, p.410). However, most writers and practitioners of such therapeutic approaches are only just beginning to engage with the issue of their comparative effectiveness.

Critiques of this issue aside, how does their practice relate to our four core therapeutic objectives? With regard to the first, some have argued that through giving children the opportunity to practise relating to another human being in an intense, interpersonal context, individual child psychotherapy certainly promotes emotional regulation and reflective thinking (Hunter 2001; Kenrick 2000). Indeed, as one therapist put it, the sessions provide a 'trial ground where new developments can be explored before they are safely taken home' (Hopkins 2000, p.346).

With regard to our second, third and fourth objectives, classic individual child-focused psychotherapy can only claim to achieve these indirectly. The hope is that with increased trust and attachment to the therapist comes an ability to broaden out these positive experiences to other carers, and to take better advantage of experiences in the world at large. More critically, one might argue that direct work with children which focuses exclusively on the 'inner world' might actually undermine our fourth objective, facilitating social participation.

However, with the current emphasis on multi-disciplinary and collaborative working so much to the fore, it may be that many child psychotherapists do not practice in the manner of traditional child psychotherapy. Nevertheless, published accounts of child psychotherapy have rarely addressed the social relations of adoption. As such they may not yet have caught up with changes in actual practice (but see Bartram 2003).

Accounts of 'clinical' case studies in adoption tell us that positive shifts occur in individual children through child-focused work (Hopkins 2000; Hunter 2001; Ironside 2001; Kenrick 2000). However, to date there are few research studies which have systematically, and comparatively, explored these issues. The one published effectiveness study of classic psychoanalytic psychotherapy with adopted children took place with very small cohort numbers, and therapy was compared to a waiting list cohort rather than to those receiving a different intervention (Lush, Boston and Grainger 1991). Nevertheless, this study demonstrates a positive effect of therapy on most of the twenty children followed through over two years. An earlier review of psychotherapy with severely deprived children comes to similar conclusions (Boston and Szur 1983). Nevertheless, we are still none the wiser as to the relative effectiveness of this particular combination of mode and method in the adoption context.

In the absence of conclusive research, there are clearly some circumstances in which exclusive direct work with children may be indicated, despite our claim that in general it does not fulfil our core therapeutic objectives. Some children or young people may need a therapeutic space well away from their adoptive parents (Hodges 1984). For example, in relation to our third objective, opening family communication, it may be the case that having the opportunity to explore identity issues with somebody outside the adoptive family home will eventually impact on openness of communication within the family

(Hopkins 2000). In any case, children should always feel that they have access to someone external to the family if they have specific worries about family life and the care that they are receiving. In this respect it should be remembered that adoptive children are no different to any others. All children should have access to other adults in their lives (through, for example, school). However, the rights to this kind of personal support for adoptive children should not be confused with whether or not they should participate directly in therapeutic interventions.

In order for direct therapeutic work not to impede the formation of attachments within the family, it may be most appropriate for it to take place once early work on increasing attachment behaviours with the whole family, or through the parents, has been undertaken. Thinking back to our case example it is hard to see how, at this point in their family life together, Alan would be facilitated by intensive individual therapy with no parental involvement, unless Lucy and Bill were themselves psychologically defended to the point of refusing any interaction with formal therapeutic resources themselves. The practice of adoptive parents sending children to therapists to have them 'fixed' certainly goes on. Despite the best efforts of practitioners, some parents really may be impossible to engage (Bartram 2003).

Given Alan's feelings of isolation and his experiences of racism which add further injury to his legacies from an abusive birth family and the care system, it is worth Lucy and Bill trying to work with his therapist. Unsurprisingly, children's therapy appears to work better if parents understand and support its purpose (Schuman and Shapiro 2002; Tsiantis 2000). In this particularly attachment-insecure situation, family support worker Isabel will need to work hard with Alan's therapist to help him see that appropriate communication with Alan's parents needs to occur. She may also have work to do with Lucy and Bill to recognise their potential defensiveness in order to avoid them sabotaging his therapeutic relationship (Bartram 2003). Another reason that the adults in his life need to work together is so that angry, grief-stricken and disorganised Alan does not succeed in splitting them.

Having considered classic psychotherapy with children we now move on to holding and related attachment therapies. These methods, which are particularly informed by the attachment theory and neurological research we explored in Chapter 2, constitute our second orientation of psychotherapeutic approaches. They aim to provide a 'corrective emotional experience' for children with attachment disorders (Howe and Fearnley 1999, p.25) through intensive therapy and often physical holding. For Howe and Fearnley this type of therapy '...aims to approximate, through experience, what should have occurred in the child's formative years' (1999, p.25). These therapies (along with many in the adoption context) have not been subjected to rigorous comparative evaluation. However, there are some published practice cases (Cline 1979; Fearnley 1996; Howe and Fearnley 1999; Keck and Kupecky 1995) and one research study (Myeroff and Mertlich 1999) which claims success with them in specific circumstances.

Might Lucy and Bill's family benefit from Alan, and indeed other children in the family, having this intensive (and costly) treatment which is largely unavailable in the statutory sector? Certainly it has often been used in cases where adoptive parents simply cannot bear to live with their 'attachment disordered' child. Lucy and Bill are approaching such feelings of desperation. Traditionally, such therapies have removed the child from the family context completely and attempted to 'fix them'. However, the general trend in contemporary approaches veers more towards the involvement of other family members. Many of them might be better classed as a form of conjoint family therapy, rather than exclusive child-focused work.

The holding of the child by the therapist is seen as a controversial intervention in the adoption context for two main reasons. First, the therapeutic logic has been questioned as having 'no support in contemporary developmental theory or research' (O'Connor and Zeanah 2003, p. 237). The argument here is that there is no theoretical case for the assumption that secure attachment relationships can be kick-started simply through one-off dramatic catharsis. From the traditional psychosocial perspective on attachment therapy (Bowlby 1988), holding relates to the capacity of the therapist and/or parent to 'hold in mind or be sensitive to' (Steele 2003, p.219) the child's internal working models of self and others. Holding children down (especially forcibly), plays no part in this therapeutic schema for (re-)establishing attachment.

From a conventional psychiatric perspective, with its primary focus on observed child behaviours and conduct disorders, it is suggested that holding therapies are probably focused inappropriately in any case. For proponents of such approaches, it is the behaviour itself rather than the relational context in which it is established and sustained that needs therapeutic and/or parenting attention (O'Connor and Zeanah 2003). In both cases commentators point regularly to the potential traumatic and demeaning experience of the child who is held. Alongside these theoretical critiques, academic researchers such as Rushton (2003) and Barth and Miller (2000, p.452) point to the lack of any rigorous empirical research evidence of effectiveness of holding and related therapies.

A second allegation is that holding therapies are unethical as well as ineffective precisely because they are intrusive and potentially traumatising (Dozier 2003).

Nevertheless, within accounts of holding therapies and their critiques, there are significant differences between the nature and intensity of the holding experiences described, as well as whether or not the child's permission for the therapy was sought, and whether or not parents/carers were directly involved in treatment and holding. These distinctions are not always made entirely clear in the literature or the critique.

In the light of the lack of positive outcome studies, caution in the use of holding therapies is appropriate. Attachment therapists will also have to account more rigorously for the therapeutic logic of this work. Arguably, O'Connor and Zeanah's (2003) theoretical critique of holding therapy is too narrowly conceived (Howe 2003). Research undertaken on the work of the Keys Attachment Centre by Salford University is certainly optimistic about the method of holding therapy in this residential setting. (Huntington *et al.* 2004). In the absence of conclusive evidence, an ethical rather than a theoretical base line should arguably be applied. This is our view. Children should never be physically forced into and trapped in therapy of any kind.

There are then reasons why direct work with adopted children should continue to be considered as legitimite therapeutic options. However, returning to our focus on Lucy and Bill's family, some major concerns remain. The first is that in the absence of secure attachments to Lucy and Bill, Alan and the other children may attach to the therapist rather than to the new parent (Hart and Thomas 2000; Hoyle 1995; Hughes 1997; Keck and Kupecky 2002). In Alan's case part of the problem too may be that therapist Jason himself may be having difficulty in letting go, or in sharing Alan with others (Lanyado 2001).

A second issue which Lucy, Bill and Isabel will need to consider is that like many other adopted children, Alan and his siblings already have many adults, including new professionals, involved in their lives (Hart and Thomas 2000). Better then, if possible, to work with those already involved, rather than add others in. This would be one very sound reason for Lucy and Bill, possibly via Isabel as therapeutic-broker, to engage Alan's therapist in working alongside them. If successfully managed, Jason could even act as an adoption supporter in their wider kinship network – a symbolic third parent even – rather than as a threat to the formation of an attachment relationship between Lucy, Bill and Alan. However, we do not know for sure whether children with attachment difficulties can use direct and intensive relationships with therapists in the clinic to enhance their relationship with adoptive parents back home. To our knowledge there is no research on this issue. And reports of practice experiences are divided on the matter (Bartram 2003; Hart and Thomas 2000; Hopkins 2000; Hughes 1997).

We have one final point, which supports a cautious approach to individual therapy for adopted children as an exclusive strategy to follow in respect of any one family. It can put too much emphasis on the child to change or be changed. As we saw in Chapter 2, the research of Steele and colleagues demonstrates that adoptive parents themselves have therapeutic work to do if they are to help their children settle (Steele *et al.* 2003). It is to a focus on exclusive work with parents that we now turn.

Parent-focused interventions

Therapeutic interventions in families are increasingly being targeted at parents. In general terms, this help with parenting seems to be very effective in improving family relationships and children's behaviour (Barlow, Coren and Stewart-Brown 2001; Scott 2002). To address parents' difficulties in relation to their children's problems, parenting skills programmes have consistently been found to be superior to most other forms of support in child and adolescent mental health (Brestan and Eyberg 1998; Chorpita *et al.* 2002; Fonagy 1998; Foote, Eyberg and Schuhmann 1998; Kazdin 1996). However, two reviews have shown that their effect is most strong with younger children (Dishion and Patterson 1992; Ruma, Burke and Thompson 1996).

Key components of such skills training are outlined by Scott (2002). One very large study by Brestan and Eyberg (1998) shows that videotape modelling parent-training programmes and parent-training programmes based on a manual are the most effective forms of therapy analysed. A recent meta-analysis has demonstrated that when it comes to improving attachments between parents and children, relatively short-term behavioural interventions which quite specifically focus on increasing parental sensitivity are more effective than longer term ones with more diffuse aims (Bakermans-Kranenburg *et al.* 2003). However, there are few research studies which show whether or not parenting programmes have anything more than a short-term effect (Barlow *et al.* 2001).

It remains unclear whether training is best administered in a group situation or individually, and whether there are differences in effectiveness in relation to ethnicity. However, in relation to gender we now know that programmes including fathers are significantly more effective than those that do not include them (Bakermans-Kranenburg *et al.* 2003). Also, unsurprisingly, effectiveness depends crucially on sensitive engagement of parents in the first place.

These meta-analytic outcomes studies rarely incorporate a study of process and thus we cannot categorically account for reasons behind the changes in family function. However, from other research we know enough about parenting to approach a good enough understanding of why they work. The content of successful parenting programmes involve a combination of helping parents change their own behaviours and their own feelings about their children. Of course these two objectives will be combined in different ways, with some interventions clearly more behavioural in orientation and others more relational. However, in general terms what occurs is that as a result of a shift in parenting, children's behaviour modifies, as does their capacity to function reflectively (Riksen-Walraven and Van Aken 1997; van Ijzendoorn, Juffer and Duyvesteyn 1995).

If this general theory of change applies in the adoption context, the first two of our core therapeutic objectives are fulfilled, suggesting a promising future for Lucy and Bill's family if they find a suitable parenting intervention. So does it? The few research studies that have been conducted suggest this to be the case. For example, preliminary evaluations of interventions designed to address parents' attachment styles demonstrate an enhancement in both adoptive mothers' sensitivity and mother–child security of attachment as a result of the intervention (Dozier, personal communication 2002). Studies of both psycho-educative group parenting programmes run by experienced foster carers, and individual attachment-enhancing work in the homes of carers where baby-sitters were provided, both seem to be effective (Chase Stovall and Dozier 1998, 2000; Dozier, personal communication 2002). The Circle of Security Project (Marvin *et al.* 2002) is a further example of interventions to enhance parental sensitivity. And although it has not been subjected to a systematic evaluation, both mothers and fathers have found the psycho-educative programme 'A Piece of Cake' run in this country by Adoption UK to be very helpful (Hart *et al.* 2002). Delivered by experienced adopters in small local groups, it covers such issues as the expectations of adoptive parents, childhood trauma, attachment and creative parenting strategies.

Others report on the positive reception by parents of similar programmes (Beek 1999; Gordon 1999; Swaine and Gilson 1998). Coram Family are developing a supplementary manual of material which is sensitive to the adoption dimension, which can be used alongside parenting skills programmes such as Webster-Stratton (1999) if the parents attending the programme are adopters. The manual addresses issues such as play which is based on earlier traumatic experiences; regression; and various attachment issues where adopted children are likely to be particularly sensitive to specific interventions because of their history. They are also conducting an evaluation of its effectiveness (Kanuick, personal communication 2003).

The degree to which the feelings and behaviours of parents, are specifically addressed varies from programme to programme and thus we cannot say that they all categorically meet our first core objective. The intervention of Dozier and colleagues is very strong on educating the care-giver in the effects of their own upbringing and attachment orientation on the children in their care. Training manuals for therapeutic workers point to the difficulty of this task and the need to approach it with great sensitivity (Dozier *et al.* 2002).

Dozier *et al.* (2002) advocate the use of experienced foster carers or adoptive parents as therapists in order to reduce parental defences. Their training manual includes instructions to the therapist to include references to their own difficulties with parenting, particularly when the parent they are working with demonstrates resistance to exploring difficulties with her own care-giving. In relation to our second objective, enhancing behaviour management skills, many courses offer parents help with behavioural strategies.

All of the above approaches recognise the importance of establishing a strong therapeutic alliance with and (in group contexts) between parents. Many also recognise the relevance of including experienced foster carers or adopters as lead therapists. A further related approach which one of us has developed together with a family therapist, explicitly values adoptive parents as co-therapists. It has begun to be applied in fostering and adoption (Golding 2003; Hart and Thomas 2000). Inspired by attachment theory, this approach advocates keeping children away from formal therapy contexts during the early stages of adopted family life, in order to avoid unnecessary attachments to professionals and to concentrate on building relationships between children and their substitute primary care-givers (Hart and Thomas 2000). In this model, a lead therapist works with the children indirectly, i.e. through the adoptive parents. This perspective is respectful of parents as experts on their children in their own right, and acknowledges the necessary place of therapeutic work by adoptive parents with children placed in their care.

However, the model has not been subjected to comparative evaluation. Furthermore, research by Steele and others presents some challenges to this perspective since they show that the care-giving styles of adoptive parents can have more of a swift and profound impact on the children placed with them than was previously acknowledged (Steele *et al.* 2003).

Such work demonstrates that is important to consider the impact on family practices of the emotional capacity of adoptive parents and prospective adoptive parents. In relation to our case study, we know very well that Alan, Brian, Katie and Ellen have come to their new family with open sores, so to speak. But might Lucy and Bill themselves have some old wounds that need healing if their family life is to be given the best chance of success? We know of old that infertility can leave painful emotional scars (Wegar 2000). However, in recent years other issues – most particularly unresolved losses (not necessarily associated with infertility) and a lack of close, supportive relationships – have come to the fore. Attention to these issues may help explain which adoptive parents are in the best position to help children settle.

There are currently two main approaches to assessing the care-giving capacity of adoptive parents currently being developed for use in practice. We summarise them in Table 5.1 on the following page.

The first method, inspired by psychoanalytical thinking, involves the Adult Attachment Interview (AAI), which was created as a research tool to measure adult attachment per se (Hesse 1999). The AAI is being used by Miriam Steele and her colleagues in the Coram Family/Anna Freud Centre Research Study on the impact of adoptive parents' attachment representations on child attachment in placement (Hodges *et al.* 2003; Steele *et al.* 1999, 2003).

The second, based in social psychological rather than psycho-analytical thinking, makes use of an Attachment Style Interview (ASI) to measure the style of relating brought by adoptive parents to the task in relation to the use made of

Table 5.1 Two approaches to the assessment of the emotional capacity of adoptive parenting

	The adult attachment interview	The attachment style interview
Format	Questions to elicit descriptions of childhood memories, experiences and relationships and their effect on current personality and relationships	Questions to establish supportiveness of relationships and attachment categories
Theory	Attachment/psychoanalytic	Attachment/social psychology
Focus	Coherence of narrative account of experiences and effects; mental representations of emotions (mentalisation) rather than accounts of behaviour or attitudes	Style of relating; accounts of behaviour and attitude rather than mental representations
Classification	Four categories of attachment as coherence of narrative: • Autonomous-secure: good fit between memories and evaluations of attachment, succinct yet complete picture, provision of relevant details, clarity and orderliness • Insecure-dismissing: brief and incomplete account with lack of fit between memories and evaluations • Insecure-preoccupied: neither succinct nor brief account with irrelevant details and passive speech or current anger • Unresolved: loss or trauma referred to in way that suggests minimisation or continued absorption	Five categories of attachment as relationship style and effect: • Secure: confiding relationships with partner and friends • Insecure-fearful: no partner or close confiding relationships • Insecure-enmeshed: low partner support, many friends but not confiding • Insecure-angry/dismissive: poor partner support and high conflict, no confiding friend, conflict with family of origin • Insecure-withdrawn: no partner of confiding relationships, socially isolated

supportive relationships. The ASI, designed by their team, is being used by Antonia Bifulco and Geraldine Thomas in the Parents for Children/Royal Holloway Study on family assessment in adoption (Bifulco and Thomas 2003).

Insights such as these can be usefully drawn on to further refine the co-therapy model. Therapy trainings have long recognised the need for students to explore the impact of their own difficulties on the way they work with clients, with most courses requiring trainees to engage in personal therapy.

Encouraging exploration of parental difficulties can be seen as part of the supervisory role of the lead therapist, much in the way that trainee therapists are encouraged to explore their own difficulties so that they do not impact too greatly on their relationship with clients.

During the early stages of adoptive family life, for parents experiencing difficulties such as those of Lucy and Bill, one or a combination of parent-oriented therapeutic approaches would go some way towards directly tackling our first two core objectives. The other two should also be met, at least in part. Regarding our third objective, that of opening family communication, as we saw above, research suggests that parents who have been helped to reflect on their parenting respond better to their children's needs. In the adoption context the need for open family communication must be established as we will see in the following chapter. Our fourth objective, that of facilitating social participation, will partially be met if Lucy and Bill attend a group parenting programme. This would provide them with valuable peer support and help them to generate social connections for their children.

However, sensitivity to family practice suggests that Lucy, Bill and Isabel need to think carefully about how to make parent-focused therapy really work for them. Here, practical issues such as local availability of appropriate services, distance to travel to therapeutic groups and child care need to be considered. If general trends of attendance at such events are anything to go on, only one of them may be able to go, and it is most likely to be Lucy. This practice contributes to women in heterosexual partnerships taking the greater responsibility for dealing with family difficulties which, as research now clearly tells us, might be better shared with their partner (Bakermans-Kranenburg et al. 2003).

Yet the real problem remains that Lucy and Bill are likely to find it tricky to find someone willing to look after Alan and his siblings. Their desperation for help may mean that they find it difficult to take the attachment needs of the children into consideration when seeking out child care. Social workers and others planning group training programmes should take these difficulties into consideration, and demonstrate to adoptive parents that they are aware of the need for support to work with rather than against their broader family needs. One response is to provide site-based child care during training programmes. One voluntary agency, for example, capitalised on the enthusiasm of prospective adopters by recruiting them to run the creche whilst adoptive parents received training (Kaniuk, personal communication 2003). Another is to actively recruit other adults in the family's network to undertake child care on a regular basis for such events, as part of an integrated short break scheme, for example.

Parent-focused therapeutic interventions, then, whether they are conducted in the home or elsewhere, are clearly an important resource, and go some way towards fulfilling our four core objectives. However, practical matters need consideration. The final section of this chapter considers the value of interventions which include both parents and children as participants.

Parent–child and family-focused interventions

The general effectiveness of family therapy approaches has certainly been demonstrated in many different situations, including conduct disorder, hyper-activity and bereavement (Carr 2000a and 2000b; Cottrell and Boston 2002; Woolfenden and Williams 2000). In recent years the net has been thrown rather more widely with ecological and systemic approaches pioneering the inclusion of long-term therapeutic work with schools, friends and extended family (Blum and Ellen 2002; Oyserman, Terry and Bybee 2002; Twemlow *et al.* 2002). Less intensive therapeutic work in schools, where teachers are given advice on strategies to use in class with children with attachment difficulties also seems beneficial (Chapman 2002). Regarding formal therapeutic interventions, multi-systemic and family preservation approaches have been shown to be effective in families whose problems are complex and long standing (Chafflin, Bonner and Hill 2001; Cunningham and Henggeler 1999). However, recently there has been some dispute about their relative effectiveness (Westat, Chapin Hall Centre for Children and James Bell Associates 2002). Surprisingly more focused, shorter-term therapies now seem to be demonstrating at least equal, if not more effectiveness (Bakermans-Kranenburg *et al.* 2003).

As with other general studies of therapeutic effectiveness we do not know the extent to which these cohorts include adoptive families. However, we do know that specific interventions aimed at working with adoptive parents and children together, as well as with others in their networks, have been developed in therapeutic settings. These include traditional family therapy, systemic family preservation work, parent–child dual therapy approach and what we term conjoint attachment and development orientated narrative approaches used in agencies such as Family Futures in London and the Attachment Project in Brighton and Hove (Archer and Burnell 2003; Hart *et al.* 2002). Whilst these are all relatively well-established methods, and some have been evaluated, to our knowledge none of them has been subjected to robust comparative research within the context of adoption.

Positive practice accounts of traditional family therapy in adoption are very thin on the ground. Most accounts in the literature concern its negative reputation amongst adoptive families (McDaniel and Jennings 1997; Winkler *et al.* 1988). Here the neglect by family therapists in recognising the impact of children's past legacies on adoptive family life has been explored, as has the practice of crudely blaming adoptive parents for their children's difficulties. As one study demonstrates, rather than family therapy as a general approach being at fault, the problem lies more in the lack of adoption-sensitive skills and awareness of individual practitioners (McDaniel and Jennings 1997). We have yet to see whether more adoption-sensitive traditional family therapy will emerge in future accounts of practice.

In the meantime, there are other parent–child focused interventions about which more positive things have been written. The 'family preservation' tradition is well established in the US, and it has made some inroads in this country, although published evaluations on its effectiveness feature more in fostering than in adoption (Chamberlain and Weinrott 1990; Livingston Smith and Howard 1999; Walker *et al.* 2002). Family preservation is intensive and relatively costly. It involves drawing on a variety of support methods, of which direct therapeutic methods are just one part, albeit a vital one. Emphasis is also placed on alleviating practical problems, including those relating to finances and housing, and on promoting positive mental health within the family, with the long-term availability of the service of key concern. Work is generally undertaken with all family members as well as, in some cases, others in the network, for example teachers and social workers, to enhance family functioning and social participation. Often parents are given the status of therapists and thus they draw heavily on some of the parent-focused interventions we discussed earlier (Walker *et al.* 2002).

Family preservation interventions generally enhance the behavioural management skills of parents. And of all the therapeutic approaches we have considered in this chapter, family preservation interventions are most likely to fulfil our fourth objective since they integrate a focus on relationships beyond the immediate family. However, they may not in themselves be that effective at achieving our first core objective. A recent meta-analysis has suggested that in cases of severe attachment difficulty, such broad interventions, whilst necessary to clear the way for more focused therapeutic work, cannot replace it.

In such cases, behavioural interventions which focus quite specifically and systematically on addressing parental sensitivity towards their children are necessary. It is likely then that in addressing the difficulties of Lucy and Bill's family, the broad tasks of helping them with practical issues in their daily life needs to be enhanced by a focus on their own competencies as parents. This can either be achieved through a parent-focused mode of therapy or through one of the family-focused modes we discuss below. The precise method chosen will depend on the needs and wishes of family members. Unfortunately, it will also depend on local availability of particular expertise.

In adoption, Hughes' dual-therapy model is well-known and popular although it remains to be subjected to research evaluation. It involves parents and children with severe attachment problems in the therapy room together with a therapist (1997; 2003). Hughes is explicit about the theory of change behind his choice to abandon working as a traditional child psychotherapist. As we said earlier, in child psychotherapy, the child's relationship with the therapist is the critical foundation for change. However, for Hughes the therapeutic relationship is 'too circumscribed and too brief and it lacks the crucial quality of 24-hour-a-day engagement that a parent has with a child' (1997, p.7). In his earlier work, the importance of the relationship between child and therapist lay in its ability to serve as a working model for the child's relationship with the parent in the room. Thus the parent would be expected to emulate the therapist's interventions leading to change in the child. In more recent work Hughes brings parents into a more explicit and sustained co-therapy role (2003). Hughes' emphasis on the inter-subjectivity between the parent-therapist partnership and the child places his work somewhere between the physical holding of alternative therapists and the holding in mind of traditional psychotherapy.

In fulfilling our first three objectives, Hughes' approach has much to recommend it. Without enhancement in the form of offering consultations to others in the family network, the fourth objective, as in most of the therapies we have considered in this chapter, is only indirectly fulfilled. A major issue with his approach is that its dual parent–child focus means that siblings are likely to have to access therapy separately. In the case of families such as those of Lucy and Bill, this would entail four separate sets of appointments with parents, children and therapists.

Conclusion

This chapter has explored various approaches to the enhancement of care-giving and receiving between adoptive parents and their children. As we have shown, this is a vast and complex terrain.

The first part of the chapter emphasised how an understanding of family practices can help make therapy really supportive to families. We set out the argument for an integrative approach to formal therapeutic practice in adoption drawing on the insights of attachment theory in relation to methods of intervention inspired by other knowledge bases. Here we outlined four core objectives to be held in mind when making decisions about therapy for adoptive families.

Using Lucy and Bill's family as a case example, we then went on to highlight the benefits of an evidenced based approach to tailoring formal therapeutic support to the needs of individual families and children. In doing so we adopted a family practices approach to thinking about the mode, method and timing of therapy to be drawn on. Our review of effective therapies led us to caution against the exclusive use of child-focused therapies, and highlighted parenting interventions as an important component of post-adoption therapeutic support. We went on to consider the effectiveness of working with parents and children together, and demonstrated that broadly speaking such interventions are well supported by efficacy and effectiveness studies, although in adoption specifically the evidence base is thin.

In our discussion, we explored the concern that child-focused therapies can locate the problem of behaviour and emotional distress in the child alone. As a consequence, the origins of difficulties in the care-giving aspect of the attachment relationship can remain unexplored as professionals and parents focus on changing the child. One way of dealing with this is for parents to undertake therapy of their own which enhances their sensitivity to their children, and to explore the impact of their own psychological processes on their care-giving styles. We have also highlighted the important role of the adoption support worker in both knowledgeably facilitating therapeutic interventions, and wherever possible, delivering them.

However, changes in the care-giving and care-receiving behaviour of parents and children alike are unlikely to endure without paying some attention to the external stresses and broader contexts which affect the chances of adoptive parents and their children to form a successful relationship. In the final chapter of this book we explore in a much broader sense how children can be helped by all those involved in their care to achieve their full potential, both within the home and beyond. In the meantime, it is to the support that is needed to maintain connections and helpful relationships for children within the wider adoptive kinship system that we now turn.

Chapter 6

'Holding Multiple Families in Mind'
Enabling Open Communication in Adoptive Kinship

Introduction

Promoting secure fresh attachments is the foundational task for parents and their adoption supporters. It is the necessary condition for a settled and successful adoptive family life. However, it is not a sufficient condition in itself. The distinctive nature of family formation in adoption requires that attachments be established within many relationships and affiliations inherited from a different family past. We have long known from research that adopted adults have a more secure sense of personal identity and well-being if they were told as children where they came from and why they were adopted (Triseliotis 1973). We also know that there can be a mutually reinforcing relationship between the achievement for children of a sense of belonging in the adoptive family and discussion between children and parents about the different origins and reasons behind their adoptive family life (Howe and Feast 2000; Howe *et al.* 2001).

Equally, though it is all too easy to see why parents might avoid the tricky tasks of both 'talking and telling' (Feast and Howe 2002) and keeping alive links with birth families and former carers as they simultaneously struggle to help their troubled children settle and attach. Take Lucy and Bill for example. It is hard to imagine how they could find space in their lives right now to do anything like this. And exactly how, when and what should be openly talked about when the truth is often so painful and upsetting? It is hardly surprising that in both theory and practice it is ambivalence, confusion and dispute that prevail when it comes to deciding exactly what approach should be taken to supporting 'openness' in adoption.

In this chapter we consider how the apparent tension between the twin objectives of reparative attachment and a settled identity based in continuity of ties might be eased. We do this by proposing a new approach to 'life story work' in adoption, in which openness about talking and telling, and plans and arrangements for contact, are placed centre-stage in adoptive family life. By seeing family life and new attachment relationships as being constructed through a process of story telling as well as love and care we can begin to understand how crucial openness is. And contact itself, over which there remains so much uncertainty, becomes important because it contributes to continuity of communication *about* the past rather than just continuity of relationships *with* people from that past. These relationships may remain significant in themselves but the primary purpose of contact, from the narrative perspective we take here, is to fill gaps in the family story. In this way it is possible to ensure personal identity and family life in adoption become coherent. As narrative coherence is at the heart of both secure attachment and a sense of family belonging it is an essential aspect of family life to be supported. Practice should, therefore, be guided by the two core principle of 'family scripting' and 'open family communication'.

In relation to the idea of 'family scripting' the aim for adoption supporters is to enable parents and children to establish and live by their own distinctive family story or script. As we said in Chapter 2 the conventional way of thinking about adoptive childhood and family life is to see them as normal lifecycle processes in which additional adoption-specific tasks have to be overcome. But instead of seeing the process of one mainly of 'adjustment' (Brodzinsky, Smith and Brodzinsky 1998) we look on it as one of 'construction'. Each family makes its own way and if things are going to work out well (or well enough) it is best if parents and children do that working out together. Things go wrong when set scripts get prescribed and people try to follow them rigidly. Adoptive parents sometimes try to stick to idealised notions of what 'family' must be. Children often get trapped in attachment patterns whose original protective purpose in the birth family past is wholly inappropriate for the adoptive family present and future. Professionals can bring sets of assumptions about what rules should be followed, for example in relation to contact arrangements.

This is why the joint commitment to securing 'open family communication', that we identified earlier as one of the core therapeutic objectives of adoption support, is so important. The capacity for mutual reflection at the heart of open communication is closely linked to the quality of the attachment/care-giving relationship (Fonagy *et al.* 2002). So successful work on attachment provides the primary context for a dialogue about the difference of family life in adoption. However this is a dialogue which requires people to be able and willing to 'hold multiple families in mind', as Margaret Rustin so beautifully put it (1999). This can seem a particularly difficult thing to do together for children and parents whose own relationship feels fragile. It is often in the early stages of placement and again later, perhaps in adolescence, that bringing to mind and discussing displaced family experiences and expectations can prove most unsettling.

Rethinking practice

Any effective support strategy designed to help parents and children develop and discuss their own family script will require some rethinking of current practice in relation to contact arrangements and 'life story work' in adoption. As we saw in Chapter 3 there is an obligation on agencies to provide specified information and to practically support contact arrangements. However there is a virtual silence in current policy and guidance on how these crucial aspects of practice ought to be integrated into any family support strategy in adoption.

In the case of contact there is a danger that discussion about the general principle of open communication in adoption is confused with debates and decisions about specific arrangements for contact. Hence arguments for openness can be automatically conflated with arguments for continued contact, direct or indirect. However the two are not necessarily linked at all. Contact can enhance communication in adoptive families, about identity issues for children and about the nature of adoptive family life in general, as recent research has shown (Grotevant and McRoy 1998). But it does not necessarily do so. David Brodzinsky (2003) has cautioned that in what he calls 'structurally open adoption' contact can be used as a reason for avoiding rather than developing the primary process of wider 'communicative openness'.

The life story process needs fresh attention too. As presently practised 'life story work' (Ryan and Walker 2002) is something that is done (or not) with children to help them make better sense of their 'adoptive identity' (Grotevant 1997), that is to understand from where they originate and why they have been adopted. In the 'family practices' perspective on adoption this is too narrow and individual an approach to take, both to the concept of identity and to an understanding of how a life story gets scripted. A settled personal and social identity for children placed from public care requires more than just coming to terms with the fact and meaning of the status of adoption. Arguably, this traditional view needs to be updated to take account of the dynamics of dual (or serial identification) by children across a wider adoptive kinship network (including foster carers, and perhaps even former social workers) and the implications this has for their parents' image of the adoptive family identity.

And the 'life story' in question needs to be seen as one jointly constructed over time by family members themselves. To this extent we agree with Barbara Yngvesson and Maureen Mahoney when, as a result of their research into inter-country adoption in the US and Scandinavia, they say that 'identity is not a thing but a process' (2000, p.102). The suggestion of John Triseliotis that it might help to think of 'a hierarchy of identities' in adoption (2000, p.92) is similarly relevant here. Fresh attachment is foundational because it provides children with a core sense of self. However, beyond this the autobiographical life story process is one of incorporating and settling differing sources of identification rather than of taking on any singular 'adoptive identity'.

In the second half of the chapter we set out the key elements of a new model of 'adoptive family life story work' that is informed by our core propositions about open family communication and the joint scripting of adoptive family life. This includes a reconsideration of the place of contact in this process. In order to do this we first discuss two contrasting approaches currently taken to the task of helping families reconcile the tension between establishing reparative attachment and retaining continuity of ties. We then briefly remind ourselves about the fragmented and diverse family and kinship context in which children develop their 'autobiographical self' (Damasio 2000) in adoption.

Keeping things open: disengagement and continuity in adoptive family life

The unusual nature of adoptive family life following placement from care is neatly exposed by the reflection of one adoptive mother on the placement of a sibling group in her family. 'I wonder,' she said, 'if we've adopted the children or they've adopted us.' It would be wise to accept her own conclusion that, 'at any rate, it's clearly a two-way process' (Fergusson 2003, p.26).

This kind of open recognition from the start that adoption is inherently an ambiguous, even paradoxical, family situation in which to construct a settled life story should surely guide practice. Further on in this chapter we suggest a number of different ways in which this might be achieved. The following is just one example. With the idea of a two-way process in mind, it may even be appropriate for Lucy, Bill and the other parents to make a symbolic gesture, such as enabling their children to keep their former surnames on their birth certificates, or perhaps combining the family names of the children and the adoptive parents to make a new one. This would constitute a powerful commitment to really making it a two-way process.

Maintaining symbolic ties is important. It may seem paradoxical, then, that the ultimate achievement of a sense of permanence and belonging for both children and adoptive parents requires sufficient disengagement from past family affiliations. Fresh primary attachments are the key to success in this. Yet when children first arrive it can feel to both them and their new parents that the adoptive home is little more than an outpost added in to an already well-established if often frightening and transient family landscape. Keeping some things from the past can be essential to moving on.

Case study: Bryony Hall, Rachel Cunningham, and Luke and Debbie Forster

Take, for example, the situation of Luke and Debbie. Three weeks into placement and adoptive family life, one might say, remains far from familiar, for parents and children alike. Luke may be six years old already, big enough for his little sister Debbie to cling onto for her own comfort, but he is clearly in need of the love and emotional care adoptive couple Bryony and Rachael have signed up to give him. But his yearning for the lost family life and relationships of foster care, and the upset it causes, keep him closed off from any feelings he might have for these strange new parents. His palpable, visceral grief and longing, lurking behind which is the long, cold shadow cast by his scary original father, also stop Luke from being able to think. He cannot think about himself in the present, and about the people around him now, let alone consider his future in his new school, family and neighbourhood. In order to arrive emotionally in his new home Luke will need to confront those demons that come to mind whenever thoughts about his father slip back into his head or when he feels odd in various ways. Most importantly, he will have to shift from having a rather anxious primary attachment to temporary parents Lindsey and Dave to having a secure primary attachment to Bryony and Rachael.

So it seems sensible to suggest that Bryony and Rachael find a way of helping Luke move on and settle into his adoptive family home. But Bryony and Rachael are already struggling to grasp exactly what is going on, not quite getting it right over helping these vulnerable children with props to ease the transition. Clearly they have no idea of the importance of transitional objects. And Rachael, perhaps almost as much as Luke himself, has started to hold back her real feelings, of bewilderment and irritation with Luke and his refusal to settle and connect. The interested nursery worker is already biting her lip, although she could be a real asset in helping Debbie settle. There is no sign of the social worker. So the stage is set early for avoidance and alienation, the price on all sides too high, so to speak, of saying what is really felt. Fragile identities, of 'adopted child', 'adoptive parents' and 'permanent family', exposed so soon. And exactly what would be the aim anyway, of exposing Luke's feelings and helping him work through his upset and resistance at letting go of his overwhelming pre-occupation with his foster relationships? Certainly, to help free him up emotionally to make new primary attachments, but for good now. But what can Luke take with him meanwhile, what really has to go and what ought to stay part of who he is – and who he will want to become?

In circumstances like these it is not surprising that splitting rather than integration in thinking about the contrasting needs of children in transition might occur. This can happen as much in theory and research as it does in practice. What kind of adoption support practice might help Bryony and Rachael, Luke and Debbie find a way of starting to talk openly together and tell each other their new story of adoptive family life and kinship? How can Luke and Rachael's 'multiple family' experiences be held in mind in the adoptive family without being a continuous and disruptive intrusion? What role should contact play in particular? These are vexed questions and Bryony and Rachael may well receive contradictory advice on how to help Luke and Debbie accommodate their old and new family lives.

Two competing perspectives can be detected in theoretical texts and practice accounts. The first, which we call the *'disengagement/reconnection' model* of adoptive childhood, family life and kinship originates in the traditional view, that a settled 'adoptive identity' would be achieved when children came to terms with their adoptive status and with the losses that implied. We discussed this theoretical perspective in some detail in Chapter 2. In practice accounts the well-known work of Vera Fahlberg (1994) exemplifies this approach as applied to contemporary adoption.

The second approach, described here as the *'extended kinship' model*, draws on systems theory and the idea that children can cope with and benefit from continuous multiple family affiliations. The Review of Adoption Law published shortly after the enactment of the Children Act 1989 was influenced by this latter perspective (Department of Health and Welsh Office 1992).

Fahlberg insists that 'full disclosure to the adoptive parents about the child's past is absolutely necessary' (1994, p.210). But the life story process in general, and contact in particular, play no more than a residual role in the day-to-day life of the adoptive family home. The 'life story book' itself is a device to help with what is called 'disengagement work' (1994, p.325), helping children resolve the grief caused by the loss of previous family relationships, and thereby move on and settle in their substitute home.

Fahlberg's own practice examples (1994, pp.353–373) provide a reminder to social workers and adoptive parents of the potential relevance of the 'life story book' through childhood. Gaps in information may need to be filled and the grieving process itself may take time. 'Adaptive grieving' (Brodzinsky 1987), for example, occurs later where children placed as infants only come to understand adoption and what they have lost on reflection rather than from the experience of separation itself. Nonetheless the underlying emphasis is on using the 'life story book' to facilitate the severance not the sustenance of relationships. In adolescence, reconnection with birth parents, with or without direct contact, will probably be necessary because the achievement of an independent sense of identity requires that separation from parent figures (birth as well as adoptive) be reworked. In the meantime, though, it is assumed that the process of open communication will need to exclude them.

Although Fahlberg's classic text on the child's 'journey through placement' has had enormous influence on practice, a shift in assumptions about contact between children in public care and their birth relatives during the early 1990s gave practitioners a different message about openness in adoption. An inclusive approach to family placement and contact was embodied in the Children Act 1989 and repeated in the Review of Adoption Law (Department of Health and Welsh Office 1992). This was consistent with evidence from research (Fratter *et al.* 1991) that the severance of relationships and contact in permanent placement was associated with disruption and instability. It is also informed by systemic ideas about kinship and family belonging in which relationships are supplemented and adapted rather than substituted and displaced. Hence adoption can be understood to have created an 'extended family system' (Reitz and Watson 1992, p.12) in which two families are linked forever through the child, 'who is shared by both' (1992, p.11). Some go one step further than this. Rustin's (1999) notion of 'multiple families' leaves open the potential to include others, such as former foster carers, within the family system. In this 'extended kinship' model it is the expectation of continuity of relationships rather than their severance and re-engagement that drives practice in relation to both life story work and contact.

These are clearly quite different theoretical and practice scripts for managing the process. Hence Bryony and Rachael will be advised by some practitioners to make sure Luke and Debbie stay in touch, directly or indirectly, with both their foster and birth parents. This is because children, they will be told, can be expected to be able 'to juggle with several family circles and feel quite comfortable in all of them' (Argent 2002, p.2), whilst 'a main circle' evolves. But they may be advised by others, especially in relation to the maintenance of links with birth parents, that 'in the majority of contemporary adoption situations, direct contact represents contamination and re-traumatisation' (Archer and Burnell 2003, p.204). In the first case the 'extended kinship' approach argues for openness and communication in the context of continuity of relationships. In the second case a strong disengagement approach is employed to argue that the primary focus of contact is therapeutic and the main objective may be to help Luke and Debbie say 'a long goodbye' (Burnell 2003, p.206) to their past, at least for the time being.

We propose that the most important advice for Bryony and Rachael is simply to 'keep things open'. There are two aspects to this advice. First, is their primary responsibility to establish the conditions in which Luke and Debbie can give voice to their feelings and fears about their transient and difficult family experiences. What is being kept open here is communication itself. This is the foundational general condition for any subsequent specific decision about contact and its nature and purpose.

Second, there is the proposition that such decisions themselves should also be kept open. That is, no external set family script should be taken off the peg and applied by Bryony and Rachael to their lives with Luke and Debbie. It may well be that continuity of relationships and ties through contact will help things settle and that the 'adoptive kinship network' thereby formed will enhance personal identity and a common sense of family belonging. A growing amount of research evidence can be provided to support this family story (Grotevant and McRoy 1998; Neil 2002a, 2002b, 2003; Wrobel *et al.* 2003). It may equally be the case that any continuous relationship and tie will prove disruptive or insignificant. Contact might undermine, or be of marginal relevance to, rather than underpin a sense of permanence and interrupt the task of achieving an integrated and settled identity for the children. The same research invariably identifies specific cases where contact has not been helpful, although it has to be said that in the absence of reliable and effective support systems it is difficult to determine whether it is contact itself or the way it is set up and supported that cause things to go wrong when they do.

'Keeping things open' is consistent with the idea that decisions about contact in adoption should be made on a case by case basis. More than this though is the principle that they should be made in a way that enables children themselves, in time, to decide on their own definition of continuity and identity.

By 'keeping things open' in this way Bryony and Rachael, with the help of their keyworker and through formal therapeutic support where necessary, will be reducing the inherent tension between attachment and identity in adoption. They will be enabling discussions about links and identifications with past family lives to be tied into the process of forming those secure fresh attachments required for the permanent new family future. Any decision taken about contact arrangements may or may not be helpful, in the event, to the achievement of a sense of settled identity and family belonging. However, what is most important of all, from this perspective, is that the process of making such a decision, seeing it through, checking out its impact and changing things as necessary, is as fully shared as possible.

From the point of view of the family all this is much easier said than done. The process of giving shape and meaning to their distinctive family lives and personal identity depends on the capacity of children to develop an 'autobiographical' stance or self. In adoption from care this capacity is impaired by the traumatic and transient nature of early experience. It is further challenged by the fragmented family context in which a coherent and settled sense of self must be established. This makes the communicative task required of parents Bryony and Rachael particularly challenging and the adoption support role especially important. The dynamics of avoidance in adoption can be extremely powerful and support for open communication will need to be well embedded. The timing and pacing of children's engagement with their adoptive family narrative, and the context in which it takes place, need to be thought about carefully. As Keefer and Schooler (2000) argue, age and developmental stage are crucial considerations here. The nature and function of the information that must be made available and accessible to children and their parents is a central question for practice, as we see later.

Owning experience: developing an autobiographical self and life story identity in adoption

Normally children construct the story of who they are and where they belong in the context of greater or lesser continuity of parenting, family life, kinship and culture. The individual life story is an integral part of family life and heritage. At least one parent is almost invariably available throughout childhood to help children from birth to give voice to experience, to use language to construct narratives about what has happened and how they, and others, feel about it (Oppenheim et al. 1997). All being well this builds attachment and an emotionally secure sense of self in relation to others. It also enables children to develop a coherent sense of family belonging and social identity. This 'autobiographical project' (Nelson 2001, p.27) produces a family life story that links the child's sense of who they are in the here and now with both their past and their anticipated future. Children normally develop the 'autobiographical self' that Damasio (2000) and others (Fonagy et al. 2002) see as the culmination of early optimal development by the time they are four or five years old.

Through taking an autobiographical stance children are enabled to feel increasingly in control of, and responsible for, the process of understanding and then giving meaning and shape to their (family) lives: 'owning experience', in the helpful definition of one commentator (Fivush 2001, p.35). The autobiographical stance enables children, from their fourth year, to have a sense of continuity of self over time. For example, it encompasses the understanding by children that their gender and ethnicity are defining characteristics. It is on these early foundations that children and young people come to be able to establish for themselves a settled sense of identity as they move into adulthood. Identity, from this 'life story' perspective, is 'an internalised and evolving self-story, an integrative narrative of self that provides modern life with some modicum of psychosocial unity and purpose' (McAdams 2001, p.101).

The autobiographical stance is established fairly early but only in late adolescence, current research suggests, do children acquire the full cognitive capacity to draw together in an integrated way the elements that make up a coherent narrative (Habermas and Bluck 2000). This includes being able to make links between past events and present experience, to identify causes and patterns in one's life and, crucially, to tell the story in a way that make sense to oneself and others. And of course, as we saw in Chapter 2, the individual life story gets constructed in a family setting. A 'family narrative' (Fiese *et al.* 1999) emerges when family is the reference point. From this narrative perspective we can say that children take on the family story for themselves. This is how they achieve a sense of kinship and belonging. They do this, McAdams suggests, by using the 'little stories' (2001, p.104) of their early years as a foundation for coherent and integrated accounts of themselves and their family lives later on.

In adoption this life story process is disrupted. According to the conventional account, in traditional baby adoption early placement enables the initial development of the autobiographical self to be readily achieved. In this view it is usually in middle childhood, when children are normally fitting the pieces of their (family) life together, that the capacity to understand the concept of adoption first disrupts the process (Brodzinsky 1987).

However, from the trauma and attachment perspective outlined in Chapter 2, any separation will have huge reverberations across adoptive childhood. It is claimed that the rupture of the intense relationship between biological mother and child, developed in utero, is irrevocable. This is because early relationships are somehow inscribed in the very make up of the brain (Archer 2003).

Evidence for the precise extent of the impact of early experience is still being accumulated. In the meantime, adoption is not the cultural norm, so the emerging life story narrative has to be revised, whatever perspective one takes. Significant displaced characters from the past have to be brought to mind and fitted into the story. This process still goes on in contemporary care adoptions, although it may be that the social stigma traditionally associated with adoption as a family status per se is diminishing (Leon 2002). We have seen how, in the conventional account of 'adoption psychology', children have to be helped to 'adjust' (Brodzinsky *et al.* 1998) to the fact of their adoptive status, and to take on an 'adoptive identity' (Grotevant 1997) in adolescence and beyond. In infant adoption this task is made easier because the adoptive parents and the adoptive family have been there relatively early on, providing the secure emotional base and 'conversational scaffolding' (McAdams 2001, p.104) necessary for the autobiographical self to develop.

However, the later placement of children from care regularly undermines the natural capacity of children to incorporate the fact of their adoptive status into their family life story and identity. Traumatic pre-placement experience is incapacitating of memory and reflective thought (Archer and Burnell 2003; Cairns 2002; Fonagy *et al.* 2002). With children often still defensively caught up, with anger and shame (Hughes 1997), in the personal and family scripts provided by neglectful and abusive parents, it can be extremely difficult for substitute parents to connect children to the new adoptive family story line. It is not just the fact of adoption but the realities and impact of earlier family experience and identification that have to be put in their place if the adoptive life story is to become sufficiently coherent and integrated to enable childhood and family life to be settled. Telling each other the 'little stories' of family in adoption is extremely difficult to do. By convention stories have a beginning, a middle and an end. But the start of the adoptive family story lies in the different, unfinished (and often unclear) family stories of both children and parents. These are often extremely painful to recall, let alone share and talk about together. And early experience invariably leaves children with an impeded capacity to take the calm and reflective approach necessary to own experience and put it to positive use in planning the future.

It is easy to see how the process of retrieval of memory, necessary for achievement of an autobiographical stance, can get hijacked or avoided in adoption. Very often children, such as several of those interviewed by Caroline Thomas and colleagues (Thomas *et al.* 1999) and Catherine Macaskill (2002), get stranded, having no one with whom to share their worries. They are left suppressing thoughts and feelings about their displaced birth family and wondering why decisions were taken in ways that have left them and their views side-lined. Adoptive parents can be uncertain and fearful when it becomes apparent that even the most terrible events and experiences might need to be spoken of openly. Some parents in our study spoke about their fear of 'opening a can of worms' (Hart *et al.* 2002, p.136) by allowing issues of the past to be raised with their children in therapy.

Often social workers, too, seem to need to tidy away painful realities that will demand attention one day, for example by maintaining the single fiction for the 'life story' book that rejecting and abusive parents had tried their best and loved their children really (Archer and Burnell 2003). This can only contribute to confusion and dismay in children. Shelley Mann, adopted as a teenager after half a childhood and more in foster care, is pointed in her advice. She demands that 'more credit should be given for the intelligence of children, as it is all too easy to patronise and tread lightly, when plain honesty would suffice and keep them on track' (Mann 2003, p. 46). She was left having to confront her unreliable and deceitful birth mother on her own at 12 in order to gain control over her own life story. She reflects, 'At last I felt that our relationship now had a basis in reality and truth on my terms rather than the fantasy she had created and wanted me to participate in' (2003, p.47).

Social workers, courts and adoptive parents too have their fantasy family in mind when adoption is decided on. Maintaining the fantasy may become an increasingly implausible strategy but lifting the lid on the ghosts from the past can feel even more scary. And whenever this is done, it needs to be undertaken in a way that takes proper account of the age and developmental stage of the child (Keefer and Schooler 2000). Although some guidelines on what this might actually mean in practice do exist (Keefer and Schooler 2000), it is important to make clear that such work is very complex and sensitive. Parents and professionals will need to be able to rely on good supervision if they are to take it forward in a way that really helps children. As adoptive parent Kirsty Fergusson said of her three sons, 'they had eighteen years of memories between them, which had to be delivered into our safekeeping' (Fergusson 2003, p.25). Just how to keep these memories safe, especially painful and shameful ones, is a challenge that should not be under-estimated.

Nevertheless, it is just this respectful and containing stance by adoptive parents that provides a sound base for the difficult business of beginning the dialogue with children about the past, its meaning and continued importance. Rather than wait for children themselves or their behaviour to demand that the lid is lifted and the real family story re-told, parents and support workers must get the conversation started as soon as possible from the very outset.

A patchwork of broken-up experiences: fragmentation and diversity in adoption kinship

As we saw in Chapter 2 kinship is best seen as a process by which people come to feel related to one another (Carsten 2000) rather than a categorisation based on blood relations alone. However, it is exceptionally demanding for adopted children 'to get a grasp on what a mother, father, brother or sister is, when they have such a patchwork of broken-up experiences to draw on' (Rustin 1999).

The early placement experience of Luke and Debbie illustrates some of the complexities. It reminds us how powerful a presence previous family experience and relationships can have in adoptive family life. The traditional expectation that children experience adoption individually, and develop an 'adoptive identity' (Brodzinsky 1987; Grotevant *et al.* 2000) apart from their birth family origins, is difficult to sustain when nearly four in ten children are placed with siblings. Luke not only carries memories and representations of previous and displaced family relationships into his new home, he also actually brings one of those relationships with him. And Debbie is clearly relying on her reassuringly parental brother. How Luke as the older brother processes information about and experiences from their former lives will certainly impact on how Debbie does so. There is much evidence here of continuity of both emotional relationships and personal identification anchored in the wider kinship network.

Achieving a sense of relatedness in adoption, and thinking about contact and links, requires sufficient information to allow parents and children to establish mental maps of kinship networks. As we saw in Chapter 1, these networks are marked by fragmentation and diversity. Bryony and Rachael are likely to know whether Luke and Debbie have brothers and sisters, but they will not necessarily be told much about them or where and with whom they are now living. They are unlikely to know much about the children's fathers. They will be destined to remain shadowy, even spooky, figures unless social workers have made sure to track them and their details down, and to provide the children with some photographs of them. The number, characteristics and significance of previous foster and birth relative carers of Luke and Debbie, as well as their photographs, may well have got lost down the line. And social workers (and therapists) themselves, some of whom may have been anchor points for children, have a habit of disappearing.

This tends to mean that it is birth mothers (and perhaps grandmothers too) that come first to mind when links with the past are being considered. Because it is adoptive mothers who appear almost overwhelmingly to take on a full-time caring role on placement of children, and birth mothers who are losing their emotional parenting role, the experience of mothering is usually the context through which kinship connections are forged, or not. Foster (and other adoptive) mothers too can play a crucial role, especially when siblings are in care or adopted elsewhere. This unity of mothering is both the reason why contact can be such a difficult thing to contemplate and why, when managed sensitively, it can provide the common ground on which any successful engagement can be established. However, cultural differences as well as emotional dynamics have to be accommodated if these pivotal points of contact (imagined or actual) between the two family landscapes are to provide a safe context for real communication and connection. The divergent social circumstances and cultural values and expectations of birth and adoptive mothers can mean that feelings of pity, disgust, shame and fear inhibit and disrupt the process of mutual empathy, which is the bedrock of real communication in and across the adoptive kinship network.

Adoption support, contact and the adoptive family life story: a model of effective practice

The primary task of adoption support in relation to identity is to help parents and children communicate openly as they establish and sustain their family life together within this context of fragmentation and diversity. Open family communication enables children to deal with issues of their individual 'adoptive identity' in the context of their developing attachments. It also means that family members together can find ways of talking about and telling their unique adoptive family story, what we refer to as 'scripting'. This communication about identity, kinship and relatedness needs to be continuous, as everyone involved takes their part in the scripting task as it develops over time. The questions are, what role should contact play in this process of establishing and narrating new family and kinship, and exactly how should support be provided for this expanded idea of 'adoptive family life story' work?

A model of effective practice requires the integration of aspects of adoption support that are usually seen as being separate roles and tasks. Figure 6.1 indicates the five key areas of practice that in particular need reconfiguring if 'adoptive family life story work' is to be properly supported.

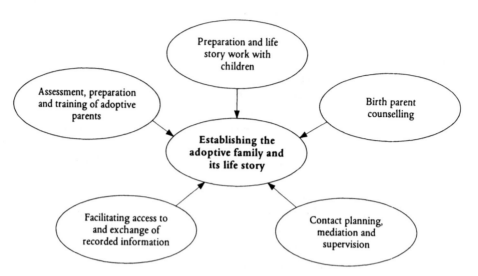

Figure 6.1 Adoptive family life story work

Whilst each of these five aspects of practice include elements that might be combined successfully in an effective model of adoptive family life story work there is little evidence that they have been routinely integrated in practice. For example, 'life story work' is seen as 'a project undertaken with a child by a sympathetic adult such as a social worker or carer' (Fursland 2002). In the words of the standard practice text by Tony Ryan and Rodger Walker it 'gives children a structured and understandable way of talking about themselves...[and]...a record which they and, with their agreement, the adults caring for them can refer to at any time' (2002, p.6). Similarly the assessment and preparation process is expected to enable prospective adopters to reflect on their own early experience and its impact. Draft guidance insisted 'The understanding by the prospective adopter of the parenting styles he (sic) has experienced and of how this has impacted on his current functioning as a parent and individual is central to assessing his (sic) suitability to adopt. He will need to demonstrate that he understands the link between what he had brought from his family of origin into his current functioning and what an adoptive child will bring with them' (Department of Health 2003f, p.132).

However, these two individual autobiographical processes are not linked in any sustained way in the practice literature. Equally it is difficult to find guidance for parents and agency workers on the use of contact and the thoughts and feelings it evokes in helping children work out where they belong and who they want to be. Counselling approaches based on loss resolution following permanent separation and termination of contact (where available) can give proper attention to birth parent grief in such cases, but they are not necessarily much help where contact continues and rather different issues arise (Sales 2002).

This lack of co-ordination results from uncertainty and contention in theory and practice about the focus and purpose of communication and contact in adoption. As much as current limitations in professional competence, it probably explains the research findings that show the very patchy quality of practice in relation to each of these five aspects in their own right. Hence social work with children prior to and during placement is limited in substance and impact (Quinton *et al.* 1998). Although they are now expected to be an essential aspect of practice, 'life story books' are not routinely produced for children (Macaskill 2002; Thomas *et al.* 1999). Even the provision by social workers to adoptive parents of basic information on the child's background cannot be guaranteed (Lowe *et al.* 1999). Lack of clarity persists about the purpose of contact in adoption (Neil 2002b), and where it is arranged professional management and support is often unreliable (Argent 2002; Lowe *et al.* 1999; Macaskill 2002).

By starting with our propositions that the primary aim of practice is to support parents and children in the process of scripting their adoption family story and that the main role of contact is to underpin that process, we can outline the key elements of an integrated approach that might help remedy confusion and ineffective practice.

Scripting the adoptive family life story

As John Byng-Hall says, 'we are all characters in each other's stories' (1999, p.132). The ultimate aim of adoption is to enable children to tell their own story in their own way. However the first consideration must be to support adoptive parents to think about the adoptive family story they intend to construct with the children they have taken on. This involves naming what kind of family life is anticipated and considering what role the placed child is expected to play in enabling things to work out as planned. Once the 'meaning' (Reder, Duncan and Gray 1993) that is being ascribed to the child is explored with adoptive parents the process of helping them find ways of talking as a family about their joint future (and deciding who should be involved in this) will be more productive. We propose three core aspects of the family scripting process that need to be integrated and supported in practice.

Core aspects of adoption support to help effective family scripting are:

- inviting prospective adoptive parents to *reflect on and reconstruct* their own family story in preparation for placement

- enabling adoptive parents and children to *know about and make sense together* of the child's family experiences and their legacy in order to integrate them in adoptive family life

- encouraging the *depiction and discussion* of the adoptive family future and who is intended to be involved in it.

The *reflection and reconstruction process* is twofold. The first aspect has to do with the emotional awareness of prospective adoptive parents and the second with their cultural expectations of family life. Both should be addressed in the assessment, preparation and continued training support of prospective adopters and then be connected to the subsequent support work on the other two aspects of the family scripting process.

Recent advances in the understanding of the dynamics of attachment have shifted the focus of assessment towards the emotional capacity of prospective adopters. As we explored in the previous chapter, research findings demonstrate that it is the mental representations by parents of close emotional relationships, rather than just their care-giving behaviour, that influence subsequent attachment security in their children. These findings have put in question a narrow, competence approach to the assessment of parenting (Berlin and Cassidy 2001; Steele *et al.* 2003).

Getting in touch with the adopted child's experience by getting back in touch with one's own is the central task. Unresolved loss is a major risk factor here, whether or not it arises from the fact of infertility. Hence it is as early as the assessment and preparation stage that the future adoptive family script has to be first explored, by helping prospective parents articulate an emotionally coherent narrative account of their past parenting and family experience. This is a challenging and sensitive task, and hence one that might be avoided on all sides.

It is important that methods of evaluation and assessment such as the Adult Attachment Interview and the Attachment Style Interview (see Chapter 5) be adapted for use in day-to-day practice and that practitioners become familiar with this developing field of research and practice methodology. Specialist consultation should be used to support and enhance routine practice. Nonetheless from the outset prospective parents have to be invited to reflect on the emotional security and coherence of the close family (and other) relationships they are making available to a child.

However, coherent reflection on emotional relationships (like secure attachment in children) is a necessary but not sufficient element in the reflection and reconstruction process proposed here. Class and culture are important, too, as we have said. It helps to identify the dynamics in advance so that adoptive parents can give voice to and re-examine their expectations and idealisations.

Thinking back to our case study, Luke's rejection of Bryony and Rachael's middle-class home is one example of the sort of thing that can occur. For adoptive parents like Bryony and Rachael, it can be socially embarrassing and isolating, as well as personally disappointing and saddening, if children such as Luke and Debbie seem to be trashing their family beliefs, values and behaviour.

Addressing this issue is partly to do with cautioning parents about predicted difficult behaviour and restricted educational and social achievement due to poor genetic inheritance and early neglect and trauma. This aspect of preparation and training is becoming a standard feature of practice (Fursland 2002). Hardly ever considered by contrast is the impact of an adoptive child's ambivalent commitment to the prescribed cultural norms and routines of family life. However, helping parents prepare for the eventuality that children may well get hooked back into associations and identifications that seem to owe more to the birth family script than the anticipated adoptive family narrative is equally important.

Parents need to be able to empathise with the culturally ambivalent as well as the emotionally ambivalent experience of children who are likely to be placed with them, who will be trying to resolve (to a greater or lesser extent) competing calls of class, ethnicity and kinship throughout their adoptive childhood. Acceptance rather than regret or blame is of enormous importance to adopted children struggling, as they invariably do in adolescence, with the contrasting sources of social identification and the class differences embodied in their family situation.

In practice, reflection on emotional relationships and on the reconstruction of cultural expectations of adoptive family life can be achieved by a simple adaptation of existing preparation and training methods. Examples of these are set out in Figure 6.3.

Methods to enable prospective adoptive parents to reflect on family life include:

- *Using 'dummy' family life story books.* Mock 'life story books' are sometimes used to coach prospective parents in putting difficult information into words to help children talk about their past (Kaniuk 2003, personal communication). This approach can be adapted by asking parents to sketch out their own life story first. The aim is to enable reflection on parents emotional and social experiences and the way they might influence their expectations of any placed child and intended family future.

- *Do it yourself matching.* Preparation and training can include invitations to prospective parents to use dummy child assessment forms (Form E and successors) to consider which children might be a good match for them and their family image.

- *Direct child care.* Arguably the best way of preparing to look after children is to do it in practice first. Inviting prospective parents to run the creche at an established adoptive family event or to help out on family or group outings provides excellent opportunities for people to see what things might really be like in reality.

- *Direct buddying/parent mentoring.* Established adoptive parents can share their experiences with new adopters in order to demystify some of the processes.

The second step in the family scripting process is enabling adoptive parents and children to *know about and make sense together* of the child's family experiences and legacy. Individual life story work cannot wait until placement. And adoptive parents are now entitled to a prescribed form of 'full written information to help them understand the needs and background of the child and an opportunity to discuss this and the implications for them and their family' (Department of Health 2002d). Nonetheless fully taking on board the reality of the birth family legacy for childhood and family life in adoption is almost as impossible for prospective parents being 'prepared' for the future as it is for children armed only with their 'life story book'. Perhaps, as Caroline Archer suggests (personal communication 2003) professionals can help adopters get in touch with children's feelings and experiences at every level, even pre-placement.

Our proposals below for approaches for talking about memories are offered with caution, and in the recognition that research findings to guide us in this field are emergent rather than established. Initial fantasies in all quarters, professional as well as parental, do need exploration from early in the process. However, things often never really hit home until the children arrive and, sooner or later, things cease to work out quite as intended. Furthermore, even when it becomes apparent that things ought to be talked about if they are not to remain intrusive, when and how to do so can be an extremely tricky decision. Maybe Luke's shadowy father is so scary because of the sexually exploitative relationship he trapped Luke into, and maybe he has hurt other children too. Above all else Bryony and Rachael will need time to think through, with a sensitive supporter, exactly what can be done to help Luke feel safe enough to get control over his feelings (perhaps of fear and humiliation) and thoughts (of responsibility) when his father comes to mind. Talking and telling in these situations only follows the (literally) painstaking emotional calming and reassurance that must become the daily routine of family life. Arguably soothing physical touch is just as important in these situations (Archer 2003). Without the creation of this kind of comfort zone for Luke, speaking the unspeakable may well feel punitive and blaming.

Nonetheless, in the end, early experience will only come back to haunt adoptive family life in other ways if it is not given some voice.

Approaches for talking about memories and their meaning include:

- *Involving foster carers Lindsey and Dave in 'life story work' with Luke and Debbie.* The process of gathering information and artefacts and talking about them in the foster home would have enabled Lindsey and Dave to be the temporary custodians of the children's experiences and memories.

- *Inviting Lindsey and Dave to help Luke and Debbie hand on this process to Bryony and Rachael.* Ensuring the introduction process is as much about introducing new parents to the children's life story, and to ways of talking openly and with acceptance about it, as it is to Luke and Debbie themselves.

- *Identifying and agreeing the right place for memorabilia, from past family experience, in the new family home and routines.* Doing this carefully but explicitly with children, including those much younger than Luke and Debbie, enables new parents to learn what matters and what is painful for children and to talk about this appropriately in the process. Certain photos should be on the mantelpiece rather than staying stuck in the life story book and put away for later. Transitional objects, including favourite clothes and toys, have a central role to play. In this way memories of past ties and affiliations are reviewed in the light of new relationships and incorporated into adoptive family life as and when it feels right, rather than left in suspended animation and unresolved, as has happened with Luke.

- *Recovering and incorporating past family memories into current family life.* Luke is more likely to be re-traumatised by being left alone with his confusing and upsetting memories of his father than he is by having these gently brought to mind and put in their place in the normal course of reparative parenting by Bryony and Rachael. So long as parents have been prepared for and are supported in the process, the raising of difficult memories will provide containment and reasssurance rather than a threat.

- *Introducing specific family life scripting techniques.* A number of methods can be used by parents to help children explore and make sense of their route to adoption. For example, Margot Sunderland's idea that children can be helped to use stories as a way of emotionally 'digesting' difficult feelings (2000). Serial story telling (i.e. taking it in turns to tell a child's or parent's life story) helps in jointly processing what has happened. Techniques from art therapy can also be usefully drawn on as tools in family life scripting work (for example, using a roll of wallpaper on which to draw a chronological account of family life and the individual journeys that people have taken to get to it). *My lifestory,* an interactive CD ROM, is a very child-centred interactive tool to help children process memories and their meaning (Hart 2003).

The third aspect of family scripting requiring encouragement and support has to do with the *depiction and discussion* of the adoptive family future. In reality this is a process that will be integrated with family reflection on the past. However, of crucial importance here is the question of who is to be counted in, where family and kinship are concerned. This is not something that can be fully determined in advance and for all time, as if family life could be pre-programmed. On the contrary the point about the scripting approach is that decisions always remain open for reflection and revision as children are helped to take increasing control over their destiny. Nonetheless it is vital that parents and children have a clear idea from the start what position in the kinship network birth relatives and previous foster carers and others occupy at any one time. Luke's distress at the move from his safe foster home will only be relieved when this work is done.

Children need to develop confidence that their new parents both understand who are the most important characters from the past and are committed to putting them in their rightful place in their future family life. In some cases this means recognising how scary some people still are when they are brought, or triggered into mind, and reassuring children that they are safe from them now. In other cases it means helping children keep still positive relationships alive in their minds as part of the adoptive family story. In either case parental confidence in orchestrating discussions and decisions is the prerequisite for the development in children of the sense that this family really is theirs for life and also that they can, when they feel able to do so, have a say in exactly which relationships might be included. Adoption support is about encouraging that confidence in parents. Below we list a few further practical ways in which the intended boundaries and relationships of adoptive family, kinship and social life can be explored together by parents and children.

EXPLORING THE BOUNDARIES OF KINSHIP RELATIONSHIPS

- *Family and kinship mapping.* Genograms and eco-maps are familiar methods for helping family members to think about networks of relationships and family connections. A useful technique is the 'field map' used with young children by researchers who want to understand child perceptions of relationships in a range of fields, such as family, relatives, friends, school, professionals (Samuelsson, Themlund and Rinstrom 1996; Sturgess, Dunn and Davies 2001). Children can be asked to help new parents understand which birth relatives/friends etc. might and might not feature in different ways in future adoptive family life by naming then placing significant people in system of concentric circles. The child placed in the centre shows which people are loved, liked, not liked and feared by putting them in the relevant circle. A more actively therapeutic approach to this involves drawing life-size body maps of each family member whilst they physically lie on top of the paper on the floor. A large heart is drawn on each body map and people held dear by each individual can be named or depicted inside.

- *Family drawings.* The simple technique of inviting children to draw 'me and my family' (Dunn, O'Connor and Levy 2002) will enable adoptive parents to understand better how children are picturing their family life following serial moves between homes and relationships. This provides the basis for making sense of why people are included and excluded and for helping children fit their family script together with the one unfolding in the adoptive home.

- *Generating symbolic representations of the adoptive family.* The concept of a family shield can be introduced. Planning what elements might be included in it, and then drawing one together engages family members in a joint enterprise and helps individual family members negotiate what kind of a family they aspire to be. Hobday, Ollier and Kirby(2002) provide other examples of ways to help children think about and explicitly construct family identity.

- *Talking about names and their meaning.* Enabling children to bring their former surname with them into adoptive family life is one option that can be thought about. On adoption, the children's birth surname can be retained as part of their name, even if this is simply on their birth certificate. In later life children can choose whether or not to use the surname actively as part of their identity. Another approach which symbolises that adoptive parents are open to changing their identity too, would see the entire adoptive family adopting a new surname, for example by joining together the surname of each family member.

For each of these three aspects of family scripting the objective must be to prevent what family therapists Kirsten Blow and Gwyn Daniel have referred to as the 'frozen narratives' (2002) that can occur when family stories are contested and people retreat into the defence of their mutually exclusive scripts. In their case the context is divorce but the potential is similar in adoption. By seeing adoptive family life, kinship and identity as processes to be worked at rather than simply structures for children to be fitted into, the focus of adoption support should be on helping parents and children find practical ways of keeping the discussion open.

Supporting contact as an aid to communication and a settled family life and identity

The expanded approach to supporting what we have called the 'adoptive family life story' process has implications for decisions about contact. Contemporary practice is marked, as we have seen, by uncertainty and contention. Research evidence on the merits or otherwise of specific contact arrangements is thin.

Academic debates (Quinton and Selwyn 1998; Quinton *et al.* 1997, 1999; Ryburn 1998, 1999; Selwyn *et al.* 2003) have tended to add as much heat as they have light to the continuing practice debate about disengagement and continuity in adoption. Yet the experience of contact is likely to be intrinsically unsettling unless there is sufficient consensus in each case, amongst the adults involved, about the meaning to be communicated to the child of any arrangements made. Hence it is helpful if questions both about the purpose or role of contact in adoption and about how contact decisions and arrangements should be made and supported are revisited from the open family communication and scripting perspective we have developed in this chapter.

The purpose of contact

The purpose of contact is defined by the contribution it is likely to make to the dual process of achieving fresh attachment, family belonging and identity and doing so through open communication about the adoptive family past and future. An opportunity for continued links and contact enhances the capacity of adopted children to take greater control of their destiny not primarily because it sustains relationships or ties but because it prevents the avoidance of communication about the past and its legacies in the adoptive home. Although some retained relationships will be important in their own right, it is the quality of engagement with the implications of these relationships and their salience in the present and future that is at the heart of a settled adoptive family childhood. Contact is helpful in these respects when it facilitates effective information exchange and understanding and when it enables emotional relationships and family roles to be appropriately renegotiated across the adoptive kinship network. To this extent contact can have a therapeutic function for children, as is now increasingly recognised in therapeutic practice (Archer and Burnell 2003).

Conventionally these two elements – access to information and maintenance of emotional links – tend to be seen as rather separate. For example, John Triseliotis (2001) has suggested the distinction should be made between two different types of continuity. On the one hand 'generational continuity' is ensured by enabling children to have access to recorded information about their origins and their adoption, on the other 'emotional continuity' is sustained where contact is maintained with people where there was a significant relationship before placement. In recent practice, ambivalence about the right decisions to be taken about contact have led to a corresponding split. 'Indirect' or mediated arrangements, usually through a 'letterbox' system, have become ubiquitous whilst 'direct' or 'face-to-face' contact, especially with birth parents, is still rarely established. This divided practice is defended as a sensible compromise: 'letterbox' arrangements ensure information exchange takes place whilst prohibition or avoidance of face-to-face meetings and phone calls is intended to protect children against the persistence of emotionally unsettling or traumatising relationships.

However, as David Brodzinsky (2003) argues, structural arrangements for contact do not necessarily lead to a process of open communication about the meaning of the contact. The limited amount of research on 'letterbox' and other mediated forms of contact provide some supporting evidence for this view (Berry *et al.* 1998; Kedward, Luckock and Lawson 1999; Logan 1999). Birth parents and relatives usually need a great deal of support and encouragement to sustain their active involvement in the process and adoptive parents can see any information provided as something to be set aside in order not to unsettle things at home. Thus there is no guarantee at all that the common practice of dealing with the contentious issue of contact by setting up a 'letterbox' arrangement will lead to increased communication and openness in adoptive family life.

At the same time the concern to restrict direct contact can unnecessarily suspend the difficult but important process of helping children and adoptive parents achieve a proper sense of control over the relinquishment or re-negotiation of displaced emotional ties. This can happen when an over-protective stance is taken by adults. For example Maureen Crank reports the words of one 14-year-old girl who not only had no direct contact but also had her birth mother's letters opened and inspected before she got them. 'Why do they do this? I lived with Eileen for my first eight years – I know better than anyone that she lies sometimes. I know it's because she feels she let me down and it still hurts and sometimes she is just plain stupid. It hurts me too, but not as bad as someone I don't know opening my letters all the time' (Crank 2002, p.103). Alternatively, as Beth Neil (2003) has pointed out, direct contact is usually considered where children have a prior attachment to birth parents and relatives rather than where they have none. Yet it is in the latter cases of early placement of very young children that normalising and unthreatening relationships with birth relatives can be most successfully established, as the main US research study has shown (Grotevant and McRoy 1998; Wrobel *et al.* 2003).

Thus in themselves neither increased indirect, or restricted direct, contact are necessarily sound strategies for achieving the goal of open family communication. Instead, as outlined in Table 6.1, a more precise set of considerations about the purpose and conditions of effective contact should be borne in mind when decisions are to be taken about the nature of arrangements that might be agreed in any particular case.

Table 6.1 Thinking about the purpose of contact for Luke and Debbie

What are the purposes of contact?	• To contribute to fresh attachments and adoptive family belonging and identity through open communication facts and feelings about the family, past and future • To maintain previous relationships in themselves The objective in this case and at this stage is to get Luke and Debbie talking about their feelings of loss, grief, confusion and fear so they can start to settle and attach.
How can contact fulfil this role?	In two ways: • By facilitating effective information exchange and understanding • By enabling emotional relationships and family roles to be renegotiated across the adoptive kinship network
What conditions should apply if arrangements are to be successful?	There are three core conditions: • The parents/adults involved have the potential capacity and motivation to participate in the process of (re) negotiating agreements over arrangements • The children have a developmentally appropriate means of expressing feelings and views about arrangements • In any case child safety is guaranteed
How might direct 'face-to-face' contact help at this stage in the case of Luke and Debbie?	• *With foster carers Lindsey and Dave:* meetings and phone calls are crucial. Luke and Debbie can then see all is well with them and be helped to understand their move. Both foster and adoptive parents can reconsider the kinship role Lindsey and Dave might take so that Bryony and Rachael can discuss this with the children • *With birth parents and relatives:* on the evidence available, now is not the time for direct contact because it will not help Luke and Debbie manage their anxiety and confusion
How might indirect/mediated 'letterbox' contact help at this stage in the case of Luke and Debbie?	• *With foster carers:* mediation is only necessary if Lindsey and Dave have difficulty endorsing Bryony and Rachael as parents to the children • *With birth parents and relatives:* it is important that Bryony and Rachael have continued access to information that can be used to help Luke and Debbie start to talk about their past and to help them all decide whether and when to invite direct contact

Supporting contact decisions and arrangements

Things should have been sorted out earlier in the case of Luke and Debbie. If contact arrangements are going to work well it should be adoptive parents like Bryony and Rachael who are ultimately left feeling most in control of the process, and from the earliest opportunity. However, because decisions about contact are supposed to be for the long-term benefit of the children and not for any short-term advantage for parents, agencies and courts on the one hand, and children themselves on the other, claim a right to a say in the process.

The Adoption and Children Act 2002, as we demonstrated in Chapter 3, has settled the debate about the balance of influence in favour of maintaining the right of adoptive parents to make their own way in respect of contact once the adoption order is granted. However, agencies must present any proposed plans for contact to the court for consideration when a placement order is applied for, and the court can make orders of contact for the period of the placement (s26, Adoption and Children Act 2003) and on adoption itself (s8, Children Act 1989). Hence the expectation is that decisions and plans about contact arrangements should be negotiated and agreed so far as possible between all those involved but the court can have the final say if necessary. The wishes and feelings of the children concerned must be heard and taken into consideration by the court and they too can apply for orders of contact.

This approach is not consistent with the argument, put by Nigel Lowe (1997) and supported by others (Bridge and Swindells 2003; Ryburn 1998), that adoptive parenting should be seen as a contractual relationship with the state. This would give professionals too much control over contact decisions and could undermine the confidence of adoptive parents in their own judgements. However, it is consistent with research findings, which show that the contact arrangements that work best are those that are jointly agreed and planned by those involved (Neil 2003) and that this should include children as they become able to participate (Macaskill 2002; Thomas et al. 1999). The task for the keyworker and the agencies is to find ways of *preparing* birth and adoptive parents (and children and others as appropriate) for making decisions about contact, to develop an approach to *planning* that is inclusive, and to provide continued *practical and emotional support* where that is necessary to help share the work involved in making arrangements succeed. Other adoptive, foster and birth parents who have positive experiences of contact arrangements could usefully get involved in this work.

Preparation: cultivating empathy and the long view

The 'family scripting' process is the proper context for adoptive parents and children to consider contact. For birth parents and relatives the task of involving them falls to their own keyworker. In either case the primary goal is to help the adults put themselves in the shoes of the children at the point when they reach 18. It is from this point of looking back on childhood that the most balanced judgements can be made about the potential long-term benefits of any continued contact. This does not mean that fixed assumptions should be made about the details of current and future contact arrangements. What it does do though is encourage people to stand outside their current parental and adult preoccupations and anxieties and take the long, child-centred view about adoptive kinship relations.

In preparation groups prospective adopters where possible should be introduced to birth parents and adopted adults. They should also be given access to the research findings on the experience of older children and adopted adults who are asked to look back on their family experience. This is because these throw light on what is lost in childhood when contact is not carefully thought through. The work of David Howe and Julia Feast (Howe and Feast 2000; Feast and Howe 2003) and John Triseliotis (1973, 2000) on adult views of their adoptive childhood is important here. The main message for prospective parents is that, although the children to be placed may be as anxious as they are about considering staying or getting in touch with people from the past it is essential to grasp the nettle early, get decisions made either way and then keep them under review.

A second preparation objective also has to do with empathy. The evidence is that contact arrangements work best when the adults involved, adoptive parents and birth relatives alike, have the capacity to empathise with the emotional experience of the other party to any arrangement (Berry *et al.* 1998; Neil 2003). Mutual empathy is likely to contribute positively to the process of getting a shared understanding and agreement so its achievement should be a central objective for agency practitioners.

Birth relatives should be involved in preparation and training sessions. However, it is important to remember that over-identification with the distressing situation of the birth parents and relatives can be as disabling of clear thinking as can under-identification or emotional detachment. This is particularly so for mothers in adoption who, as we have seen, are almost invariably the parents who get brought so uneasily together by the process. There is evidence that the greater the cultural and class differences between birth and adoptive mothers the more difficult it might be to achieve mutual empathy and understanding about contact (Berry 1991). The assessment of adult attachment outlined earlier can help mothers and fathers alike get in touch with the extent to which they are likely to be either enmeshed in or dismissive of birth parental experience.

Planning: towards an inclusive consultation and mediation model of support

Contact planning is an attitude of mind to be incorporated into day-to-day family life not a one-off event orchestrated by professionals. The conventional bureaucratic model of adoption support planning has to be used only as a framework for helping family and adoptive kinship members gain confidence in judging what arrangements might best be put in place at any one time and in negotiating agreements.

The core principles of 'keeping things open' and enabling family members themselves to write the script particularly apply to decision-making about contact. Crucial here is the active participation of children and young people, in accordance with their developmental capacity. Those who spoke to Caroline Thomas and Verna Beckford (Thomas *et al.* 1999) and to Catherine Macaskill (2002) reinforced the core message: that continuous dialogue between adoptive parents (and social workers) and children about contact decisions is more important than particular decisions themselves. Children generally seem to want the option of more contact rather than less but mostly they want to be kept involved in discussions in the meantime. They also need adults to make the often scary process of contemplating and making contact feel manageable. As Sonia (11 years old) said, hugging her adoptive mother after meeting her birth mother, 'You're a big strong mummy that can keep me safe' (Macaskill 2002, p.57).

The adoption support role is thus one of inclusion, consultation and mediation rather than professional decision-making and case management. Because they now acquire parental responsibility on placement adoptive parents have a right to expect that their views on contact are formally respected. This may dismay agency practitioners who are suspicious of the motivations of adoptive parents, expecting them to renege on earlier agreements about continued contact once they gain the authority to do so. It is this fear that seems to cause social workers to hang onto control for as long as possible and prescribe approved arrangements for parents.

In contrast, we suggest this is an appropriate shift in the balance of say and influence. It will cause support workers to take much more seriously the preparation role, outlined above, and to develop the capacity to offer informed advice and mediation skills in addition to their formal advocacy role on behalf of children, for as long as they remain 'looked after' by the local authority.

We know that contact works best when the parties involved feel confident enough to move beyond formal mediation structures (Grotevant 2003; Neil and Young 2003). This is partly because participants feel constrained by such formal arrangements and partly because formal mediators have tended to make administrative mistakes which confound, rather than facilitate, communication.

Other than this we know very little about effective practice in contact mediation.

The work of the Post-Adoption Centre Contact and Mediation Service has been described by Sally Sales, who set it up. She has made a powerful case for using an independent agency to undertake the task 'outside the adversarial adoption process' (2002, p.28) and within the 'extended family' model of continuity discussed earlier in this chapter. However, initial evaluation (Kedward *et al.* 1999) showed that very few agreements were being achieved and suggested that mediation would be more effective if it were incorporated into practice much earlier. This is more easily done now that formal adoption and placement decisions have been brought forward in the protection and care planning process, and the ground on which battles are often fought between birth parents and agencies shifted to an earlier stage of court proceedings. Hence there seems no reason, other than lack of imagination and commitment, why mainstream agencies should not introduce a consultation and mediation model of practice in contact planning.

Practical and emotional support: being there to help manage contact and encourage communication

Both face-to-face contact and 'letterbox' arrangements are usually hard for people to manage and sustain. Two aspects of support are necessary. First, adoptive and birth parents and others involved should have access to responsive and reliable practical help in establishing and managing agreed arrangements. Second, this practical help needs to be provided in the context of the kind of efficient therapeutic key work support discussed in Chapters 4 and 5. The careful integration of the two is important if the complexities and anxieties engendered by contact are to be prevented from derailing the process. In the case of 'letterbox' arrangements the conventional focus on co-ordination of the exchange of information can produce a largely administrative solution unless the primary objective, of using the information exchanged to underpin the family scripting process, is held in mind. Even in well-established and managed services a significant proportion of arrangements appear to lose direction or lapse (Vincent and Graham 2002).

This may partly be due to the very odd and contrived nature of the process itself. A curiously formal and largely redundant mode of communication (letter writing) is expected to provide the main means of helping people who are fearful or uncertain of each other to re-organise their mutual family ties and relationships. The fact that so many birth parents have learning difficulties and find it a struggle to write letters is also relevant here (Selwyn *et al.* 2003). Maybe, as Pam Hodgkins suggests, the bureaucratic response of 'letterbox' arrangements may have more to do with avoidance of responsibility for supporting people through the complex and painful process of real communication. She says, 'Perhaps it is the fear of what could go wrong with direct contact that sways the vast majority of workers into favouring the ubiquitous letterbox. Are they trying to convince themselves that it is any more possible to have indirect contact without consequences than it would be to have direct contact or no contact?' (2003, p.151). This is the heart of the matter, because indirect contact may be neither one thing nor another, not a proper relationship and not a way of ending a relationship.

Direct contact is arguably easier to support, once the conditions outlined earlier are satisfied. However the evidence is that professional responses are not always attuned to the needs of the case. The research undertaken by Beth Neil (2002a, 2002b, 2003) on face-to-face contact for early-placed children confirmed the view that agencies tend to guide families towards formulaic approaches to contact and to match their methods of support to those expectations. This lack of responsiveness to the particular circumstances of each case and to the way these circumstances are likely to change as adoptive family life proceeds leaves people stranded. For example, Catherine Macaskill found several adopters in her study who were 'deeply disappointed' when they discovered, on returning to agencies for backup, 'that the initial enthusiasm that social workers had expressed about the theoretical concept of contact during the preparation and assessment period did not extend to a long term, practical commitment to implement essential changes in contact arrangements that reflected the child's best interests' (2002, p.29).

One way of improving support for openness in adoption, including the management of contact, is to extend the conventional agency case management and commissioning approach. This should ensure that a keyworker is more reliably available to help family members deal with the feelings provoked as well as their practical needs. The Adoption and Children Act 2003 sees things in this way. In contrast is an approach based on changing the culture of support practice for all adoptive families rather than just tightening up protocols and procedures for the few who are deemed to be entitled to an adoption support services plan. Through our discussion about developing communities of adoptive practice, in the final chapter we now turn our attention towards this alternative vision.

Chapter 7

Developing Communities of Adoptive Practice

Introduction

In previous chapters we have had much to say about adoptive family life and about the support needs of adoptive families. However, our focus has mainly been on the nature of internal family and kinship relations of adoptive family life and aspects of their formal support. Not much has yet been said about the social and organisational contexts in which the relationships of family and formal support are embedded. In this final chapter we widen our perspective to include these contexts. However, we want to do this in a way that reinforces our concept of adoptive family practice and support as something based in collaborative allegiances between everyone involved, rather than as simply a set of external professional interventions. In this way family members, friends and agency workers are together best seen as the 'practitioners' of family life in adoption.

This way of thinking about adoption support is rather different from the framework promulgated by the Adoption and Children Act 2002 and its disappointingly traditional model of corporate service delivery. It is also rather different to discussions in the family and social support literature (Featherstone 2004). The usual approach to discussing the wider context of family is to separate two perspectives. On the one hand, the role of informal social support networks (Ghate and Hazel 2002) or self-help and community development (Milne 1999; Wann 1995) is considered. On the other, analyses of organisational structures and relationships for effective formal support are made (Brown, Crawford and Darongkamas 2000; Ovretveit 1995; Payne 2000).

In this chapter we want to look at the context of support by adapting the concept of 'communities of practice' (Wenger 1998; Wenger *et al.* 2002) so it fits with our idea of family and its support as being a collaborative practice. So far as service development is concerned the vision here is cultural as well as structural (Cooper, Hetherington and Katz 2003). The starting point is still with the nature and quality of relationships rather than the details of the organisational arrangements that might be developed in each local area. The social infrastructure of adoption support depends on both. The aim in this chapter is to establish the principles underpinning the achievement of communities of adoptive practice and sketch out some practical examples of the operational implications.

However in order to remind ourselves once again of the view on all this from one adoptive home front window we return to the early family experiences of Bryony, Rachael, Luke and Debbie. Who shares an interest in helping this adoptive family get settled? Who will rise to the challenge, who will refuse to get involved and who, despite their best intentions, will fade quietly into the background?

Case study: Bryony Hall, Rachel Cunningham, and Luke and Debbie Forster

Let us assume it is now six months into placement, several weeks since the last cursory placement (and adoption support) review and by now time for Bryony and Rachael to face up to the alarming recognition that they are stranded. Their social worker Dave has hardly helped. He's never really asked the right questions to enable them to tell him how desperate and isolated they really felt. And he was never entirely clear about what they might actually do, for example to help Luke beyond his sadness and continual mourning when his old foster carers said they would rather not continue to stay in touch. Dave was also at a loss when it came to advising them on how to manage Debbie's endless tantrums. But worse still is the dawning sense that perhaps they had not really helped themselves from the start, by being so optimistic about the future joys of their new family and social life and so dismissive of offers of help. It all sounded so patronising and bureaucratic – who else has to organise their family life through written agreements and plans through social services? Somehow intrusive too, as if they were just another set of foster parents. And maybe even discriminatory, given the obvious ambivalence of some of the people they met, parents and professionals, en route to their approval as same-sex adopters, and the placement of the children.

Right now the signed copy of their plan is lost in a pile of stuff in the hall. In fact it is buried under the worrying letters from the school and the education authority and the latest, unread edition of the local 'adoption support network' newsletter. If anybody were to read that plan now, they would see that it promised a rather different family life. This was to be a family that would have relatives and friends to call upon as necessary. Numerous friends indicated as potential baby-sitters. Bryony's sister and her three children just 30 miles down the road, Rachael's parents a good deal further but offering to have the kids during the holidays and sometimes coming to stay themselves to help out. Six grandchildren already, so lots of experience there.

But the cousins and Luke and Debbie never got on. To the cousins their new relatives seemed odd, Luke sullen and withdrawn and Debbie a drama queen the moment she had to join in anything. The cousins made Luke and Debbie feel worse, asking why they didn't know their birthdays and where their 'real' parents were. Rachael's mum hadn't offered to have the children again after a difficult Easter weekend. And her constant references to Luke as 'strange' and 'not all there' hardly helps. Meanwhile Bryony's best friend has asked them if there are any other people that might be called on to cover the monthly baby-sitting arrangement. Debbie's refusal to go to bed, opting instead for screaming outbursts on the floor was the final straw. But nobody else seems to be returning calls just now, no volunteers to help out forthcoming. At present it really is difficult for relatives and friends to see what they might be getting in return when they offer to help out.

And Bryony's friend has now decided she'd rather not have those mad kids at her birthday do. Rachael has just learnt too from her sister that she doesn't want Luke to come to her wedding. So just when the family could do with a bit of fun, just when they really need to feel loved and supported, there are no invitations falling through the letterbox, and no cheerful messages of support on the answerphone.

And their social exclusion stretches way beyond the networks of family and friends they have already established. The plan also included lots of positive things about Luke and his education, special needs and statement. In fact there are actually two plans, one especially to do with schooling because he is still formally 'looked after' by the local authority. But school feels distant too, partly because it is actually nine miles away and reached in the taxi that calls for Luke, and partly because neither Bryony, Rachael nor their social worker had any real idea how special education worked anyway. This makes family and social life feel even more fragmented, little space emerging for normal neighbourhood encounters and routines as these two parents struggle largely alone to manage the problems the children provoke. Debbie is still without a new nursery place after she had to be withdrawn following complaints about her aggressive behaviour. That too has put a further barrier up between other local parents and children and the new family of adoption trying to find its place in the community.

The idea of community in adoption

There is not much research at all on informal support networks in adoption. For example, we know very little about how kin and friendship relations work on a daily basis, and the norms that govern them. Research, then, gives us little insight into how people go about supporting families like those of Bryony and Rachael. There are some accounts of the role of professionals in providing support groups for adoptive parents (Livingston Smith and Howard 1999; Nelson and Parrish 1993). However, there is not much in the adoption literature on organisational structures and professional roles that might facilitate wider inclusion for adoptive families. Thus we cannot claim that the discussion of the adoption-specific working culture we aspire to in this final chapter is particularly evidence-based. Rather it has an experimental edge to it. It can be seen as an optimistic, perhaps even slightly idealistic endnote. A cautious reader might proceed with some hesitance. There is no robust and well-established body of research findings extolling the virtues of community working in adoption to publicise in the pages that follow.

And even the concept of community itself invites caution. Critiques of the power inequalities that get hidden beneath the veneer of mutuality in communities could similarly be applied to the idea of 'communities of practice' as we intend to use it here (Balloch and Taylor 2001; Canavan *et al.* 2000; Crow and Allan 2000; Duncan and Edwards 1997). There is nothing about the practice of adoption that excludes it from this critique. As we have seen, the fact that adoptive family life is established under an official gaze is a constant reminder all round that relations of power are being played out when parents, professionals and children form supportive alliances. For example, as we have argued in previous chapters, Bryony and Rachael's difficulties in opening up to Dave about just how hard it really is, need to be carefully worked with. Surveillance is inevitably some part of the deal when the state places a vulnerable child. So difficult, then, in some ways for adoptive parents to feel on an equal footing with social workers, even if collaboration is firmly on the agenda.

Other dynamics are perhaps even more tricky. In contemporary care adoption there are few birth parents, for example, who would see themselves as being in the same club as the adoptive parents who now have their children. And adoptive parents themselves might be relieved at this. Thinking back to our case example, Luke and Debbie's former foster carers are similarly way out of reach of the new family. No cosy joint club membership there then, either.

A further danger also exists. 'Community' is as likely to be used as a label imposed from outside as it is to be self-assigned. For every adoptive parent who is a member of Adoption UK there are probably many others who really do not see the need, content, perhaps, to take their place in the relative anonymity of the broader community of families.

Back in the office, school and clinic the dynamics of power and anxiety also resonate. The risk of conflict is inherent here too, poorly disguised by the rhetoric of 'partnership working' (Aldgate and Statham 2001), and a 'common philosophy' (Miller *et al.* 2001) in inter-agency and inter-professional practice. Professional turf wars (Eraut 2002), agency politics (Roaf 2002; Simpson *et al.* 2003a, 2003b) and unconscious organisational processes (Granville and Langton 2002; Obhoizer and Roberts 1994) routinely derail the best of intentions for 'service user' and 'child-centred' joint practice. We recognise these risks and know them to be real. But our concern here is less with dilemmas about the organisational structure of practice and more with the spaces that can always be found in any institutional arrangements, local and national, for the development of a more collaborative culture of working. It is this emergent, metaphorical quality of adoptive community practice that we want to capture.

Communities of adoptive practice

The idea that the social and organisational context of support in adoption might best be understood by using the concept of a 'community of practice' is compelling. Unlike more conventional categorisations the emphasis on 'practice' as the basis for community allows normally divided worlds and discourses to be integrated. Hence questions about the relationship between the nature of social support on the one hand and those about inter-professional working on the other can be brought together. And discussions too about 'service user' participation in the design and delivery of services (Department of Health 1999a; Harrison and Mort 1998) can be moved on. We first explore the key dimensions of the concept. What is a community of practice and who might belong to one in the case of adoption? We then consider what needs to be done to help such communities emerge.

What is a community of (adoptive) practice?

The concept of communities of practice was introduced as a way of thinking about knowledge management, reflection and learning within commercial organisations (Blair 2002; Wenger 1998; Wenger *et al.* 2002). People are now beginning to use the idea as a framework to think about public sector relationships and organisational structures (Buyss *et al.* 2003; Kerfoot 2002; Roos 2001; Wenger *et al.* 2002a). We hope to extend the use of the concept a little further.

At first the focus of texts on communities of practice was on the way workers organised their lives with colleagues, and (to a lesser extent) with agency clients or customers in order to get their jobs done. These practices took on a community dimension according to Wenger and colleagues (Wenger 1998; Wenger and Snyder 2000; Wenger *et al.* 2002) when different people, with different expertise, worked together on common tasks and learned from each other in so doing. Wenger and colleagues provide the example of engineers who design a certain kind of electronic circuit finding it useful to compare designs regularly and discuss the details of their speciality (Wenger *et al.* 2002). From the start the potential of such communities of practice was seen to be enormous. In the words of Wenger, 'As a locus of engagement in action, interpersonal relations, shared knowledge, and negotiation of enterprises, such communities hold the key to real transformation – the kind that has real effects on peoples lives' (1998, p.85).

For Wenger and colleagues, communities of practice differ from other ways of organising work about which much has been written. The customary concern has been with institutional forms of collaboration and teamworking (Brown *et al.* 2000; Ovretveit 1995; Payne 2000). In contrast the communities of practice approach is more anthropological, being about the way local, national and international social groupings form and provide an experience of membership, belonging and identity. The emphasis here is on the voluntary origins of such practice. People in such communities want to do things together; 'the click factor' (Thomas 2003, personal communication). Hence communities of practice are 'groups of people informally bonded together by shared expertise and passion for a joint enterprise' (Wenger and Snyder 2000, pp.139–140). They may meet face to face, but some function through virtual (text or electronic) communication. It is suggested that such self-direction will enable them to 'share their experiences and knowledge in free-flowing, creative ways that foster new approaches to problems'. This informal culture of collaboration may then take on a more procedural character as the 'unique perspective' that is created gets expressed in the development of 'a body of common knowledge, practices, and approaches...and established (ways) of interacting' (Wenger *et al.* 2002, p.5).

The concept of communities of practice has developed quite separately from writing on informal communities and networks. Of course it is this latter approach that has been most influential in conventional discussions of self-help, community development, mutual aid and family support (Milne 1999). However the idea of practice, as we have argued, can be construed more ambitiously than this, and communities of practice identified and developed across diverse boundaries. The formation of a community of practice in relation to adoption support represents a challenge to these conventional boundaries and creates the possibility of a new 'landscape of practice' (Wenger 1998, p.118). Table 7.1 summarises the distinctions between communities of adoptive practice and other structures of interaction.

Wenger and colleagues are particularly interested in the way 'boundary crossing' (2002, p.153) causes people to look afresh at their own assumptions. The aim is inclusive, to make connections and consolidate learning across

Table 7.1 Distinctions between communities of adoptive practice and other modes of practice

	What's the purpose?	Who belongs?	How clear are the boundaries?	What holds them together?	How long do they last?
Communities of adoptive practice	To create, expand and exchange knowledge To develop individual/organisational and family capacity To develop helping and advocacy relationships	Self-selection based on expertise or a passion for helping children settle	Fuzzy	Passion, commitment, the 'click' factor	Evolve and end organically (last as long as there is relevance to the topic and interest in learning together)
Formal departments	To deliver a service	Everyone who reports to the group's manager	Clear	Job requirements and common goals	Intended to be permanent but last until the next re-organisation
Operational teams	To take care of an on-going operation or process	Membership assigned by management	Clear	Shared responsibility for the operation	Last as long as the operation is needed
Project teams	To accomplish a specific task	People who have a direct role in accomplishing the task	Clear	The project's goals and milestones	Predetermined ending when the project has been completed
Communities of interest	To be informed To lobby and advocate	Interested service users	Fuzzy	Access to information and sense of likemindedness	Evolve and end organically
Networks	To receive and pass on information To know who is who	Professionals, parents, children	Undefined	Mutual need and relationships	Never really start or end (exist as long as people keep in touch or remember each other)

potential lines of division in relation to the joint enterprise. These interactions are animated in two particular ways.

First, in order that differing perspectives are effectively co-ordinated there need to be 'boundary objects' (Wenger 1998, p.105) through which people can connect. Boundary objects include the language and terms used to describe joint perspectives as well as concrete artefacts such as documents that unite different individuals in a common purpose or give them cause for discussion. Had it been written in a way that emphasised mutual collaboration across lay and professional worlds, the plan buried under the pile of papers in Rachael and Bryony's hall might have served as a useful boundary object. Even more helpful would have been a specific emphasis in the plan on how such collaboration might actually occur, rather than being simply assumed.

Second a process of 'brokering' is helpful (Wenger 1998, p.109) whereby individuals, who are members of multiple constituencies, introduce elements of one practice into another. Brokers need to be able to manage their ambivalent position operating across practice boundaries in order to translate and align differing perspectives. And they need sufficient legitimacy to carry influence as well as to address conflict effectively. In adoption support, social workers like Dave have the potential to fulfil this role, for example helping to keep alive links between Bryony and Rachael, the former foster carers and Luke's new teacher nine miles down the road so that they can all do their best to help Luke settle in school. More generally, broker roles are also being taken up by adoptive parents. They are increasingly working as paid practitioners, and some have published accounts of their work (e.g. Archer and Burnell 2003).

A key task is to accommodate a tension that is familiar in any group process as the practice community both consolidates its core work and identity, and explores new connections at the periphery. As Wenger and colleagues neatly put it, 'Community development tends to turn a community within; boundary work turns it outward' (2002, p.153). Communities of practice are said to be at their most effective when their core and boundaries evolve in complementary ways. This is difficult to achieve, but when it happens it creates deep expertise at the core, and constant renewal at the boundary. It is through this 'balancing act' that the best kind of learning occurs (2002, p.154).

However, there are threats to this way of working too. For Wenger and colleagues the balance of learning is said to be threatened where practical issues such as geographical distance come to dominate (Wenger et al. 2002). Important too are psychosocial issues such as too amorphous an identity and the exclusivity of 'groupthink' (Janis 1972; Wenger et al. 2002). The network of connections created in a community of practice should be neither too loose nor too tightly drawn. In the case of Bryony and Rachael's family, such concerns seem far from relevant at the moment. The immediate task here is to establish a micro community of adoptive practice with them, drawing in as many relevant people as possible, and supporting them in what is certainly not a simple project. Here, making Luke's teacher feel a part of it, and committed to the process of helping him settle, will be as crucial as engaging his adoptive grandmother. Given Bryony's and Rachael's isolation, the potential difficulties of 'groupthink' and insularity seem more of a luxury than a concern at the moment when thinking of generating a community of adoptive practice with them. However, the concern might become relevant if Bryony and Rachael find themselves on the periphery of a community of adoptive practice which they experience as cliquey and unwelcoming. As we saw earlier, for the optimistic vision of community embedded in the plan of Bryony and Rachael's family to be recovered, or to be rendered workable and more realistic, a lot of work is needed. This will include making them feel welcome in the wider, established community of adoptive practice.

It is crucial too, however, in any expanded model of 'communities of adoptive practice', to understand that connections operate on more than one level. In fact a dual process of practice has to take place. The joint enterprise is clearly the establishment of a settled adoptive childhood and family life. For us this means the capacity of adoptive family life to provide for play and fun as well as secure attachment and a measure of child achievement in the outside world. From the perspective of the individual child, parent or family this enterprise, or common task, concerns their family life and the network of people in the community of practice constituted in the context of child placement. For Bryony and Rachael, how to keep the troupe of supporters they identified at the beginning mutually engaged over time could usefully have been identified as an explicit challenge on the plan. The image of fellow travellers being helped to stay together through thick and thin on a shared 'journey through placement' (Fahlberg 1994) and well beyond captures this perspective.

However the individual journey of families like that of Bryony and Rachael is taken within a 'landscape of practice' (Wenger 1998) comprising all adoptive families. In the language of policy there has to be 'capacity' built in general to enable the joint practice of support in particular cases to be effective. This wider community building task is our main concern here. Of course the bigger picture also affects the smaller one. For example, were such a vibrant and inclusive wider community of practice in place, Dave might well have had more energy, commitment, expertise and enthusiasm to draw on in his support of Bryony and Rachael. Also, Bryony and Rachael might have felt part of the bigger picture to start with, rather than needing to be drawn in much further down the line.

Current debates about integrated organisations focus mainly on the structural or institutional aspects of effective joint practice. By contrast the 'communities of practice' concept addresses the cultural dimensions of the terrain, expressed in specific collaborative ways of joint working. Inter-professional teams may be formed in adoption support and this may indeed be a positive way forward. Early indications are that new forms of organisation can stimulate practice innovation (Hart *et al.* 2002). But most important is the way people involved in adoption work together.

Practical matters are of central importance in this respect. Thus a sense of common allegiance depends for its development on a 'shared repertoire' (Wenger 1998, p.83) of routine activity. In the case of adoptive families this largely means having an accessible way of communicating across the gap between the office, clinic, school and home. Newsletters, websites, e-mail groups, telephone trees and chat rooms are the life blood of cross boundary communication. A virtual community of adoptive practice can operate very successfully (Williams 2003, pp. 307–315). On a self-help basis the Adoption UK members experience resource bank Parents Are Linked (PAL) is a good example, as is their Internet Adoption Community initiative which, amongst other things enables adopters to engage in on-line web-chats hosted by parents and professionals (www.adoptionuk.com). To help reduce Bryony and Rachael's feelings of isolation, and to help them become better informed, Dave could certainly point them in some of these directions. For example, a message to PAL about their difficulties with Luke would undoubtedly yield advice from more experienced adoptive parents on contact with foster carers.

Equally important as points of connection are the opportunities to meet and spend time together in various ways that both characterise and cultivate a sense of belonging and community. These are often related to specific aspects of support, such as groups, courses, workshops and the like. As any evaluation will show, whilst the content of these kinds of gathering may or may not be celebrated for its quality and relevance, it is the experience of the process of being together with others in the same boat that is almost invariably the cause for celebration. In this connection rituals are important too, just as they are in family life itself. Hence experience has shown that regular parties and picnics, outings and other purely social events help knit people together in both anticipation and remembrance. They also remind everyone that fun is as noble an aim as any other where family life is concerned. Some of the longer established voluntary adoption agencies are particularly well practised in sustaining a culture of joint celebration along these lines.

Thinking back to our case example, developing local connections with other adoptive parents and wider adoption supporters might be really useful for Bryony and Rachael right now. There is certainly evidence to support the effectiveness of this approach to supporting adoptive parents (Livingston Smith and Howard 1999; Nelson and Parrish 1993).

What might it achieve in the specific case of Bryony and Rachael though? First, it has the potential to give Bryony and Rachael the feeling that they wanted – to be parenting as part of a larger community – even if it is not the community of friends and family they had hoped for. Second, they may find comfort in seeing with their own eyes that they are not the only ones who have difficulties. Third, other adoptive parents and adoption supporters might help them think through ways of re-engaging family and friends. And fourth, by making connections with adoption supporters in professional networks they might be helped to negotiate for their children in the wider community of school.

For Luke and Debbie other pay-offs are also possible. With their parents participating in a community of adoptive practice, the children themselves may be introduced to other adopted children bringing opportunities for friendships with children in similar situations. In some areas more structured activities may be set up directly for the children themselves. For example, After Adoption in Manchester run many successful groups for adopted children and young people.

Distinctive in all this is the idea that this culture of joint working should transform customary boundaries within and between agencies and professionals on the one hand and family members and informal networks on the other. In a community of practice different expertise is recognised, accountability is reciprocal and learning is mutual. So, for example, traditional roles in peer support groups can be changed around and new prospective adopters can be paid to run the creche for the children of experienced group members. When the charismatic adoption specialist is invited over from America to run training sessions for the adoption and fostering team, adoptive parents, and other central people in the lives of adopted children, such as teachers or grandparents, can be invited to attend too, as a matter of course. Adoptive parents can themselves lead on, or advise social workers about, revisions to the official parenting skills manual used by the professionals, or (properly paid) co-run the course themselves. Already adopted children can organise the activities for those newly placed when the summer camping weekend is arranged. In these ways deeper engagements develop as experience is shared and learning maximised.

This is not really about 'user involvement' in running services or the denial of professional expertise. We fear that these approaches run the risk of being either exploitative or neglectful. If parents (and children) do share the work, they should be paid and rewarded properly for doing so wherever possible. And it has been parents themselves who have demanded more authoritative professionalism from formal services (Adoption Today 2003a, p.23; Benton 2000). People will always form self-help groups in recognition of a common interest, and often in response to professional neglect or ineptitude. In adoption these groups have also played a significant role in challenging formal services and forcing them to get their own act together. Adoption UK is the prime example here on a national basis. Locally, self-help groups have strongly influenced service development too (Luckock 2002). But 'communities of practice', as we use the idea in this book, are different because of their emphasis on a culture of mutuality across boundaries of role and status. This should apply as much to services as a whole as to the individual case in question.

Of course it is important not to romanticise this vision. For there are likely to be more tensions and conflicts to be managed in any expanded concept of communities of practice than are allowed for in the conventional account of internal organisational learning through voluntary association developed by Wenger and others. Some of these are to do with the dynamics of inter-agency and inter-professional working, where opportunity and space for shared expertise and passion is usually limited and conditional. Hence in the case of adoption support the actual emergence of the concept itself, along with new duties, powers and guidance, provides the 'boundary objects' necessary for practice to be integrated in new ways. And the Adoption Support Services Adviser (ASSA) can helpfully be seen as a broker with the necessary organisational legitimacy. Yet, as we saw in Chapter 3, the actual drift of the policy context is conventional rather than innovative. It focuses on the administration of restricted rights and resources in individual cases, not on the culture of inter-professional and interpersonal working in general.

Other tensions are those to do with the interpersonal experience of giving and getting support as we have discussed in previous chapters. Here we are reminded of Everett's analysis of mental health reform in Canada:

> Certainly the entire reform process has strained traditional helping relationships in unexpected ways as mental health professionals encounter their former and current patients in planning meetings and consumers and survivors meet their daytime political foes in the emergency room as they seek crisis admission after hours. (Everett 1998, p.91)

Everett talks of relationships between users and professionals as being *strained* by such new forms of social encounter. Equally however, they might be constructed as shifted or even transformed, although in the moment it may not seem like it. However one constructs the dynamic, there is no doubt that working at the interface of these boundaries stirs up some very powerful emotions and sometimes quite bad feelings (Lofgren 1978; Shaping Our Lives 2003).

A good deal of care must be taken, as we have seen, if mutual understanding, joint commitment and trust within and across the family and agency boundaries created through adoption is to be achieved. Here some of the classic texts on teamworking, as well as resources in the literature on service user involvement can be drawn upon to help avoid some of the pitfalls (Department of Health 2003e; Payne 2000; Werrbach, Jenson and Bubar 2002).

Take for example the idea of joint multi-professional and parent training. As Werrbach *et al.*'s evaluation (2002) of a collaborative parent-professional training initiative shows, effective mutual participation needs to be cultivated rather than simply assumed. Their study found professional workers to have more difficulty adjusting to joint training than did the parents. Here, boundary issues and self-consciousness on their part were issues that needed to be addressed. In the case of Bryony's and Rachael's new family, attendance at a joint training event for new adoptive parents, their children's teachers, social workers, health visitors and other adults involved in their lives might well be helpful.

Whilst Werrbach and colleagues are very optimistic about the potential for parental involvement in such joint training, thinking back to our case study, at this point in their family lifecycle Bryony and Rachael might be less than enthusiastic. With their confidence at rock bottom, a pre-briefing and offers from Dave to accompany them might help smooth the way. Organisers of the joint training would preferably themselves be brokers, in the terms of Wenger and colleagues. They would need to take care with ground rules to ensure that an agenda of mutual respect is set and jargon explained. Appropriate child care for adoptive parents would need to be thought through so that children like Debbie and Luke are properly cared for, with their attachment needs properly considered. Events need to be structured at the right time of day to enable Bryony and Rachael to attend. Important, too, in considering the structure of the event are opportunities for all voices to be heard, even those of unconfident, struggling parents.

Who might belong in a community of adoptive practice?

Having defined the concept of a community of practice in adoption we can now turn briefly to the task of mapping out the membership in more detail. We need to see the picture through the eyes of an individual family like that of Bryony and Rachael, Luke and Debbie, which is struggling to establish its particular network of support. And we have to consider the wider local landscape of adoptive community practice and who we might expect to feel a sense of belonging and commitment to it.

In thinking about community membership we must start by deciding exactly who it is that might feel a sense of identification with, and responsibility for, the joint enterprise in question – that of establishing settled adoptive childhood and family life. Wenger and colleagues have emphasised the voluntary nature of the associations formed in communities of practice. They speak of shared passion and free will as the basis of mutual engagement and a preparedness to negotiate across boundaries in order to learn and develop together. We have already reminded ourselves that, in adoption, passions are as likely to be in contention as they are to be shared, and that any sense of self-determination can be diminished, not enhanced.

Katz has spoken about 'the geometry of complexity' (2000, p.215) that emerges when the conventional shaping of adoption as a triangular relationship is scrutinised more carefully. His approach is to name what he sees as the 'multi-triangular dynamics of adoption' (p.216). Consistent with this way of thinking about adoptive relationships, in Figure 7.1 we use the idea of an 'adoption star' as a figurative representation of the different groups with an investment in any community of adoptive practice.

The beauty of a star is that, unlike a triangle, as many different points as necessary can be added or deleted as new participants join or withdraw from the frame. This flexibility is a hallmark of any effective practice community.

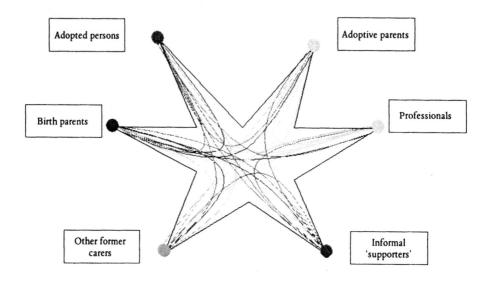

Figure 7.1 The adoption star

However the danger still remains that the different roles and positions people are grouped together in might be seen as too fixed and separate. This is not the intention. The six groups included here do indeed incorporate distinct positions in relation to the shared task. Parents are parents and professionals are professionals in any encounter. And clearly some relationships of support will be permanent (for example, those between related parents and children) whilst others will be far more transitory (for example, the involvement of a particular special needs teacher in a specific case or in the local service community as a whole). But in a community of practice parents are also supporters (of other parents) and educators (for example of helping professionals). And professionals can accept support and guidance from many different sources too.

Thinking back to our practice example, Dave, the social worker for Bryony, Rachael and the children, will need the sensitivity, skill and energy to help the family make those connections of social support so far unrealised. It will help if he has the capacity to see the available sources of support as constituting a potential community of practice. More than this though, and our central concern here, is the need for his own engagement with the family to itself be supported by a larger infrastructure of adoptive community practice in the area. Individual families and their members will move in and out of the frame over time according to need and interest. The intensity of their involvement in the organised world of adoption support is a matter for them. However the initiation and maintenance of a local adoption support culture that facilitates participation and allegiance in the ways outlined requires continual work. As we have seen in Chapters 3 and 4, this is a professional responsibility that should not be avoided. The cultivation of this infrastructure is of central importance if any local adoption plan is to be successful.

Cultivating communities of adoptive practice

Attention is now turning to ways of stimulating the development of communities of practice as organisational building blocks. Our proposals for the cultivation of communities of adoptive practice are based on the factors that have encouraged communities of practice elsewhere, and aspects of current reported practice in adoption support that exemplify the emergence of this new way of thinking.

Below we provide a summary of tasks to be undertaken to enable a culture of community practice in adoption support to become established in any local area.

Cultivating communities of practice:

- Identify champions and sponsors.

- Develop a visual map of patterns of relationships.

- Establish a support team.

- Launch the community of practice in the way that is most appropriate for the context.

- Provide opportunities for people to collaborate around different aspects of adoption support.

- Pay attention to cultivating the community through its different stages of development.

Champions and sponsors

To get communities of practice off the ground, champions and sponsors are identified as having key roles to play (Wenger *et al.* 2002, p.214). Given that the practice of adoption support is now statutorily prescribed, a role of champion must be allocated to one or more persons employed by the local authority. The

ASSA is the obvious candidate at this formal level. However, it is the essence of the idea of a community of practice that engagement is passionate rather than dutiful. Local authorities have not always been renowned for imaginative innovation in the development of services in adoption, a defensive caution has sometimes characterised practice. Leadership in relation to new approaches to support has more often been seen to emerge from adoptive parents' self-help groups in the form of Adoption UK, or from voluntary agencies such as The Post Adoption Centre, Parents for Children or Coram Family, and private consortiums such as Family Futures.

The ASSA in each area will need to consider where the lead will come from in that locality; who is best placed to bring enthusiasm and imagination to the task. This is because it is the ASSA in the first instance who will command the local authority funds necessary for community practice to be supported either directly or on commission. Nonetheless champions will also need a broader base of authority and legitimacy stretching across the boundaries of adoptive family life and agency services. And champions can and will emerge from any and all points on the adoption star and practice in all sorts of ways. The field of adoption support in particular has been marked by the advocacy and proselytising of adoptive parents and adopted people, some of whom have made significant contributions in changing service cultures locally and nationally. They have done so from both outside and within professional roles, reminding us too that common experience regularly transcends organisational divisions. The argument here is that it is exactly this tradition that must be valued and built on if dismal bureaucratic service cultures are to be avoided. A good example of such innovation is that of the partnership entered into by Essex County Council and Adoption UK. Essex fund one year's free membership to Adoption UK and three local support groups run by Adoption UK. A 'buddy' scheme in which new adopters are put into contact with experienced adopters who support them during the early weeks of placement is also being developed (Adoption Today 2003b, p.3). Schemes such as these certainly need champions and sponsors to get them started.

If champions provide the lead and give voice and visibility to community practice, sponsors are crucial for the support and resources they offer. In the field of adoption support it makes sense for sponsors to be understood as those people in governance and managerial roles in mainstream service agencies such as the education authority and health trust and local voluntary and independent organisations. Where local services are now becoming integrated in children's trusts there may a reduction in formal boundaries between services but there will still be competition for scarce resources of time and money to be devoted to different areas of child-centred practice. Wenger and colleagues (2002) value the scepticism of sponsors because it is this reality which will cause any emergent practice community, and its champions, to be driven on to demonstrate their worth. The operational means by which advocates of adoption support will be able to champion this cause will vary by area. But it is of the essence that the ASSA in each case has political skill in articulating demands as well as personal authority and commitment to the task.

Mapping the landscape

The landscape of community practice in adoption support is constituted by a pattern of relationships. The visual mapping of these relationships is a key task in the development of any new culture of working (Cross, Borgatti and Parker 2002). We have already discussed, in Chapter 6, the importance of the mapping of adoptive kinship relations for effective communication and contact in individual families. Much the same applies to the topography of the more extensive networks of contacts we have in mind here. A list of people who might potentially be included in the mapping of a community of adoptive practice can be found below.

- Adopted children
- Adoptive parents
- Former foster carers
- Birth parents
- Friends
- Extended adoptive family
- Social workers
- Class teachers
- Youth workers
- Special needs teachers
- Educational psychologists
- Health visitors
- Therapists
- GPs

From the perspective of family members such as Bryony, Rachael, Luke and Debbie a sense of being connected is essential not simply in relation to specific sources of support in themselves but also to a common experience shared by other adoptive families like their own. If they are going to decide whether to join this new adoption support club they will need to have in mind, as well as on paper, who the members are and what they have to do to sign up and get involved. As we discuss more fully below we think this sense of belonging is best cultivated from the start, adoptive parents and their family and friends especially being encouraged to think of themselves as joining a club from the moment they decide to go through with their plan to adopt.

From the perspective of the agencies Bryony and the family should represent another opportunity for strengthening relationships of support through additional interactions in an existing or newly forming community of practice. A basic mapping exercise, using frameworks such as those suggested by Cross *et al.* (2002), will capture actual and potential members, their expertise and their learning requirements in respect of adoption and its support. Affiliations that are collegial and reciprocal are likely to be more important than those that derive from institutional roles alone, but mapping illuminates where participation is peripheral and where gaps in resources might usefully be filled.

It has for some time now been the practice of policy makers and managers to test the likely accessibility and responsiveness of services by tracking the typical pathways people take through them as they move across the service landscape. This approach is helpful in adoption, too, especially if it is incorporated into the preparation and support process from the start so that Bryony, Rachael and prospective parents like them can have in mind their own personal mental map of connections and possibilities.

The general community of practice for adoption support in any area will be built up from the constellation of micro communities that form around each newly established adoptive family. But the model we propose here does not just see people as 'service users' for whom a clearer and better sign-posted path must be beaten by the professionals. Instead Bryony and Rachael, particularly later down the line, are as much resources for other parents, as they are reliant on the support service networks that community membership should provide. This is similarly the case for Luke and Debbie in relation to other children. And Luke's teacher, struggling to make sense of and manage his withdrawal and resistance, will be a much more effective source of family support if he is better connected. In his case, connected to those other teachers, educational psychologists and social workers locally who have in common their need to share and enhance their knowledge and skills in working with adopted children. Any mapping should capture this dual dynamic of participation. It is precisely this that builds capacity and competence within a vibrant local culture of adoption support.

Support teams

Support teams which provide continuity and which nurture the development of communities are emphasised in the literature (Wenger *et al.* 2002; Brown and Solomon-Gray 1995). Team members have time and expertise to offer. They raise awareness as well as providing coaching, education and administrative support (Wenger *et al.* 2002). Support team members conduct workshops, stage conferences, develop toolkits, organise mechanisms to connect with other communities and teams, and meet with people – co-ordinators, community members and sponsors – to lay a foundation on which communities can build for the future.

In the adoption context, the role of the ASSA will be key in building a support team. However, bearing in mind what we have said in this book about the importance of understanding and working with adoption across contexts, it will be important to recruit members of support teams from all points on the adoption star. Essential here is the recognition that representatives from different groups, professional and family, should be included in support teams. To avoid tokenism, parents and children should be included in sufficient numbers to enable the development of mutual support and they should be paid and rewarded for participating. Training should be available for all support team members. Support teams will play a central role in launching, maintaining and developing the kind of community practice we have in mind.

Launching a community of practice

Launching is a key consideration that needs careful attention. Wenger and colleagues distinguish between high-visibility and low-visibility approaches (2002). The former involves a well-publicised launch, for example an adoption support conference, a major training event or an adoption fair. The latter constitutes a more incremental approach with community development occurring in the context of face-to-face meetings, newsletters and e-mail discussion groups. The high-visibility approach is preferred in contexts where a dramatic promotional effort is likely to be treated seriously. By contrast, the latter approach gives the initiative leaders time to learn from experience and to build momentum through early results and word of mouth.

In adoption support, however impoverished the local capacity for community practice, some patchwork of emergent micro communities of support will exist. Not everyone will feel as stranded as Bryony and Rachael and their children. The process of launching may most usefully be encapsulated in a public event that announces the move towards explicit agency commitments to establishing a new culture of adoptive practice. But the business of launching new ways of working must not be detached from the longer haul of maintaining and developing practice.

Opportunities for collaboration and stages of community development

Two final considerations are necessary in respect of this process of consolidation and growth. The first has to do with the different aspects of adoption support and the second with the stages of development in community practice. We have already said the domain of adoption support has as its focus the achievement of a settled and happy family life. Within this overall objective, however, we can tease out those aspects of family life and its support explored in previous chapters. Providing around these different aspects of adoption support will be an essential task for those people championing and supporting adoptive community practice.

Our primary concern in this book has been with the promotion of family and kin relationships because the attachments and communications through which they are (re) formed are foundational. But experience and relationships in the wider social world of adoptive childhood are crucial too. Luke and Debbie are struggling to find their place in the school, playground and local streets as well as in their new home. Particular attention must therefore be paid to interactions centred on these social settings for children and families, which are so often experienced as being difficult and challenging.

One approach is to identify specific workers who can undertake boundary-crossing practitioner roles both in individual situations and on behalf of the adoption support community as a whole. In the Brighton and Hove Attachment Project, social workers, education counsellors and psychotherapists had a brief to take on these roles as a context for direct therapeutic intervention with permanent foster and adoptive families (Hart *et al.* 2002). For example, the education counsellors sought to form a team around a particular child with behavioural or learning difficulties in school, enhancing contact and communication between parents, children and teachers and sharing knowledge and strategies. They were also expected to disseminate around the education authority, developing understanding and skills in relation to this work with permanently placed children. Social workers and therapists, in relation to children's social services and CAMHS respectively, had similar roles. In the event the impact of the Attachment Project in this respect was limited, partly as a result of uncertainty about its priorities (Hart *et al.* 2002). No champions of the bigger picture emerged to take the necessary lead to improve the work and to drive the process on. But the potential is great for developing learning and skills by identifying practitioners who have the role of pooling experience and connections within the constellation of micro communities formed around each child when things are unsettled and troubling at school or on the streets.

Another boundary-spanning role is strongly indicated for the birth family social worker in relation to any participation by original family members in any community of practice. In adoption from care the boundary that marks the connection between the adoptive and birth family is usually the most divisive of them all. If the work of communication and contact discussed in Chapter 6 is to be enhanced in the individual case, by being incorporated in the general practice community of adoption support in the local area, formal support roles are crucial. Whether the lead is taken by local authority workers or by independent agencies such as the Post Adoption Centre, perhaps offering mediation (Kedward *et al.* 1999; Sales 2002), the task will involve particularly skilled and attentive approaches to the making of connections. Emerging good practice in the individual case was discussed in the previous chapter. However we have not found any examples reported of practice that has successfully widened links to include groups of birth and adoptive parents and relatives coming together for mutual learning and support. Arguably, of course, this might be seen as a step too far for everyone.

A third example of collaborative connections concerns the approach that might be taken to enabling short breaks from care-taking and the relentless intensity of family life for parents and children alike. From a community of practice perspective 'respite care', so conceived, can be both a service, provided as part of the local framework of adoption support and an opportunity for expanding relationships and a sense of belonging to the wider adoptive practice community. Hence friends and family, in addition to people drawn from any existing local pool of short-break foster carers, can be conceived of as potential carers and recruited early on. This helps ensure that attachment relationships are taken account of in planning any short breaks. Some time into placement parents like Bryony and Rachael may well need a break from kids like Debbie and Luke and vice versa. They may feel so desperate that they will palm the children off on anyone who can be found to have them. However, unless the break is planned with the attachment and stability needs of Debbie and Luke firmly in mind, rewards are unlikely to be reaped from it, however much everybody concerned convinces themselves that the break may stave off a disruption. Up and running Direct Payment Schemes in other areas of social care are important sources of ideas to help develop good practice in the adoption context (Flynn 2002; Glasby and Littlechild 2002).

And underpinning all these will be an unwavering commitment to the practical and apparently mundane, those arrangements that must always be made to facilitate access and participation. Professionals will be less likely to avoid the commitment of time and thought to community practice (rarely will adoption support be their sole concern) unless the agency permits, encourages and rewards such a culture of working. Over-stretched parents may need financial support and help with child care to participate effectively. We repeat our initial caution about the inflated claims often made for the benefits of community as the solution to personal and social problems. Community membership can be burdensome, either if it feels like an imposition or if it demands more than is given back as the price of participation.

The final consideration in the process of cultivation of any community of adoptive practice concerns *sustaining* them. In the original formulation of Wenger and colleagues and the focus on knowledge and its management in organisations, a key task was seen to be one of sustaining interest at times of low momentum. The situation is a good deal more complex when it comes to the kind of community practice we are sketching out for adoption support. As we have said adoptive communities of practice, in our formulation, have a micro and a general constitution. Individual children and families move through and beyond the landscape of communal support in accordance with the unfolding of adoptive childhood and family life whilst the infrastructure of the adoptive community locally has its own lifecycle. Very little is yet known about either pattern. What can be asserted however, is that the point of entry and participation for each person should be when a decision is taken that leads subsequently to the formation of a new adoptive family. This is of course in line too with the official policy commitment to a seamless approach to adoption support (Department of Health 2003b).

For children the encouragement of a new sense of community belonging starts when the decision is taken that they are to be placed for adoption. For birth family members and their support workers the conversation will also start at this point. For prospective parents their own decision to proceed with preparation and assessment is the key moment. Leaving things any longer, for example to matching and placement, is really too late. Opportunities for facing up to and thinking about the coming reality of adoptive childhood and family life alongside existing practitioners and their experience and expertise should be available from the start. This should help people from wandering off in isolation, so to speak, in odd directions across unfamiliar terrain.

To this end we propose that the nature of the 'preparation' process in adoption might usefully be rethought. Currently the emphasis is almost solely on the task of assessing the suitability of children and potential adoptive parents for adoption. Preparation in this context involves helping both make sense of what to expect from adoptive family life and steering them towards an officially preferred 'match'. Adults get a chance, on reflection, to decline the opportunity of adoption generally and any placement in particular. In the case of children this option is far less available. Regrettably it appears that the opportunity for them to have a proper say is far more circumscribed (Cashmore 2002; Department of Health 2002b; Thomas et al. 1999). Achieving this for children with learning and communication difficulties is even more problematic.

By 'having a proper say', however, we do not intend that distressed and vulnerable children should be further burdened by responsibility for determining their own future, under some pretence that real choice and control does or should apply in their situation. This does not mean either that children should be excluded from the process of deliberation on grounds of this being generally for their own good. The way in which children are enabled to participate is the central issue, not whether they should have a right to do so at all. This right is foundational. Failure to help children exercise it contributes significantly to the bewilderment and additional distress of children whose lives and relationships feel transient and out of control already.

From an adoptive community practice perspective, preparation would take on an additional aspect. Not only would prospective parents and children be steered, first towards the idea of adoption and then to each other, but they would also be introduced to the local community of adoptive families, professional workers and others on our adoption star.

Elements of this community induction process are already present in customary practice in assessment and preparation or can be adapted from what is currently done. For example the concept of 'introductions' is now well established in relation to arrangements for helping in the actual move of children to their new home. Good practice involves the active participation of foster carers in this process. Birth family members will play some role where possible and advisable. Consistent with the general research finding (Thomas *et al.* 1999) children themselves are too often not fully involved in 'the preparation and presentation about themselves for their families (1999, p.133). However effective and inclusive the process, in this way a micro community of adoptive practice is being formed for the purpose of the transition. It is our suggestion that this emergent process be extended.

In the first place it seems sensible at the matching and placement stage to consider involving additional potential members of this incipient support community. For school-age children, like Luke, a major complaint concerns the disruption to schooling and associated social life and relationships on placement, especially if this takes place in term time. Whether or not schools need to be changed it is important that the relevant teacher and, where appropriate, educational psychologist, speech therapist and any other educational support worker, also be involved. The introduction is to the wider social life of the child, not only to the family in question.

Furthermore, if the idea of introductions is applied to the process of preparation as well as placement, opportunities are opened up for interesting links and associations from the outset. For example, Bryony and Rachael will be much less likely to exhaust the goodwill of their family and friends, if the key members of this informal support network were invited in from the start to participate formally in aspects of the preparation process. A simple idea here would be to put on an information session for the friends and families of prospective adopters like Bryony and Rachael and provide an information pack for them. In this way they will not only get a much better sense of what to expect but also the micro community of practice created around Luke and Debbie at subsequent placement will be enhanced by their active involvement. The nature and extent of the support commitment can be explored and to some extent agreed in advance of placement. Effective arrangements for sharing care, through baby-sitting and short breaks and the rest, can be sketched out.

Introducing potential members of the micro community of practice to the task and each other through the preparation stage should be the basis of new support strategies in adoption. In turn prospective adoptive parents in particular, and others including children themselves, should also be connected from the outset in the wider adoption community in the area. To the conventional case management approach of 'providing information' to new parents about the individual use of services should be added the idea of 'offering invitations' to participation as a member of the adoption club.

We favour an element of formality to mark rites of passage in this respect. An information pack, with all the details of people, events and services locally and nationally, should obviously be provided. But most important is the way this is done, which should foster a sense of engagement and belonging in a collective endeavour and experience. For example if the ASSA is the official face of the adoption support service his or hers is a face that must be seen on the doorstep. Perhaps the ASSA should be the person who welcomes the new prospective parents. The preparation group should be organised and led by representatives from all points of the adoption star, helping new applicants to really appreciate the communal, interdependent nature of adoption and its support. Membership might be ritualised through the use of cards and attendant rights, for example, full access to the local adoption support website. And, crucially, Luke's teacher should be invited to join too so that he is not isolated either from the infrastructure and culture of the adoption support community.

If the initial point of engagement and entry to a community of adoptive practice is well managed, and champions, sponsors, support teams and the rest are in place and active, we suspect collaborative practice thereafter will be sustained. This is a practice community that will always be self-regenerating, so long as a culture of participation is created, because it can be guaranteed that new members will be increasing in number for the foreseeable future.

Conclusion

Cultivating communities of adoptive practice requires work on the part of many different people and organisations. Perhaps there is no one person represented on our adoption star who will be immune from finding this kind of work a real challenge. Everyone needs to work at seeing and doing things differently.

However, as we have seen in this chapter, collaborative allegiances and partnership working in adoption are certainly emerging. Whether these shifts will lead to the establishment of communities of adoptive practice as we understand them is yet to be seen. And, as we made clear at the beginning of this book, there are real threats to, and difficulties with, the giving and receiving of adoption support and therapy. We started out in Chapter 1 by explaining that the ambivalence about adoption which is embedded in law, policy, professional and adoptive family practice, is at the heart of these threats and difficulties.

Using the sociological concepts of family practices and narratives as tools to think about meaning and experience, Chapter 2 offered the opportunity to understand more about the ambivalent nature of adoptive family life. As we have argued throughout this book, one major step on the road to adoption competence is really understanding and engaging with what goes on in families such as those of Lucy and Bill, Bryony, Rachael and Bella.

As well as exploring the ambivalence of adoptive family life, Chapter 2 also laid out the main legacies of adopted children, which as we saw in our three case studies, have a considerable impact on how adoptive family life is lived. In this chapter too we touched on the legacies that adoptive parents themselves bring to adoptive family practice.

Always with one eye still firmly on the case studies of adoptive family life which we introduced in Chapter 1, Chapters 3 and 4 turned towards a consideration of policy and professional practice. Discussion within both chapters centred on our critique of the Adoption and Children Act 2002 as it related to support provision. We set out the potential threats and promises of the new act, including a consideration of the role of the ASSA.

In Chapters 5 and 6 we honed our discussion down further to professional practice in the world of adoption therapy and support. Chapter 5 set out a model of effective therapeutic practice in adoption as well as providing a critique of the evidence base regarding the effectiveness of different modes and methods of therapeutic intervention.

In Chapter 5 we also explored the current practice of looking to formal therapeutic intervention for the answers to the difficulties of adoptive family life. And we sounded a warning that this might yet lend itself to a model of working which identifies adoption with pathological status rather than community of practice. The increasing recognition that adoptive parents have their own histories and difficulties which must be dealt with if children are to settle, should of course, as we did in Chapters 5 and 6, be acknowledged. However, it would indeed be regrettable if we saw a return to the bad old days of adoption 'support' in which adoptive parents were blamed for the difficulties of their children. Adoption competence really needs to move on and we have given many different examples in this book of how this might occur.

The focus in Chapter 6 was on communication and contact, and on how children can be helped to develop a coherent 'autobiographical self' in the context of adoption. Here we offered a new model of effective practice, and considered the pain and complexity of supporting adopted children to move on from, yet stay connected to, their very difficult histories. Fundamental to this was the need for adoptive families to develop a shared family narrative into which shared understandings of past legacies of both children and parents become embedded.

Chapter 6 also included a discussion of practical ways in which children can be helped to do the 'talking and telling' that is essential to adoptive family life. Whilst we suggested that much of this work can be embedded into everyday adoptive family practice, clearly some of it will have a more formal therapeutic component.

As we have argued in this book, formal therapeutic initiatives have their place in adoption support, and they are certainly increasing in popularity. Our own passion however, is for more inclusive models of service provision to develop which always hold adoptive family practices firmly in mind. Hence we see financial, social and community support as important as formal therapeutic assistance. And, as we have argued, any therapeutic support offered must have an accurate conceptualisation of adoptive family practice firmly at its heart.

In this book we have explored the nuances of the Adoption and Children Act 2002 as it applies to adoption support. The Act certainly has its limitations, not least of which is the weak model of collaboration embedded within it. Nevertheless, it certainly has provided an impetus, as well as a loose framework, for the kinds of new ways of working we have outlined in this final chapter to be developed. Families like those of Lucy, Bill, Bryony, Rachael and Bella deserve the energy and commitment that creative interpretations of the Act are beginning to foster. Let us hope that in the coming years, at both a national and a local level, creative responses to adoption support will continue to be firmly on policy and practice agendas.

References

Adams, M. (2002) *Our Son, A Stranger: Adoption Breakdown and its Effect on Parents.* Montreal: McGill-Queen's University Press.

Adoption Today (2003a) 'CAMHS (Child and Adolescent Mental Health Services): Your questions answered.' *Adoption Today 103*, 23 (February).

Adoption Today (2003b) 'Our friends in Essex.' *Adoption Today 112*, 30 (October).

Ainsworth, M.D.S., Blehar, M., Waters, E. and Wall, S. (1978) *Patterns of Attachment: A Psychological Study of the Strange Situation.* Hillsdale NJ: Erlbaum.

Akhtar, S. and Kramer, S. (eds) (2000) *Thicker Than Blood/Bonds of Fantasy and Reality in Adoption.* Northvale, NJ: Jason Aronson.

Aldgate, J. and Statham, J. (2001) *The Children Act Now.* (Prepared for the Department of Health, Studies in Evaluating the Children Act 1989.) London: The Stationery Office.

Alexander, L.B. and Dore, M.M. (1999) 'Making the Parents as Partners principle a reality: the role of the alliance.' *Journal of Child and Family Studies 8*, 255–270.

Anon (1989) 'A parent's diary.' In A. Brechin and J. Walmsley (eds) *Making Connections: Reflecting on the Lives and Experiences of People with Learning Difficulties.* London: Stoughton/OUP.

Archer, C. (1999a) *First Steps in Parenting the Child Who Hurts: Tiddlers and Toddlers.* London: Jessica Kingsley Publishers.

Archer, C. (1999b) *Next Steps in Parenting the Child Who Hurts: Tykes and Teens.* London: Jessica Kingsley Publishers.

Archer, C. (2003) 'Weft and warp: Developmental impact of trauma and implications for healing.' In C. Archer and A. Burnell (eds) *Trauma, Attachment and Family Permanence: Fear Can Stop You Loving.* London: Jessica Kingsley Publishers.

Archer, C. and Burnell, A. (eds) (2003) *Trauma, Attachment and Family Permanence: Fear Can Stop You Loving.* London : Jessica Kingsley Publishers.

Argent, H. (ed) (2002) *Staying Connected: Managing Contact in Adoption.* London: British Association for Adoption and Fostering .

Audit Commission (1994) *Seen But Not Heard: Co-ordinating Community Child Health and Social Services for Children in Need.* London: HMSO.

Audit Commission (1999) *Children in Mind: Child and Adolescent Mental Health Services.* London: HMSO.

Bachrach, L. (1993) 'Continuity of care and approaches to case management for long-term mentally ill patients.' *Hospital and Community Psychiatry 44*, 465–468.

Bakermans-Kranenburg, M.J., van Ijzendoorn, M.H. and Juffer, F. (2003) 'Less is more: meta-analyses of sensitivity and attachment interventions in early childhood.' *Psychological Bulletin 129*, 195–215.

Balloch, S. and Taylor, M. (eds) (2001) *Partnership Working: Policy and Practice.* Bristol: Policy Press.

Barlow, J., Coren, E. and Stewart-Brown, S. (2001) *Systematic Review of the Effectiveness of Parenting Programmes in Improving Maternal Psychosocial Health.* Oxford: Health Service Research Unit, University of Oxford.

Barratt, S. (2002) 'Fostering care: the child, the family and the professional system.' *Journal of Social Work Practice 16*, 163–173.

Barth, R.P. and Berry, M. (1988) *Adoption and Disruption: Rates, Risks, and Responses.* New York: Aldine Publishing Company.

Barth, R.P. and Miller, J.M. (2000) 'Building effective post-adoption services: What is the empirical foundation?' *Family Relations 49*, 447–455.

Bartram, P. (2003) 'Some Oedipal problems in work with adopted children and their parents.' *Journal of Child Psychotherapy 29*, 21–36.

Beck, A. and Beck-Gernsheim, E. (1995) *The Normal Chaos of Love.* Cambridge: Polity Press.

Beck-Gernsheim, E. (2002) *Reinventing the Family.* Cambridge: Polity Press.

Beek, M. (1999) 'Parenting children with attachment difficulties: Views of adoptive parents and implications for post-adoption services.' *Adoption and Fostering 23*, 16–23.

Bell, M. (2002) 'Promoting children's rights through the use of relationship.' *Child and Family Social Work 7*, 1–11.

Belsky, J. (1999) 'Interactional and contextual determinants of attachment security.' In J. Cassidy and P. Shaver (eds) *Handbook of Attachment.* New York: Guilford Press.

Bennett, D.S. and Gibbons, T.A. (2000) 'Efficacy of child cognitive-behavioral interventions for antisocial behavior: A meta-analysis.' *Child and Family Behavior Therapy 22*, 1–15.

Benton, A. (2000) 'Towards the reality of reunion: An adoptive mother's journey through the fantasies and realities in adoption and birth mother reunion.' In A. Treacher and I. Katz (eds) *The Dynamics of Adoption.* London: Jessica Kingsley Publishers.

Berlin, L.J. and Cassidy, J. (1999) 'Relationships among relationships. Contributions from attachment theory and research.' In J. Cassidy and P. Shaver (eds) *Handbook of Attachment.* New York: Guilford Press.

Berlin, L.J. and Cassidy, J. (2001) 'Enhancing early child-parent relationships: implications of adult attachment research.' *Infants and Young Children 14*, 64–76.

Bernard, C. (2002) 'Giving voice to experiences: parental maltreatment of black children in the context of racism.' *Child and Family Social Work 7*, 239–251.

Berry, M. (1991) 'The practice of open adoption: findings from a study of 1396 adoptive families.' *Children and Youth Services Review Special Issue 13*, 379–395.

Berry, M., Cavazos, D., Barth, R. and Needell, B. (1998) 'The role of open adoption in the adjustment of adopted children and their families.' *Children and Youth Services Review 20*, 151–171.

Bifulco, A. (2002) 'Attachment style measurement: A clinical and epidemiological perspective.' *Attachment and Human Development 4*, 180–188.

Bifulco, A. and Thomas, G. (2003) 'Assessing families using methods from attachment theory.' Conference paper for *Old and New Blends of Adoption Practice.* (27 February) Dublin.

Bjorkman, T. and Hansson, L. (2000) 'What do case managers do? An investigation of case manager interventions and their relationship to client outcome.' *Social Psychiatry and Psychiatric Epidemiology 35*, 43–50.

Blair, D.C. (2002) 'Knowledge management: hype, hope, or help?' *Journal of the American Society for Information Science and Technology 53*, 1019–1028.

Bland, R.E. (1997) 'Keyworkers re-examined: good practice, quality of care and empowerment in residential care of older people.' *British Journal of Social Work 27*, 585–603.

Blow, K. and Daniel, G. (2002) 'Frozen narratives? Post-divorce processes and contact disputes.' *Journal of Family Therapy 24*, 85–103.

Blum, R.W. and Ellen, J. (2002) 'Work Group V: Increasing the capacity of schools, neighborhoods, and communities to improve adolescent health outcomes.' *Journal of Adolescent Health 31*, 288–292.

Boston, M. and Szur, R. (eds) (1983) *Psychotherapy with Severely Deprived Children.* London: Routledge.

Bowlby, J. (1980) *Attachment and Loss: Vol 3 Loss, Sadness and Depression.* London: Hogarth Press.

Bowlby, J. (1988) *A Secure Base. Clinical Applications of Attachment Theory.* New York: Basic Books.

Brestan, E. and Eyberg, S. (1998) 'Effective psychosocial treatments of conduct-disordered children and adolescents: 29 years, 82 studies, and 5,272 kids.' *Journal of Clinical Child Psychology 27*, 180–189.

Bridge, C. and Swindells, H. (2003) *Adoption: The Modern Law.* Bristol: Family Law.

Brodzinsky, D.M., Schechter, M.D. and Marantz Henig, R. (1992) *Being Adopted: The Lifelong Search for Self.* New York: Anchor Books.

Brodzinsky, D.M. (1987) 'Adjustment to adoption: A psychosocial perspective.' *Clinical Psychology Review 7*, 25–47.

Brodzinsky, D.M. (2003) 'Risk and resiliency in adoption: a multidimensional stress and coping model.' In The Anna Freud Centre (ed) *Conference: Attachment Issues in Adoption: Risk and Resilience Factors.* London: The Anna Freud Centre.

Brodzinsky, D.M., Smith, D.W. and Brodzinsky, A.B. (1998) *Children's Adjustment to Adoption: Developmental and Clinical Issues.* Thousand Oaks, CA: Sage.

Brown, B., Crawford, P. and Darongkamas, J. (2000) 'Blurred roles and permeable boundaries: The experience of multidisciplinary working in community and mental health.' *Health and Social Care in the Community 8*, 425–435.

Brown, J.S. and Solomon-Gray, E. (1995) 'The people are the company.' *Fast Company* (November), 78–82.

Burnell, A. (2003) 'Contact as therapy.' In C. Archer and A. Burnell (eds) *Trauma, Attachment and Family Permanence: Fear Can Stop You Loving.* London: Jessica Kingsley Publishers.

Burnell, A. and Briggs, A. (1996) 'The next generation of post-placement and post-adoption services: A complementary contract approach.' *Adoption and Fostering 19*, 6–10.

Burnell, A. and Briggs, A. (1997) 'Partnership in post-adoption services: Evaluating the first year of a complementary contract.' *Adoption and Fostering 21*, 50–56.

Burns, T. (1997) 'Case management, care management and care programming.' *British Journal of Psychiatry 170*, 393–395.

Butler Sloss, E. (1988) *Report of the Inquiry into Child Abuse in Cleveland 1987.* Cm 412. London: Stationery Office.

Buyss, V., Sparkman, K.L. and Wesley, P.W. (2003) 'Communities of practice: connecting what we know with what we do.' *Exceptional Children 69*, 263–278.

Byng-Hall, J. (1999) 'Creating a coherent story in family therapy.' In G. Roberts and J. Holmes (eds) *Narrative Approaches in Psychiatry and Psychotherapy.* Oxford: Oxford University Press.

Bynner, J. (2001) 'Childhood risks and protective factors in social exclusion.' *Children and Society 15*, 285–301.

Cairns, K. (2002) *Attachment, Trauma and Resilience.* London: British Association for Adoption and Fostering.

Canavan, J., Dolan, P. and Pinkerton, J. (eds) (2000) *Family Support: Direction from Diversity.* London and Philadelphia: Jessica Kingsley Publishers.

Carr, A. (2000a) 'Evidence-based practice in family therapy and systemic consultation – II: Adult-focused problems.' *Journal of Family Therapy 22*, 273–295.

Carr, A. (2000b) 'Evidence-based practice in family therapy and systemic consultation – I: Child-focused problems.' *Journal of Family Therapy 22*, 29–60.

Cars, G., Healey, P., Madanipour, A. and de Magalhaes, B. (eds) (2002) *Urban Governance, Institutional Capacity and Social Milieux.* Aldershot: Ashgate.

Carsten, J. (ed) (2000) *Cultures of Relatedness: New Approaches to the Study of Kinship.* Cambridge: Cambridge University Press.

Carter, E. and McGoldrick, M. (eds) (1998) *The Changing Family Lifecycle: A Framework for Family Therapy.* New York: Guildford Press.

Cashmore, J. (2002) 'Promoting the participation of children and young people in care.' *Child Abuse and Neglect 26*, 837–847.

Cassidy, J. and Shaver, P. (1999) *Handbook of Attachment.* New York: Guilford Press.

Chafflin, M., Bonner, B.L. and Hill, R.F. (2001) 'Family preservation and family support programs: Child maltreatment outcomes across client risk levels and program types.' *Child Abuse and Neglect 25*, 1269–1289.

Chamberlain, P. and Weinrott, M. (1990) 'Specialized foster care: treating seriously emotionally disturbed children.' *Children Today 19*, 24–27.

Chapman, S. (2002) 'Reactive attachment disorder.' *British Journal of Special Educational Needs 29*, 91.

Chase Stovall, K. and Dozier, M. (1998) 'Infants in foster care: An attachment theory perspective.' *Adoption Quarterly 2*, 55–58.

Chase Stovall, K. and Dozier, M. (2000) 'The development of attachment in new relationships: Single subject analysis for 10 foster infants.' *Development and Psychology 12*, 133–156.

Cheal, D. (2002) *Sociology of Family Life.* Basingstoke: Palgrave.

Chorpita, B.F., Yim, L.M., Donkervoet, J.C., Arensdort, A., Amundsen, M.J., Yates, A., Burns, J.A. and Morelli, P. (2002) 'Towards large-scale implementation of empirically supported treatments for children: a review and observations by the Hawaii Empirical Basis to Services Task Force.' *Clinical Psychology: Science and Practice 9*, 165–190.

Cigno, K. and Gore, J. (1999) 'A seamless service: Meeting the needs of children with disabilities through a multi-agency approach.' *Child and Family Social Work 4*, 325–335.

Cleaver, H., Walker, S. and Meadows, P. (2004) *Assessing Children's Needs and Circumstances: The Impact of the Assessment Framework.* London: Jessica Kingsley Publishers.

Cline, F. (1979) *Understanding and Treating the Severely Disturbed Child.* Evergreen, CO: Evergreen Consultants in Human Behavior.

Close, N. (1999) 'Drowning not waving: The parent as co-ordinator of inter-agency support for a child with mental health problems.' *Journal of Mental Health 8*, 551–554.

Cohen, J.A. and Mannarino, A.P. (1998) 'Interventions for sexually abused children: Initial treatment outcome findings.' *Child Maltreatment 3*, 17–26.

Cooper, A. (2002) 'Keeping our heads: preserving therapeutic values in a time of change.' *Journal of Social Work Practice 16*, 7–13.

Cooper, A., Hetherington, R. and Katz, I. (2003) *The Risk Factor: Making the Child Protection System Work for Children.* London: Demos.

Cottrell, D. and Boston, P. (2002) 'Practitioner review: The effectiveness of systemic family therapy for children and adolescents.' *Journal of Child Psychology and Psychiatry 43*, 573–586.

Crank, M. (2002) 'Managing and valuing contact with contesting birth families.' In H. Argent (ed) *Staying Connected: Managing Contact in Adoption.* London: British Association for Adoption and Fostering.

Cross, R., Borgatti, S.P. and Parker, A. (2002) 'Making invisible work visible: Using social network analysis to support strategic collaboration.' *California Management Review 44,* 25–46.

Crow, G. and Allan, G. (2000) 'Communities, family support and social change.' In J. Canavan, P. Dolan and J. Pinkerton (eds) *Family Support: Direction from Diversity.* London and Philadelphia: Jessica Kingsley Publishers.

Cunningham, P.B. and Henggeler, S.W. (1999) 'Engaging multiproblem families in treatment: Lessons learned throughout the development of multisystemic therapy.' *Family Process 38,* 265–281.

Damasio, A. (2000) *The Feeling of What Happens: Body, Emotion and the Making of Consciousness.* London: Vintage.

Dance, C. Rushton, A. and Quinton, D. (2002) 'Emotional abuse in early childhood: Relationships with progress in subsequent family placement.' *Journal of Child Psychology and Psychiatry 43,* 3, 395–407.

Delaney, R.J. and Kunstal, F.R. (1993) *Troubled Transplants: Unconventional Strategies for Helping Disturbed Foster and Adopted Children.* Portland, ME: National Child Welfare Resource Centre for Management and Administration.

Department for Education and Employment (1999) *Sure Start. A Guide for Trailblazers.* London: DfEE Publications.

Department for Education and Skills (2003a) *Every Child Matters.* (Green Paper.) London: Stationery Office.

Department for Education and Skills (2003b) *The Children Act Report 2002.* Nottingham: Department for Education and Skills.

Department for Education and Skills (2003c) *Together From The Start. Practical Guidance for Professionals Working with Disabled Children (Birth to Third Birthday) and Their Families.* London: DfES Publications.

Department of Health (1998a) *Quality Protects Programme: Transforming Children's Services.* LAC(98)28. London: Department of Health Publications.

Department of Health (1999) *Patient and Public Involvement in the New NHS.* London: Department of Health Publications.

Department of Health (2000a) *Adoption: A New Approach. White Paper.* Cm 5017. London: Department of Health Publications.

Department of Health (2000b) *Framework for the Assessment of Children in Need and Their Families.* London: Department of Health Publications.

Department of Health (2000c) *The NHS Plan.* London: Department of Health Publications.

Department of Health (2001a) *Inspection of Adoption Services.* London: Department of Health Publications.

Department of Health (2001b) *National Adoption Standards for England.* London: Department of Health Publications.

Department of Health (2002a) *Children Adopted From Care in England 2001/2002.* Statistical Bulletin. London: Department of Health Publications.

Department of Health (2002b) *Providing Effective Adoption Support: A Consultation Document.* London: Department of Health Publications.

Department of Health (2002c) *The Exemplar Records for the Integrated Children's System.* London: Department of Health Publications.

Department of Health (2002d) *Adoption: Draft Practice Guidance to Support the National Adoption Standards for England.* London: Department of Health Publications.

Department of Health (2003a) *Adoption Register for England and Wales. Annual Report 2003.* London: Department of Health Publications.

Department of Health (2003b) *Adoption and Children Act 2002: Adoption Support Services Guidance.* To Accompany the Adoption Support Services (Local Authorities) (England) Regulations 2003. London: Department of Health Publications.

Department of Health (2003c) *Adoption: The Draft Adoption Support Services (Local Authorities) (Transitory and Transitional Provisions) (England) Regulations 2003. Draft Accompanying Guidance.* Consultation Document. (Adoption and Children Act 2002). London: Department of Health Publications.

Department of Health (2003d) *Adoption and Children Act 2002: Adoption Support Services (Local Authorities) (England) Regulations 2003.* London: Department of Health Publications.

Department of Health (2003e) *Strengthening Accountability: Involving Patients and the Public. Policy and Practice Guidance, Section 11 of the Health and Social Care Act, 2001.* London: Department of Health Publications.

Department of Health (2003f) *Draft Adoption Regulations and Guidance for Consultation: Arranging Adoptions and Assessing Prospective Adopters.* London: Department of Health Publications.

Department of Health and Welsh Office (1992) *Review of Adoption Law: Report to the Ministers of an Independent Working Group: A Consultation Document.* London: Department of Health Publications.

Department of Trade and Industry (2003) *Civil Partnership. A Framework for the Legal Recognition of Same Sex Couples.* London: Women and Equality Unit, Department of Trade and Industry.

Dishion, T.J. and Patterson, G.R. (1992) 'Age effects in parent training outcome.' *Behavior Therapy 23,* 719–729.

Douglas, A. and Philpot, T. (eds) (2003) *Adoption: Changing Families, Changing Times.* London: Routledge.

Downing, A. and Hatfield, B. (1999) 'The Care Programme approach: Dimensions of evaluation.' *British Journal of Social Work 29,* 841–860.

Dozier, M. (2003) 'Attachment based treatment for vulnerable children.' *Attachment and Human Development 5,* 253–257.

Dozier, M., Chase Stovall, K., Albus, K.E. and Bates, B. (2001) 'Attachment for infants in foster care: the role of caregiver state of mind.' *Child Development 72,* 1467–1477.

Dozier, M., Higley, E., Bernier, A., Albus, K.E. and Nutter, A. (2002) *Partners in Relationships: An Invention Targeting the Relationship Between Foster Parent and Child.* [Training Programme]. Delaware: University of Delaware.

Dryden, W. (ed) (1992) *Integrative and Eclectic Therapy: A Handbook.* Buckingham: Open University Press.

Duncan, S. and Edwards, R. (1997) 'Single mothers in Britain: unsupported workers or mothers?' In S. Duncan and R. Edwards (eds) *Single Mothers in an International Context: Mothers or Workers?* London: UCL Press.

Duncan, S. and Edwards, R. (1999) *Lone Mothers, Paid Work and Gendered Moral Rationalities.* Basingstoke: Macmillan.

Dunn, J., O'Connor, T. and Levy, I. (2002) 'Out of the picture: A study of family drawings by children from step-, single-parent, and non-step families.' *Journal of Clinical and Child Adolescent Psychology 31,* 505–512.

Durlak, J.A. (1979) 'Comparative effectiveness of paraprofessional and professional helpers.' *Psychological Bulletin 86*, 80–92.

Eaton, T., Abeles, N. and Gutfreund, M. (1993) 'Negative indicators, therapeutic alliance, and therapy outcome.' *Psychotherapy Research 3*, 115–123.

Edwards, J. (2000) 'On being dropped and picked up: Adopted children and their internal objects.' *Journal of Child Psychotherapy 26*, 349–367.

Elkin, I. (1999) 'A major dilemma in psychotherapy outcome research: Disentangling therapists from therapies.' *Clinical Psychology – Science and Practice 6*, 10–32.

Engels, R., Dekovic, M. and Meeus, W. (2002) 'Parenting practices, social skills and peer relationships in adolescence.' *Social Behavior and Personality 30*, 3–17.

Eraut, M. (2002) 'Conceptual analysis and research questions: do the concepts of "learning community" and "community of practice" provide added value?' In paper presented to Annual Conference of the American Educational Research Association, New Orleans.

Everett, B. (1998) 'Participation or exploitation? Consumers and psychiatric survivors as partners in planning mental health services.' *International Journal of Mental Health 27*, 80–97.

Fahlberg, V. (1994) *The Child's Journey Through Placement.* 2nd edition. London: British Association for Adoption and Fostering.

Farmer, M. and Pollack, S. (1998) *Sexually Abused and Abusing Children in Substitute Care.* Chichester: Wiley.

Farrell, C.M. and Morris, J. (2003) 'The "neo-bureaucratic" state: professionals, managers and professional managers in schools, general practices and social work.' *Organization 10*, 129–156.

Faulkner, A. and Layzell, S. (2000) *Strategies for Living: A Report of User-led Research into People's Strategies for Living with Mental Distress.* London: Mental Health Foundation.

Faust, D. and Zlotnick, C. (1995) 'Another dodo bird verdict? Revisiting the comparative effectiveness of professional and paraprofessional therapist.' *Clinical Psychology and Psychotherapy 2*, 157–167.

Fearnley, S. (1996) *The Extra Dimension: Making Sense of Attachments – Both Positive and Negative.* Lancashire: Keys Child Care Consultancy.

Feast, J. and Howe, D. (2002) 'Talking and telling.' In A. Douglas and T. Philpot (eds) *Adoption: Changing Families, Changing Times.* London: Routledge.

Featherstone, B. (2004) *Family Life and Family Support: A Feminist Analysis.* Basingstoke: Palgrave.

Fergusson, K. (2003) 'Adoption's rich tapestry unfolded: A family life in the 21st century.' In A. Douglas and T. Philpot *Adoption: Changing Families, Changing Times.* London: Routledge.

Fiese, B.H., Sameroff, A.J., Grotevant, H.D., Wamboldt, F.S., Dickstein, D. and Fravel, D.L. (1999) *The Stories Families Tell: Narrative Coherence, Narrative Interaction, and Relationship Beliefs.* Oxford: Monographs of the Society for Research in Child Development.

Finch, J. (1989) *Family Obligations and Social Change.* Cambridge: Polity Press.

Finch, J. and Mason, J. (1993) *Negotiating Family Relationships.* London: Tavistock/ Routledge.

Fivush, R. (2001) 'Owning experience: developing subjective perspective in autobiographical narratives.' In C. Moore and K. Lemmon (eds) *The Self In Time: Developmental Perspectives.* New Jersey: Erlbaum Associates.

Flynn, R. (2002) *Short Breaks: Providing Better Access and More Choice for Black Disabled Children and their Parents.* York: Joseph Rowntree Trust.

Fonagy, P. (1998) 'Prevention, the appropriate target of infant psychotherapy.' *Infant Mental Health Journal 19*, 124–150.

Fonagy, P. (2001) *Attachment Theory and Psycholanalysis.* New York: Other Press.

Fonagy, P. and Target, M. (1997) 'Attachment and reflective function: Their role in self-organisation.' *Development and Psychopathology 9*, 679–700.

Fonagy, P., Gergely, G., Target, M. and Junst, E. (2002) *Affect Regulation, Mentalization, and the Development of the Self.* New York: Other Press.

Foote, R., Eyberg, S. and Schuhmann, E. (1998) 'Parent-child interaction approaches to the treatment of child behavior problems.' *Advances in Clinical Child Psychology 20*, 125–151.

Fraley, R. and Shaver, P. (1999) 'Loss and bereavement: Attachment theory and recent controversies concerning "grief work" and the nature of detachment.' In J. Cassidy and P. Shaver (eds) *Handbook of Attachment.* New York: Guilford.

Fratter, J., Rowe, J., Sapsford, D. and Thoburn, J. (1991) *Permanent Family Placement: A Decade of Experience.* London: British Association for Adoption and Fostering.

Fursland, E. (2002) *Preparing to Adopt: A Training Pack for Preparation Groups.* London: British Association for Adoption and Fostering.

Ghate, D. and Hazel, N. (2002) *Parenting in Poor Environments: Stress, Support and Coping.* London and Philadelphia: Jessica Kingsley Publishers.

Giddens, A. (1992) *The Transformation of Intimacy: Sexuality, Love, and Eroticism in Modern Societies.* Cambridge: Polity Press.

Gilligan, C. (1982) *In a Different Voice: Psychological Theory and Women's Development.* Cambridge, MA: Harvard.

Gilligan, R. (1998) 'Beyond permanence? The importance of resilience in child placement practice and planning.' *Adoption and Fostering 21*, 12–20.

Gilligan, R. (2000a) *Promoting Resilience: A Resource Guide on Working with Children in the Care System.* London: British Association for Adoption and Fostering.

Gilligan, R. (2000b) 'Family support: issues and prospects.' In J. Canavan, P. Dolan and J. Pinkerton (eds) *Family Support: Direction from Diversity.* London and Philadephia: Jessica Kingsley Publishers.

Glasby, J. and Littlechild, R. (2002) *Social Work and Direct Payments.* Bristol: Policy Press.

Glaser, D. (1999) 'Child abuse and neglect and the brain – a review.' *Journal of Child Psychology and Psychiatry 41*, 97–116.

Glover, G., Dean, R., Hartley, C. and Foster, B. (2002) *National Child and Adolescent Mental Health Service Mapping Exercise.* London: Department of Health and University of Durham.

Golding, K. (2003) 'Helping foster carers, helping children: Using attachment theory as a guide to practice.' *Adoption and Fostering 27*, 64–73.

Gordon, C. (1999) 'A parenting programme for parents of children with disturbed attachment patterns.' *Adoption and Fostering 23*, 49–56.

Gordon, C. (2003) 'Hands on help.' In C. Archer and A. Burnell (eds) *Trauma, Attachment and Family Permanence: Fear Can Stop You Loving.* London: Jessica Kingsley Publishers.

Gordon, L. (1988) *Heroes of Their Own Lives: The Politics and History of Family Violence, Boston 1880–1960.* New York: Viking Press.

Granville, J. and Langton, P. (2002) 'Working across boundaries: Systemic and psychodynamic perspectives on multi-disciplinary and inter-agency practice.' *Journal of Social Work Practice 16*, 23–27.

Grotevant, H., Dunbar, N., Kohler, J.K. and Lash Esau, A.M. (2000) 'Adoptive identity: How contexts within and beyond the family shape developmental pathways.' *Family Relations 49*, 379–387.

Grotevant, H.D. (1997) 'Coming to terms with adoption: The construction of identity from adolescence into adulthood.' *Adoption Quarterly 1*, 3–27.

Grotevant, H.D. (2003) 'Contact in adoption: Outcomes of infant placements in the US.' Paper presented at a Research Symposium: Contact for Children in Permanent Family Placement: The Research Evidence Debated, Nuffield Foundation, London.

Grotevant, H.D. and McRoy, R.G. (1998) *Openness in Adoption: Exploring Family Connections.* Thousand Oaks, CA: Sage.

Habermas, T. and Bluck, S. (2000) 'Getting a life: The emergence of the life story in adolescence.' *Psychological Bulletin 126*, 748–769.

Handy, C. (1985) *Understanding Organisations.* Harmondsworth: Penguin.

Harchik, A.E., Sherman, J.A., Hopkins, B.L., Strouse, M.C. and Sheldon, J.B. (1989) 'Use of behavioural techniques by paraprofessional staff: A review and proposal.' *Behavioural Residential Treatment 4*, 331–357.

Harrison, S. and Mort, M. (1998) 'Which champions, which people? Public and user involvement in health care as a technology of legitimation.' *Social Policy and Administration 32*, 60–70.

Hart, A. (2003) 'Review of my lifestory: An interactive approach to life story work.' *Adoption Today*, (October) 21–22.

Hart, A. and Thomas, H. (2000) 'Controversial attachments: The indirect treatment of fostered and adopted children via parent co-therapy.' *Attachment and Human Development 2*, 306–327.

Hart, A., Luckock, B. and Gerhardt, C. (2002) *The Attachment Project in Context: Developing Therapeutic and Social Support Services for Adoptive and Long-term Foster Families in Brighton and Hove, A Research-based Evaluation.* [A report commissioned by Brighton and Hove Council and South Downs Health NHS Trust and funded by the Department of Health.] Brighton: Faculty of Health, University of Brighton.

Harwin, J., Owen, M. and Forrester, D. (2001) *Making Care Orders Work: A Study of Care Plans and Their Implementation.* London: Department of Health.

Hattie, J.A., Sharpley, C.F. and Rogers, H.J. (1984) 'Comparative effectiveness of professional and paraprofessional helpers.' *Psychological Bulletin 95*, 534–541.

Hesse, E. (1999) 'Children in control: Helping parents to restore the balance.' In J. Cassidy and P. Shaver (eds) *Handbook of Attachment.* New York: Guildford Press.

Hicks, S. (2000) '"Good lesbian, bad lesbian" …: regulating heterosexuality in fostering and adoption assessments.' *Child and Family Social Work 5*, 157–168.

Hicks, S. and McDermott, J. (1999) *Lesbian and Gay Fostering and Adoption: Extraordinary Yet Ordinary.* London: Jessica Kingsley Publishers.

Higgitt, A. and Fonagy, P. (2002) 'Clinical effectiveness.' *British Journal of Psychiatry 181*, 170–174.

Hill, C., Wright, V., Sampeys, C., Dunnett, K., Daniel, S., O'Dell, L. and Watkins, J. (2002) 'The emerging role of the specialist nurse.' *Adoption and Fostering 26*, 35–43.

Hill, J., Fonagy, P., Safier, E. and Sargent, J. (2003) 'The ecology of attachment in the family.' *Family Process 42*, 205–221.

Hill, M. (2000) 'Social services and social security.' In M. Hill (ed) *Local Authority Social Services: An Introduction.* Oxford: Blackwell.

Hill, M.J. and Hupe, P. (2002) *Implementing Public Policy: Governance in Theory and Practice.* London: Sage.

Hobday, A., Ollier, K. and Kirby, A. (2002) *Creative Therapy for Children in New Families.* Malden MA: Blackwell.

Hodge, M. (2003) Speech to the Local Government Association on wwweb dfes.gov.uk of 8 July.

Hodge, M. (2004) Presentation by the Minister for Children at *The National Evaluation of the Children's Fund* Conference. www.ne.cf.org/conferences.

Hodges, J. (1984) 'Two crucial questions: Adopted children in psychoanalytic treatment.' *Journal of Child Psychotherapy 10,* 47–56.

Hodges, J., Steele, M., Hillman, S., Henderson, K. and Kaniuk, J. (2003) 'Changes in attachment representations over the first year of adoptive placement: Narratives of maltreated children.' *Clinical Child Psychology and Psychiatry 8,* 347–363.

Hodgkins, P. (2003) 'Keeping in touch: a different way of looking at post-adoption contact issues.' In A. Douglas and T. Philpot (eds) *Changing Families, Changing Times.* London: Routledge.

Hopkins, J. (2000) 'Overcoming a child's resistance to late adoption: how one new attachment can facilitate another.' *Journal of Child Psychotherapy 26,* 335–348.

Howard, J. and Newman, J. (2000) *Stronger Families and Communities Strategy.* Canberra: Department of Family and Community Services.

Howe, D. (1996) *Adopters on Adoption: Reflections on Parenthood and Children.* London: British Association for Adoption and Fostering.

Howe, D. (1998) *Patterns of Adoption: Nature, Nurture and Psychosocial Development.* Oxford: Blackwell Science.

Howe, D. (2003) 'Attachment disorders: Disinhibited attachment behaviours and secure-base distortions with special reference to adopted children.' *Attachment and Human Development 5,* 265–270.

Howe, D. and Fearnley, S. (1999) 'Disorders of attachment and attachment therapy.' *Adoption and Fostering 23,* 19–30.

Howe, D. and Feast, J. (2000) *Adoption, Search and Reunion: The Long Term Experience of Adopted Adults.* London: The Children's Society.

Howe, D., Brandon, M., Hinings, D. and Schofield, D. (1999) *Attachment Theory, Child Maltreatment and Family Support: A Practice and Assessment Model.* Basingstoke: Macmillan.

Howe, D., Shemmings, D. and Feast, J. (2001) 'Age at placement and adult adopted people's experience of being adopted.' *Child and Family Social Work 6,* 337–349.

Howell, S. (2002) 'The kinning of persons: Transnational adoption in Norway.' Human Agency and Kinship Conference Paper, Copenhagen.

Hoyle, S.G. (1995) 'Long-term treatment of emotionally disturbed adoptees and their families.' *Clinical Social Work Journal 23,* 429–440.

Hughes, D. (2003) 'Psychological interventions for the spectrum of attachment disorders and intrafamilial trauma.' *Attachment and Human Development 5,* 271–277.

Hughes, D.A. (1997) *Facilitating Developmental Attachment.* Northvale, JA: Jason Aronson.

Hunt, J. (2003) *Family and Friends Carers: Draft Scoping Paper.* London: Department of Health.

Hunter, M. (2001) *Psychotherapy With Young People in Care: Lost and Found.* London: Routledge.

Huntington, A., Shardlow, S., Sudbery, J. 2004 *Valuing Attachment: A Research-based Evaluation of Services Provided by Keys Childcare Limited.* Salford: Salford Centre for Social Work Research.

Ironside, L. (2001) *Living In A Storm: An Examination of the Impact of Deprivation and Abuse on the Psychotherapeutic Process and the Implications for Clinical Practice* (submitted in partial fulfillment of the requirements for the award of Doctorate in Psychoanalytic Psychology). London: University of East London.

Irving, K. (2003) 'Troubled children and how to place them.' In A. Douglas and T. Philpot (eds) *Changing Families, Changing Times.* London: Routledge.

Ivaldi, G. (2000) *Surveying Adoption: A Comprehensive Analysis of Local Authority Adoptions 1998–1999.* London: British Agencies for Adoption and Fostering.

Jackson, S. (2001) *Nobody Ever Told Us School Mattered. Raising the Educational Attainments of Children in Care.* London: British Association for Adoption and Fostering.

James, A., Jencks, C. and Prout, A. (1998) *Theorising Childhood.* Cambridge: Polity Press.

James, S. and Mennen, F. (2001) 'Treatment outcome research: How effective are treatments for abused children?' *Child and Adolescent Social Work Journal 18,* 73–95.

Janis, I.J.L. (1972) *Victims of Group Think: A Psychological Study of Foreign Policy Decisions and Fiascos.* Boston: Houghton Mifflin.

Jewett, C. (1994) *Helping Children Cope with Separation and Loss.* London: Batsford.

Jones, D. and Rampchandani, P. (1999) *Child Sexual Abuse. Informing Practice from Research.* Oxford: Radcliffe Medical Press.

Jordan, B. with Jordan, C. (2000) *Social Work and The Third Way: Tough Love as Social Policy.* London: Sage.

Kaniuk, J. (1992) 'The use of relationship in the preparation and support of adopters.' *Adoption and Fostering 16,* 47–52.

Katz, I. (2000) 'Triangles of adoption: The geometry of complexity.' In A. Treacher and I. Katz (eds) *The Dynamics of Adoption: Social and Personal Perspectives.* London: Jessica Kingsley Publishers.

Kanter, J. (1989) 'Clinical case management: Definition, principles, components.' *Hospital and Community Psychiatry 40,* 361–368.

Kazdin, A.E. (1996) 'Problem solving and parent management in treating aggressive and antisocial behavior.' In E.D. Hibbs and P.S. Jensen (eds) *Psychosocial Treatments for Child and Adolescent Disorders: Empirically Based Strategies for Clinical Practice.* Washington DC: American Psychological Association.

Keck, G.C. and Kupecky, R.M. (1995) *Adopting the Hurt Child: Hope for Families with Special Needs Kids.* Colorado Springs, CO: Pinon Press.

Keck, G.C. and Kupecky, R.M. (2002) *Parenting the Hurt Child: Helping Adoptive Families Heal and Grow.* Colorado Springs, CO: Pinon Press.

Kedward, C., Luckock, B. and Lawson, H. (1999) 'Mediation and post-adoption contact: The early experience of the Post-Adoption Centre contact mediation service.' *Adoption and Fostering 23,* 16–26.

Keefer, B. and Schooler, J. (2000) *Telling the Truth to Your Adopted or Foster Child: Making Sense of the Past.* London: Bergin and Garvey.

Kenrick, J. (2000) '"Be a kid": The traumatic impact of repeated separations on children who are fostered and adopted.' *Journal of Child Psychotherapy 26,* 393–412.

Kerfoot, K. (2002) 'The leader as chief knowledge officer.' *Nursing Economics 20,* 40–43.

Kirk, H.D. (1964) *Shared Fate: A Theory and Method of Adoptive Relationships.* Port Angeles, WA: Ben-Simon.

Kirton, D. (2000), 'Race', *Ethnicity and Adoption.* Buckingham: Open University Press.

Laming (2003) *The Victoria Climbie Inquiry.* (Chair: Lord Laming) Cm 5730. London: Stationery Office.

Lanyado, M. (2001) 'Daring to try again: the hope and pain of forming new attachments.' *Therapeutic Communities 22,* 5–27.

Leon, I.G. (2002) 'Adoption losses: naturally occurring or socially constructed?' *Child Development 73*, 652–663.

Levy, T. and Orlans, M. (1998) *Attachment, Trauma and Healing.* Child Welfare Washington DC: League of America Inc.

Liotti, G. (1999) 'Disorganization of attachment as a model for understanding dissociative psychopathology.' In J. Solomon and C. George (eds) *Attachment Disorganization.* London: Guilford Press.

Livingston Smith, S. and Howard, J.A. (1999) *Promoting Successful Adoptions: Practice with Troubled Families.* London: Sage.

Lofgren, L.B. (1978) 'Organisational design and the therapeutic effect.' In A.D. Coleman and W.H. Bexton (eds) *Group Relations Reader 1.* New York: A K Rice Institute.

Logan, I.G. (1999) 'Exchanging information post adoption.' *Adoption and Fostering 23*, 27–37.

Lowe, N. (1997) 'The changing face of adoption – the gift/donation model versus the contract/services model.' *Child and Family Law Quarterly 9*, 371–386.

Lowe, N., Murch, M., Borkowski, M., Weaver, A. and Beckford, B. (1999) *Supporting Adoption: Reframing the Approach.* London: British Association for Adoption and Fostering.

Luckock, B. (1997) *Towards a Comprehensive Adoption Service: A Research Evaluation of the East Sussex Social Services Department/ Post Adoption Centre 'Complementary' Contract January 1996–March 1997.* Brighton: Centre for Social Policy and Social Work, University of Sussex.

Luckock, B. (2000) 'Changing practice in adoption: Experiences and lessons from East Sussex.' In A. Treacher and I. Katz (eds) *The Dynamics of Adoption: Social and Personal Perspectives.* London: Jessica Kingsley Publishers.

Luckock, B. and Clifton, J. (2003) *Demographics of Adoptive Family Life* (unpublished data). Brighton: University of Sussex.

Lush, D., Boston, M. and Grainger, E. (1991) 'Evaluation of psychoanalytic psychotherapy with children: therapists assessments and predictions.' *Psychoanalytic Psychotherapy 5*, 191–234.

Luthar, S.S., Cicchetti, D. and Becker, B. (2000) 'The construct of resilience: A critical evaluation and guidelines for future work.' *Child Development 71*, 543–562.

Lyons-Ruth, K. and Jacobvitz, D. (1999) 'Attachment disorganisation: Unresolved loss, relational violence and lapses in behavioural and attentional strategies.' In J. Cassidy and P. Shaver (eds) *Handbook of Attachment.* New York: Guilford Press.

Macaskill, C. (2002) *Safe Contact? Children in Permanent Placement and Contact with their Birth Relatives.* Lyme Regis: Russell House.

Macfie, J., Cicchetti, D. and Toth, S.L. (2001) 'The development of dissociation in maltreated pre-school aged children.' *Development and Psychopathology 13*, 233–254.

Magai, C. (1999) 'Affect imagery and attachment: Working models of interpersonal affect and the socialisation of emotions.' In J. Cassidy and P. Shaver (eds) *Handbook of Attachment.* New York: Guilford Press.

Main, M. and Solomon, J. (1986) 'Discovery of an insecure-disorganized/disoriented attachment pattern.' In T.B. Brazelton and M.W. Yogman (eds) *Affective Development in Infancy.* Norwood NJ: Ablex.

Mann, S. (2003) 'It can only get better, and it did!' In A. Douglas and T. Philpot (eds) *Adoption: Changing Families, Changing Times.* London: Routledge.

Manthorpe, J. and Bradley, G. (2002) 'Managing finances.' In R. Adams, L. Dominelli and M. Payne (eds) *Critical Practice in Social Work.* Basingstoke: Palgrave.

Marvin, R., Cooper, G., Hoffman, K. and Powell, B. (2002) 'The circle of security project: Attachment based intervention with caregiver-preschool child dyads.' *Attachment and Human Development 1*, 107–124.

McAdams, D. (2001) 'The psychology of life stories.' *Review of General Psychology 5*, 100–122.

McDaniel, K. and Jennings, G. (1997) 'Therapists' choice of treatment for adoptive families.' *Journal of Family Psychotherapy 8*, 47–68.

Menzies-Lyth, I. (1988) *Containing Anxiety in Institutions: Selected Essays Volume 1.* London: Free Association Books.

Miller, C., Freeman, M. and Ross, N. (2001) *Interprofessional Practice in Health and Social Care: Challenging the Shared Learning Agenda.* London: Arnold.

Milne, D.L. (1999) *Social Therapy: A Guide to Social Support Interventions for Mental Health Practitioners.* Chichester: John Wiley and Sons.

Monck, E., Reynolds, J. and Wigfall, V. (2003) *The Role of Concurrent Planning: Making Permanent Placements for Young Children.* London: British Association for Adoption and Fostering.

Morgan, D. (1999) 'Risk and family practices: Accounting for change and fluidity in family life.' In E. Silva and C. Smart (eds) *The New Family?* London: Sage.

Morgan, D.H. (1996) *Family Connections: An Introduction to Family Studies.* Cambridge: Polity Press.

Mukherjee, S., Beresford, B. and Sloper, P. (1999) *Unlocking Key Working: An Analysis and Evaluation of Key Worker Services for Families with Disabled Children.* Bristol: Policy Press, University of Bristol, and Joseph Rowntree Foundation.

Murray, A., Shepherd, G., Onyett, S. and Muijen, M. (1997) *More Than a Friend: The Role of Support Workers in Community Mental Health Services.* London: Sainsbury Centre.

Myeroff, R. and Mertlich, G. (1999) 'Comparative effectiveness of holding therapy with aggressive children.' *Child Psychiatry and Human Development 29*, 303–313.

National Health Service (2002) *Managing for Excellence in the NHS.* London: Department of Health for NHS.

Neil, B. (2000) 'The reasons why young children are placed for adoption: Findings from a recently placed sample and discussion of implications for subsequent development.' *Child and Family Social Work 5*, 4, 303–316.

Neil, B. and Young, J. (2003) 'The University of East Anglia "Contact After Adoption" Project.' Unpublished paper presented at a Research Symposium, Contact for Children in Permanent Family Placement: The Research Evidence Debated, London: Nuffield Foundation.

Neil, E. (2002a) 'Contact after adoption: The role of agencies in making and supporting plans.' *Adoption and Fostering 26*, 25–38.

Neil, E. (2002b) 'Managing face-to-face contact for young adopted children.' In H. Argent (ed) *Staying Connected: Managing Contact in Adoption.* London: British Association for Adoption and Fostering.

Neil, E. (2003) 'Accepting the reality of adoption: birth relatives' experiences of face-to-face contact.' *Adoption and Fostering 27*, 32–43.

Nelson, G. (2001) 'Language and the self: From the "experiencing I" to the "continuing me".' In C. Moore and K. Lemmon (eds) *The Self in Time: Developmental Perspectives.* New Jersey: Erlbaum Associates.

Nelson, M. and Parrish, D. (1993) *Partnership Spreads Post-legal Supportive/Educational Services Across the Hawkeye State. Final Report.* Des Moines: Iowa Department of Human Services.

Nickman, S.L. and Lewis, R.G. (1994) 'Adoptive families and professionals: when the experts make things worse.' *Journal of the American Academy of Child and Adolescent Psychiatry 33*, (on Infotrac) 753(3).

Norman, I.J. and Peck, E. (1999) 'Working together in adult community mental health services: An inter-professional dialogue.' *Journal of Mental Health 8*, 217–230.

Obholzer, A. and Roberts, V.Z. (eds) (1994) *The Unconscious at Work*. London: Routledge.

O'Connor, T. and Zeanah, C.H. (2003) 'Attachment disorders: assessment strategies and treatment approaches.' *Attachment and Human Development 5*, 223–244.

O'Connor, T.G., Marvin, R.S., Rutter, M., Olrick, J.T., Britner, P.A. and The English and Romanian Adoptees Study Team (2003) 'Child-parent attachment following early institutional deprivation.' *Development and Psychopathology 15*, 19–38.

Ogawa, J., Sroufe, A., Weinfield, N., Carlson, E. and Egeland, B. (1997) 'Development and the fragmented self: Longitudinal study of dissociative symptomology in a non-clinical sample.' *Development and Psychopathology 9*, 855–879.

Oppenheim, D., Nir, A., Warren, S. and Emde, R. (1997) 'Emotion regulation in mother-child narrative co-construction: Associations with children's narratives and adaptions.' *Developmental Psychology 33*, 284.

Orlinsky, D., Grawe, K. and Parks, B. (1994) 'Process and outcome in psychotherapy.' In A. Bergin and S. Garfield (eds) *Handbook of Psychotherapy and Behavior Change*. New York: Wiley.

Ovretveit, J. (1995) 'Team decision-making.' *Journal of Interprofessional Care 9*, 41–51.

Oyserman, D., Terry, K. and Bybee, D. (2002) 'A possible selves intervention to enhance school involvement.' *Journal of Adolescence 25*, 313–326.

Parker, R. (ed) (1999) *Adoption Now: Messages from Research*. Chichester: Wiley.

Pavao, J.M. (1998) *The Family of Adoption*. Boston, MA: Beacon Press.

Payne, M. (2000) *Teamwork in Multiprofessional Care*. Basingstoke: Palgrave.

Perry, B., Pollard, R., Blakely, T., Baker, W. and Vigilante, D. (1995) 'Childhood trauma, the neurobiology of adaptation and the "use dependent" development of the brain: how "states" become "traits".' *Infant Mental Health Journal 16*, 271–291.

Pinderhughes, E.E. (1996) 'Towards understanding family readjustment following older child adoptions: The interplay between theory generation and empirical research.' *Children and Youth Services Review 18*, 1/2, 115–138.

Quinton, D., Rushton, A., Dance, C. and Mayes, D. (1997) 'Contact between children placed away from home and their birth parents: Research issues and evidence.' *Clinical Child Psychology and Psychiatry 2*, 393–413.

Quinton, D., Rushton, A., Dance, C. and Mayes, D. (1998) *Joining New Families: A Study of Adoption and Fostering in Middle Childhood*. Chichester: Wiley.

Quinton, D. and Selwyn, J. (1998) 'Contact with birth parents after adoption – a response to Ryburn.' *Child and Family Law Quarterly 10*, 349–361.

Quinton, D., Selwyn, J., Rushton, A. and Dance, C. (1999) 'Contact between children placed away from home and their birth parents: Ryburn's "reanalysis" analysed.' *Clinical Child Psychology and Psychiatry 4*, 519–531.

Reder, P. and Duncan, S. (1999) *Lost Innocents: A Follow-up Study of Fatal Child Abuse*. London: Routledge.

Reder, P., Duncan, S. and Gray, M. (1993) *Beyond Blame: Child Abuse Tragedies Revisited*. London: Routledge.

Reitz, M. and Watson, K.W. (1992) *Adoption and the Family System*. New York: Guildford Press.

Richardson, J. and Joughin, C. (2000) *The Mental Health Needs of Looked After Children.* London: Gaskell.

Riksen-Walraven, J.M.A. and Van Aken, M.A.G. (1997) 'Effects of two mother-infant intervention programs upon children's development at 7, 10 and 12 years.' In W. Koops, J.B. Hoeksma and D.C. van den Boem (eds) *Development of Interaction and Attachment: Traditional and Non-traditional Approaches.* Amsterdam: North-Holland.

Roaf, C. (2002) *Coordinating Services for Included Children.* Buckingham: Open University Press.

Rogers, A.M. (2001) 'Nurture, bureaucracy and re-balancing the mind and heart.' *Journal of Social Work Practice 15*, 18–28.

Roos, I.A.G. (2001) 'Reacting to the diagnosis of prostate cancer: Patient learning in a community of practice.' *Patients Education and Counselling 49*, 219–224.

Ruma, P.R., Burke, R.V. and Thompson, R.W. (1996) 'Group parent training: Is it effective for children of all ages?' *Behavior Therapy 27*, 159–169.

Rushton, A. (2003) *The Adoption of Looked After Children: A Scoping Review of Research.* London: SCIE/The Policy Press.

Rushton, A. and Dance, C. (2002) *Adoption Support Services for Families in Difficulties: A Literature Review and UK Survey.* London: British Association for Adoption and Fostering.

Rushton, A. and Dance, C. (2004) 'The outcomes of late-placed adoption: the adolescent years.' *Adoption and Fostering 28*, 49–58.

Rushton, A. and Mayes, D. (1997) 'Forming fresh attachments in childhood: A research update.' *Child and Family Social Work 2*, 121–127.

Rushton, A. and Monck, E. (In progress) *Enhancing Placement Stability.* Institute of Psychiatry, Kings College, London.

Rushton, A., Dance, C., Quinton, D. and Mayes, D. (2001) *Siblings in Late Permanent Placements.* London: British Association for Adoption and Fostering.

Rushton, A., Treseder, J. and Quinton, D. (1993) 'New parents for older children: Support services during eight years of placement.' *Adoption and Fostering 17*, 39–45.

Rustin, M. (1999) 'Multiple families in mind.' *Clinical Child Psychology and Psychiatry 4*, 51–62.

Rutter, M. (2000) 'Children in substitute care: some conceptual considerations and research implications.' *Children and Youth Services Review 22*, 685–703.

Ryan, T. and Walker, R. (2002) *Life Story Work: A Practical Guide to Helping Children Understand Their Past.* London: British Association for Adoption and Fostering.

Ryburn, M. (1998) 'In whose best interests? Post-adoption contact with the birth family.' *Child and Family Law Quarterly 10*, 53–70.

Ryburn, M. (1999) 'Contact between children placed away from home and their birth parents: A reanalysis of the evidence in relation to permanent placements.' *Clinical Child Psychology and Psychiatry 4*, 505–518.

Ryle, A. (1990) *Cognitive Analytic Therapy: Active Participation in Change – New Integration.* Chichester: Wiley.

Sales, S. (2002) 'Managing post-adoption contact through mediation.' In H. Argent (ed) *Staying Connected: Managing Contact in Adoption.* London: British Association for Adoption and Fostering.

Samuelsson, M., Themlund, G. and Rinstrom, J. (1996) 'Using the five field map to describe the social network of children: A methodological study.' *International Journal of Behavioural Development 19*, 327–345.

Sang, B. (2002) 'Modernising patient and public involvement.' *British Journal of Health Care Management 8*, 380–385.

Schofield, G. (2002) *Part of the Family: Pathways Through Foster Care.* London: British Association for Adoption and Fostering.

Schofield, J. (2001) 'The old ways are the best? The durability and usefulness of bureaucratic public sector management.' *Organization 8*, 77–96.

Schore, A.N. (2001) 'The effects of early relational trauma on right brain development, affect regulation, and infant mental health.' *Infant Mental Health Journal 22*, 201–269.

Schuman, A.L. and Shapiro, J.P. (2002) 'The effects of preparing parents for child psychotherapy on accuracy of expectations and treatment attendance.' *Community Mental Health Journal 38*, 3–16.

Scott, S. (2002) 'Parent training programmes.' In M. Rutter and E. Taylor (eds) *Child and Adolescent Psychiatry.* Oxford: Blackwell Science.

Scott, S. (2003) 'Integrating attachment theory with other approaches to developmental psychopathology.' *Attachment and Human Development 5*, 307–312.

Scott, S. and Lindsey, C. (2003) 'Therapeutic approaches in adoption.' In H. Argent (ed) *Models of Adoption Support: What Works and What Doesn't.* London: British Association for Adoption and Fostering.

Selwyn, J., Sturgess, W., Quinton, D. and Baxter, C. (2003) *Costs and Outcomes of Non Infant Adoptions: A Report to the Department of Health.* Bristol: University of Bristol.

Sen, A.K. (1992) *Inequality Re-examined.* Oxford: Clarendon.

Sennett, R. (2003) *Respect: The Formation of Character in a World of Inequality.* London: Allen Lane.

Sevenhuijsen, S. (1998) *Citizenship and the Ethics of Care: Feminist Considerations on Justice and Morality.* London: Routledge.

Shaping Our Lives (2003) Shaping Our Lives National User Network, Black User Group (West London), Ethnic Disabled Group Emerged (Manchester), Footprints and Waltham Forest Black Mental Health Service user Group (North London) and Service Users' Action Forum (Wakefield) *Shaping Our Lives – From Outset to Outcome: What People Think of the Social Care Services They Use.* York: Joseph Rowntree Foundation.

Siegal, D. (1999) *The Developing Mind.* New York: Guilford Press.

Silva, E.B. and Smart, C. (eds) (1999) *The New Family?* London: Sage.

Simmonds, J. (2000) 'The adoptive narrative. Stories that we tell and those that we can't.' In A. Treacher and I. Katz (eds) *The Dynamics of Adoption. Social and Personal Perspectives.* London: Jessica Kingsley Publishers.

Simpson, A., Miller, C. and Bowers, L. (2003a) 'Case management models and the Care Programme Approach: How to make the CPA effective and credible.' *Journal of Psychiatric and Mental Health Nursing 10*, 472–483.

Simpson, A., Miller, C. and Bowers, L. (2003b) 'The history of the Care Programme Approach in England: where did it go wrong?' *Journal of Mental Health 12*, 5, 489–504.

Smart, C. and Neale, B. (1999) *Family Fragments?* Cambridge: Polity.

Smart, C., Neale, B. and Wade, A. (2001) *The Changing Experience of Childhood: Families and Divorce.* Cambridge: Polity Press.

Smith, P. (1992) *The Emotional Labour of Nursing: How Nurses Care.* Basingstoke: Macmillan.

Sroufe, A. (1996) *Emotional Development: Organisation of Emotional Life in the Early Years.* New York: Cambridge University Press.

Steele, H. (2003) 'Holding therapy is not attachment therapy: Editor's introduction to invited special issue.' *Attachment and Human Development 5*, 219.

Steele, M., Hodges, J., Kaniuk, J., Henderson, S., Hillman, S. and Bennett, P. (1999) *The Use of Story Stem Narratives in Assessing the Inner World of the Child: Implications for Adoptive Placements.* London: British Association for Adoption and Fostering.

Steele, M., Hodges, J., Kaniuk, J., Hillman, S. and Henderson, K. (2003) 'Attachment presentations and adoption: Associations between maternal states of mind and emotion narratives in previously maltreated children.' *Journal of Child Psychotherapy 29,* 187–205.

Stormshak, E.A. and Dishion, T.J. (2002) 'An ecological approach to child and family clinical and counseling psychology.' *Clinical Child and Family Psychology Review 5,* 197–215.

Sturgess, W., Dunn, J. and Davies, L. (2001) 'Young children's perceptions of their relationships with family members: Links with family setting, friendships, and adjustment.' *International Journal of Behavioural Development 25,* 521–529.

Sunderland, M. (2000) *Using Story Telling as a Therapeutic Tool with Children.* Bicester: Winslow Press.

Swaine, J. and Gilson, J. (1998) 'Meeting the needs of adoptive parents under stress.' *Adoption and Fostering 22,* 44–53.

Tait, T., Beattie, A. and Dejnega, S. (2002) 'Service co-ordination: a successful model for the delivery of multi-professional services to children with complex needs.' *NT Research 7,* 19–32.

Thoburn, J. (2001) 'Adoption and permanence for children who cannot live safely with birth parents or relatives.' *Quality Protects Briefing Paper 3.* London: Department of Health.

Thoburn, J., Norford, L. and Rashid, S. (2000) *Permanent Family Placement for Children of Minority Ethnic Origin.* London: Jessica Kingsley Publishers.

Thoburn, J., Wilding, J. and Watson, J. (2000) *Family Support in Cases of Emotional Maltreatment and Neglect.* London: Stationery Office.

Thomas, C., Beckford, V., Lowe, N. and Murch, M. (1999) *Adopted Children Speaking.* London: British Agencies for Adoption and Fostering.

Thomas, N. (1997) *When Love is Not Enough: A Guide to Parenting Children with Reactive Attachment Disorder (RAD).* Glenwood Springs: Families by Design.

Thomas, N.L. (2000) 'Parenting children with attachment disorders.' In T.M. Levy (ed) *Handbook of Attachment Interventions.* London: Academic Press.

Toth, S.L., Cicchetti, D., Macfie, J. and Emde, R. (1997) 'Representations of self and other in the narratives of neglected, physically abused and sexually abused pre-schoolers.' *Development and Psychopathology 9,* 781–796.

Treacher, A. and Katz, I. (2000) *The Dynamics of Adoption: Social and Personal Perspectives.* London: Jessica Kingsley Publishers.

Triseliotis, J. (1973) *In Search of Origins.* London: Routledge Kegan Paul.

Triseliotis, J. (2000) 'Identity-formation and the adopted person revisited.' In A. Treacher and I. Katz (eds) *The Dynamics of Adoption: Social and Personal Perspectives.* London: Jessica Kingsley Publishers.

Triseliotis, J. (2001) 'Evidence to Special Standing Committee on the Adoption and Children Bill, 21 November.' *Hansard,* Column 134. London: House of Commons.

Triseliotis, J.P., Shireman, J. and Hundleby, M. (1997) *Adoption: Theory, Policy and Practice.* London: Cassell.

Tsiantis, J. (2000) *Work with Parents: Psychoanalytic Psychotherapy with Children and Adolescents.* London: Karnac.

Tunstill, J. (2003) 'Adoption and family support: Two means in pursuit of the same end.' In A. Douglas and T. Philpot (eds) *Adoption: Changing Families, Changing Times*. London: Routledge.

Twemlow, S.W., Fonagy, P. and Sacco, F.C. (2002) 'Feeling safe in school.' *Smith Studies in Social Work 72*, 303–326.

van Ijzendoorn, M.H., Juffer, F. and Duyvesteyn, M.G.C. (1995) 'Breaking the intergenerational cycle of insecure attachment: A review of the effects of attachment-based interventions on maternal sensitivity and infant security.' *Journal of Child Psychology and Psychiatry 36*, 225–248.

Verrier, N.N. (1997) *The Primal Wound: Understanding the Adopted Child*. Baltimore: Gateway Press.

Vincent, A. and Graham, A. (2002) 'Through the letterbox: Indirect contact arrangements.' In H. Argent (ed) *Staying Connected: Managing Contact in Adoption*. London: British Association for Adoption and Fostering.

Vondra, J. and Barnett, D. (1999) 'Atypical attachment in infancy and early childhood among children at developmental risk.' *Monographs of the Society for Research in Child Development*. Oxford: Blackwell.

Walker, M., Hill, M. and Triseliotis, J. (2002) *Testing the Limits of Foster Care: Fostering as an Alternative to Secure Accommodation*. London: British Association for Adoption and Fostering.

Walkerdine, V. and Lucey, H. (1989) *Democracy in the Kitchen: Regulating Mothers and Socialising Daughters*. London: Virago.

Wann, M. (1995) *Building Social Capital: Self Help in a Twenty-First Century Welfare State*. London: Institute for Public Policy Research.

Ward, H. and Rose, W. (2002) *Approaches to Needs Assessment in Children's Services*. London: Jessica Kingsley Publishers.

Watkins, P. (2001) *Mental Health Nursing: The Act of Compassionate Care*. Oxford: Butterworth-Heinemann.

Webster-Stratton, C. (1999) *How to Promote Children's Social and Emotional Competence*. London: Paul Chapman.

Wegar, K. (2000) 'Adoption, family ideology, and social stigma: bias in community attitudes, adoption research, and practice.' *Family Relations 49*, 363–370.

Weiss, B., Catron, T. and Harris, V. (2000) 'A 2-year follow-up of the effectiveness of traditional child psychotherapy.' *Journal of Consulting and Clinical Psychology 68*, 6, 1094–1101.

Weiss, B., Catron, T., Harris, V. and Phung, T.M. (1999) 'The effectiveness of traditional child psychotherapy.' *Journal of Consulting and Clinical Psychology 67*, 82–94.

Wenger, E. (1998) *Communities of Practice: Learning, Meaning and Identity*. Cambridge: Cambridge University Press.

Wenger, E., McDermott, R. and Snyder, W.M. (2002) *Cultivating Communities of Practice: A Guide to Managing Knowledge*. Boston, MA: Harvard Business School Press.

Wenger, E.C. and Snyder, W.M. (2000) 'Communities of practice: the organizational frontier.' *Harvard Business Review 78*, 139–145.

Werrbach, G.B., Jenson, C.E. and Bubar, K. (2002) 'Collaborative agency training for parent employees and professionals in a new agency addressing children's mental health.' *Families in Society 83*, 457–464.

Westat, Chapin Hall Centre for Children and James Bell Associates (2002) *Evaluation of Family Preservation and Reunification Programs: Final Report*. Washington DC: Department of Health and Human Services.

White, S. and Stancombe, J. (2003) *Clinical Judgement in the Health and Welfare Professions.* Maidenhead: Open University Press.

Williams, L. (2003) 'Online adoption support and advice' In H. Argent (ed) *Models of Adoption Support: What Works and What Doesn't.* London: BAAF.

Winkler, R., Brown, D., van Keppel, M. and Blanchard, A. (1988) *Clinical Practice in Adoption.* New York: Pergamon Press.

Woolfenden, S. and Williams, K. (2000) *Family and Parenting Interventions for Conduct Disorder and Delinquency in Children Aged 10–17 [Protocol].* The Cochrane Library, 1–7.

Workforce Action Team (2001) *Mental Health National Service Framework (and the NHS Plan) Workforce Planning, Education and Training Underpinning Programme: Adult Mental Health Services: Final Report.* London: Department of Health Publications.

Workforce Action Team (2002) *Mental Health Policy Implementation Guide: Community Mental Health Teams.* London: Department of Health Publications.

Wrobel, G., Grotevant, H.D., Berge, J., Mendenhall, T. and McRoy, R. (2003) 'Contact in adoption: the experience of adoptive families in the USA.' *Adoption and Fostering 27,* 57–67.

Wuest, J. (2000) 'Negotiating with helping systems: an example of grounded theory evolving through emergent fit.' *Qualitative Health Research 10,* 51–70.

Yngvesson, B. and Mahoney, M. (2000) '"As one should, ought and wants to be": belonging and authenticity in identity narratives.' *Theory, Culture and Society 17,* 77–110.

Subject Index

Author Index

Printed in the United Kingdom
by Lightning Source UK Ltd.
133894UK00001B/198/A